G000155378

New Technology-Based Firms in the 1990s

Edited by

RAY OAKEY

P·C·P
Paul Chapman
Publishing Ltd

Paul Chapman Publishing Ltd
144 Liverpool Road
London
N1 1LA

British Library Cataloguing in Publication Data
New Technology-based Firms in the 1990s
 I. Oakey, R. P.
 338.06

ISBN 1-85396-274-0

Typeset by PanTek Arts, Idenden House, Medway Street, Maidstone, Kent. ME14 1JT.
Printed and bound by The Cromwell Press Ltd., Broughton Gifford, Melksham, Wiltshire.

ABCDEFGH 987654

Contents

PART IV INTELLECTUAL PROPERTY

PART V POLICY

CONTRIBUTORS

P. AUGSDORFER, Science Policy Research Unit, University of Sussex, Falmer, Brighton BN1 9RF

E. AUTIO, Helsinki University of Technology, Institute of Industrial Management, Otakaari 1, 02150 Espoo, Finland

D. J. BOWER, Heriot-Watt Business School, Department of Business Organisation, Heriot-Watt University, Riccarton, Edinburgh EH14 4AT

S. CAIRD, Centre for Technology Strategy, Faculty of Technology, The Open University, Milton Keynes MK7 6AA

J-T. CHIANG, College of Management, National Taiwan University, 1 Roosevelt Road, Sec4, Taipei, Taiwan 106, Republic of China

D. DEAKINS, Enterprise Research Centre, University of Central England Business School, Perry Barr, Birmingham B42 2SU

E. GARNSEY, Management Studies Group, Department of Engineering, University of Cambridge, Cambridge CB2 1RX

K. HARVEY, University of Liverpool, Senate House, Abercromby Square, Liverpool L69 3BX

R. HARRISON, Ulster Business School, University of Ulster at Jordanstown, Co Antrim BT37 0QB

J. HAUSCHILDT, Institute for Research in Innovation Management, University of Kiel, D-2300 Kiel 1, Germany

A. KAKABADSE, School of Management, Cranfield University, Cranfield, Bedford MK43 0AL

I. KAURANEN, Helsinki University of Technology, Institute of Industrial Management, Otakaari 1, 02150 Espoo, Finland

DAVID KEEBLE, Department of Geography, University of Cambridge, Downing Place, Cambridge CB2 3EN

M. LARANJA, Science Policy Research Unit, University of Sussex, Falmer, Brighton BN1 9RF

A. LUMME, Finnish National Fund for Research and Development (SITRA), 00121 Helsinki, Finland

M. J. MANIMALA, Administrative Staff College of India, Bella Vista, Hyderabad 500 049, India

C. MASON, Department of Geography, University of Southampton, Highfield, Southampton S09 5NH

J. S. METCALFE, Economics, University of Manchester, Manchester M13 9PL

R. P. OAKEY, Business Development Centre, Manchester Business School, Booth Street West, Manchester M15 6PB

T. PHILPOTT, Business School, Staffordshire University, Beaconside, Stafford ST18 0AD

R. ROTHWELL, Science Policy Research Unit, University of Sussex, Falmer, Brighton BN1 9RF

R. H. STEINKÜHLER, Institute for Research in Innovation Management, University of Kiel, D-2300 Kiel 1, Germany

G. STOCKPORT, Faculty of Commerce and Administration Management Group, Victoria University of Wellington, Wellington, New Zealand

E. WHITTAKER, Heriot-Watt Business School, Department of Business Organisation, Heriot-Watt University, Riccarton, Edinburgh EH14 4AT

M. WILKINSON, Technology for Industry Limited, 6 Hinton Way, Wilburton, Cambridgeshire CB6 3SE

PART 1 Introduction

CHAPTER 1

Placing the Contributions in Context

RAY OAKEY

INTRODUCTION

The rise of the NTBF

The beginning of the 1980s represented a watershed in political thinking and consequent industrial policy in both the United Kingdom and the United States of America. The basic philosophy of the incoming conservative governments in both countries was a belief in the power of 'market forces', which emphasised a reduced (and reducing) role for government in the development of the economy in general, and the manufacturing sector in particular. In the United Kingdom, the new Thatcher government, stung by the experience of failure to implement the 'no lame ducks' policy of the early 1970s, showed a strong determination to allow markets to operate and, if necessary, leave any ailing industrial sectors to their fate. With a few notable exceptions, in cases where public outcry forced 'minor U turns' (e.g. the proposed sale of Land Rover), this non-interventionist approach was followed and, indeed, continues to be the main thrust of the current United Kingdom government's industrial policy, as indicated by their negative attitude to the recent restructuring problems of Leyland-Daf.

The significance of these general contextual observations to the current consideration of New Technology-based firms (NTBFs) is that the rather negative image of the abandonment of problem industries was counter-balanced in the early 1980s by a sudden enthusiasm for two alternative aspects of manufacturing that appeared to offer a different alternative growth-based agenda for those concerned with national manufacturing performance. First, the late 1970s witnessed a flurry of interest in the employment potential of individual and aggregated small firms. The Birch study (1979), which was crudely paraphrased in the British media at the time of its appearance in the United States, appeared to show impressive job growth in US small firms. While aspects of the Birch study were later questioned at a general level (Fothergill and Gudgin, 1982), other specific work confirmed that indeed there had been impressive job growth in the new small firms of the high technology electronics industries, based on semiconductor technology in the late 1970s (Morse, 1976; Rothwell and Zegveld, 1982).

Thus, new high technology industries that were emerging in the early 1980s (e.g. software, biotechnology) became a second potential panacea for unemployment caused by the demise of other more traditional industries. Clearly, NTBFs were seen as particularly important, since they embodied both the attributes of small size and high technology status. However, in the United Kingdom case, there was a very damaging misconception that these new firms in emerging industries would reduce the need for government financial support, since their ability to generate high profits over short time spans would readily attract private sector investment from the new venture capital industry that was also emerging in the early 1980s. Probably the most misguided belief among political and media commentators during this period was that NTBFs would thrive in the non-interventionist 'free market' conditions established by the United Kingdom government. The remaining part of this introduction, and the wealth of evidence in following chapters, amply proves this assumption to be simplistic in the extreme.

Actual NTBF performance in the 1980s

Despite the clear enthusiasm for NTBFs that existed at the beginning of the 1980s, there are only two means by which NTBFs can contribute to employment growth. First, in an unspectacular manner, NTBFs in a given national or regional economy can produce employment gains through their aggregate prosperity. The small firms of more traditional industrial sectors have been shown to yield substantial employment gains in local areas when judged over a protracted time-span (Fothergill and Gudgin, 1979). However, analysis of the growth performance of high technology small firms in the United Kingdom during the 1980s has indicated that their aggregate employment growth has been unimpressive (Oakey, 1991; Keeble and Kelly, 1988), reflecting an unstable business environment in which volatile exchange rates, high interest rates, declining government support for industry and a roller coaster ride from slump to boom to slump again, has rendered business planning more an art than a science.

A second, and more spectacular form of employment gain in NTBFs is that achieved by 'winner' individual firms that grow rapidly to achieve large size and create, under one roof, a welcome contribution to the local economy of hundreds or thousands of jobs. The growth of a number of United States electronics-based firms, of which Apple is the most cited example, is the richest source of this phenomenon. However, the picture in the United Kingdom throughout the 1980s is more a case of unfulfilled promise, rather than real achievement. Much of the excitement of the early 1980s was created by the impressive early achievements of a number of 'home grown' firms that appeared to be following in the footsteps of Apple Computers. First, Sinclair Electronics made rapid progress, only to collapse by the middle of the decade. Acorn computers appeared as if it would 'take up the torch' for a few years until attempts to break into the American market caused severe financial problems, resulting in its sale to Olivetti (Fleck and Garnsey, 1987). Inmos, set up by the National Enterprise Board in the last days of the Labour administration, ran into funding difficulties, went through a number of ownership changes, and was finally sold by GEC to Thomson CSF of France. Finally a decade that had opened with great promise of indigenous high technology industrial growth in the United Kingdom ended with the sale of ICL, our only mainframe computer manufacturer, to Fujitsu of Japan.

For many concerned with research into the problems of NTBFs, the 1980s have been a 'lost decade'. This decade ended, after the departure of Margaret Thatcher, with an implicit, if not explicit, continuation of her policies in the face of the longest recession since the 1930s. The realisation by government civil servants and politicians that NTBFs were not a simple panacea for the industrial ills of the United Kingdom tended to sap interest in high technology industry. In the absence of any new 'magic bullet' solution to our manufacturing decline, the official attitude appears to have been to pay only cursory 'lip service' to the need for a strengthening of the United Kingdom's industrial base, with only a passing acknowledgement that its continued existence depends, at least in part, on the health of large and small high technology firms. However, although the 1980s may be generally judged a failure in terms of generating the new high technology industries, there are certainly a number of lessons we should learn in order that barriers to NTBF development in the 1990s can be attacked with renewed confidence and vigour in the remaining years of this decade.

What went wrong?

When analysing why NTBFs did not deliver the hoped for level of industrial growth, the first basic observation to make is that there was an initial gross over estimation of the employment potential of NTBFs. Far too much weight was given to evidence from the United States, indicating impressive growth in limited geographical, sectoral and temporal contexts (e.g. semiconductor production in the Silicon Valley of the late 1970s). Specific political, financial and economic conditions that existed in the USA at that time allowed such growth during a 'window of opportunity' for the semiconductor-based industries that had substantially closed, even for most Silicon Valley firms, by the mid-1980s. Put simply, by the time Europeans were attempting to simplistically replicate such American growth in the totally different socio-economic environments of the early 1980s, 'the party was over'. The 'Silicon Valley experience' had been a bright 'supernova' of economic growth that was substantially an exception rather than the rule, even by American standards. The belief of a number of European governments and their planning agencies that such a phenomenon was both replicable in often alien European environments, far from Silicon Valley, and that such growth was typical of general high technology industrial growth, is more a measure of their level of desperation than their appreciation of the growth needs and potentials of NTBFs!

Another reason for the failure of NTBFs to deliver the hoped for rapid industrial growth was a basic misunderstanding of the nature of the 'start of cycle' industries that have not evolved far from basic scientific discoveries of the laboratory bench. While the exploitation of semiconductors had proved to be a particularly appropriate vehicle for small firm growth in the USA, partly due to unique national conditions for innovation and growth in the 1960s and 1970s (Freeman, 1982), subsequent experiences with other technologies in other national contexts have tended to suggest that, while there remains considerable scope for the medium to long term exploitation of new technologies, the ironing out of fundamental problems with 'start of cycle' industries can be time consuming and consequently expensive in the short term (e.g. biotechnology, software, materials technology). The biotechnology industry is, in particular, an illustration of the problems that can occur in the exploitation of basic scientific discoveries that have promise, but involve the development of products, particularly in the biomedical area, where lead-times are frequently very protracted. Such developments are often of such a long duration that exploitation cannot take place within NTBFs without the external support of large financial or manufacturing enterprises (Oakey et al 1990).

These observations on the excessive length of many NTBF programmes of product development have relevance to a point made above on the original attractiveness of NTBFs as a vehicle for rapid industrial growth. A fundamental error made by commentators on the new firms of high technology industries in the early 1980s was the assumption that the anticipated rapid growth (and profits) potential would ensure that private sector capital would flood in to finance such enterprises, thus relieving government of any major financial support role. Had innovation in NTBFs been as simple and remunerative as envisaged, and had the United Kingdom capital market, largely represented by emerging venture capital firms, been as sensitive to the needs of NTBFs as these pundits wished, the envisaged growth might now be a reality. However, the increasing realisation by United Kingdom venture capital houses, throughout the 1980s, that such innovation and growth in NTBFs was fraught with difficulties, has led to a growing flight of venture capital firms from investment in new high technology ventures, to such an extent that the name 'venture' reasonably might be denied many of the firms that comprise the current venture capital industry, since most of their investment is now concerned with funding management buy-outs and buy-ins in well established non-high technology firms (Wilson, 1993).

This trend in the behaviour of UK venture capitalists might lead the novice observer to question whether there is any potential financial return from NTBF investments. The answer to this question raises the final point to be made under this consideration of 'what went wrong'. It could be argued that the main reason for the flight of venture capitalists from NTBFs is their extreme short-termist approach to investment. A more patient medium to long term approach to NTBF investments would be beneficial to the NTBFs concerned, the national economy, and probably the venture capital firms considering such investments. A risk averse, short-termist approach is likely to result in a failure to support NTBF proposals that may be very attractive in the long term. It is in the context of private sector investment finance in the early 1990s that a sense of reliving past events is strongest. The birth of the now impressively large venture capital industry owed a great deal to criticisms in the early 1980s that the private sector was not adequately making investments in NTBFs. Now, at the beginning of the 1990s, the UK venture capital industry, allegedly the second largest venture capital industry in the world, has virtually abandoned NTBF start ups as too risky and unrewarding. Currently, we have the worst of all worlds in which both the public and private sectors are largely unwilling to fund NTBF ventures. In such circumstances, it is not surprising that the conditions for innovation and growth in NTBFs is probably bleaker now than was the case in 1980, which also implies that we have failed to act upon a decade of NTBF experience. Certainly, NTBF formation and growth is not a 'soft option' for any government, which can be merely consigned to the support of the private sector in the anticipation that automatic free market growth will occur. The 1980s have at least shown us that government involvement and support is required to ensure the required long term survival of high technology industry in a developed western economy.

Perhaps the greatest reason for this confusion over the growth problems of NTBFs concerns the ill-considered speed with which the enthusiasm for this type of enterprise grew in the early 1980s. In conjunction with the belief that science parks were a reliable physical vehicle for the delivery of NTBF growth, acceptance of the assertion that NTBFs were the answer to industrial growth problems was accepted in advance of any evidence. As noted above, the need for a quick and attractive solution of problems associated with the decline of traditional sectors of industry was a greater stimulus to science parks and NTBF promotion than any hard evidence to confirm that they could actually deliver the required results. Across Western Europe, and more recently in the reforming countries of Central Europe, high technology small firms and science parks have been advocated as quick acting panaceas. However, a safer approach to industrial development policy-making would have been to gain evidence on the nature of NTBF growth and associated problems in the countries in which they are to be encouraged before development based on such enterprises was advocated on a large scale.

Through no fault of academics, political attitudes to NTBFs have fluctuated wildly from excessive enthusiasm to a relative current disenchantment, when unrealistic expectations were not met. Although, as argued above, the present conditions from a policy viewpoint appear very similar to the early 1980s (which is disappointing), one real advantage that does distinguish the early 1990s from the previous decade, is the gradual international accumulation of detailed evidence on NTBF growth and growth problems that, had it been available in the early 1980s, might have established official attitudes to NTBFs on a more realistic footing. The following chapters offer a range of detailed conceptual and empirically based papers that add specific substance to many of the general themes discussed above.

THE PAPERS

The collection of selected papers that comprise the remainder of this book were stimulated by a conference entitled 'New technology-based firms in the 1990s', which was held at Manchester Business School on 25 and 26 June 1993. Under the general headings of 'Entrepreneurship and innovation management', 'Finance', 'Intellectual Property' and 'Policy Issues', the following papers deal with problems associated with NTBF formation, innovation and growth throughout the 1980s. It is rather ironic that specific evidence that addresses NTBF growth problems is emerging at a time when political interest in improving the environment for NTBFs might be waning. The general impression gained from the following international contributions is that, while NTBFs are no short term solution to the economic growth of a nation, they continue to have considerable scope in the medium to long term for leading the manufacturing industrial performance of developed western economies in the next century. Unfortunately, the short term attitude of many UK institutions, from the public sector (represented by the government) to the private sector (principally represented by venture capital organisations), suggests that many NTBFs are in danger of extinction before they have been given a realistic opportunity to contribute to national industrial growth.

The main aim of the conference (which has now been established on an annual basis) and this edited book, is to publicise the cause of NTBFs and their growth problems, and keep the issue of NTBF formation and growth high on the government's policy agenda. We must progress from the early identification of bottlenecks to growth, to a second stage where such barriers are substantially removed, thus enabling us to solve other more complex problems associated with innovation in NTBFs. There is a danger that PhD students in the next century will continue to discover that those investing in NTBFs have a seriously damaging short-termist attitude to investment that is inhibiting NTBF growth, due to the failure of governments to seriously address the funding problems of the late 1990s. In such circumstances, academics researching the problems of NTBFs will be forced into a form of involuntary 'ivory towerism' in which they are actively seeking to communicate their findings for the benefit of their national economies, but none of the bodies with the power to act on this evidence are willing to listen! For government to ignore the clear signals on the problems of NTBF formation and growth noted below would not only be wasteful, but very demoralising for those of us personally committed to research designed to improve the performance of NTBFs.

Entrepreneurship and innovation management

It is interesting to note that an important contributory factor in the over-estimation of the growth potential of NTBFs has been a simplistically positive view of the value of entrepreneurship. It cannot be denied that the personal individual drive of entrepreneurs in general and the informal team working of engineering and R&D staff in NTBFs in general, at their best, can create considerable small firm growth. Indeed, the spirit of networking in and between firms is captured by Rothwell in Chapter 2. He points towards the emergence of the fifth generation innovation process, in which collaborating firms use new technology to exploit integrated systems of innovation from design to production. Given conducive internal management attitudes and rich external linkage environments, there is no doubt that NTBFs can achieve levels of innovation performance that are the envy of their large firm counterparts.

However, NTBF-based entrepreneurial behaviour may also produce a strong 'down side' to the innovation and growth process in NTBFs. A major problem of the entrepreneurial process is that, whatever its merits, it is not a democratic process, and Stockport and Kakabadse possibly reflect the egotism and selfishness often associated with entrepreneurship by indicating in Chapter 3 that there are both negative and positive forces that respectively repel or attract NTBF managements that exist within the close confines of a science park. Yet again, Bower and Whittaker argue in Chapter 4 that NTBFs can act as a useful catalyst in transferring basic scientific knowledge from research establishments for eventual exploitation by large firms. However, other experiences analysed in the section on Intellectual Property below (Chapter 11), suggest that NTBF involvement with large firms for the exploitation of new technology can be fraught with dangers if the valuable intellectual property of the NTBF is not adequately protected when large firms become involved. Probably the best way to describe the interaction between NTBF entrepreneurship and inter-firm collaboration is by emphasising that the establishment of an NTBF with an attractive technological base and a need for external investment is a necessary, but not sufficient, requirement for mutually beneficial inter-firm collaboration to take place. For sufficiency to be achieved, a good match must be made between the aspirations and requirements of the NTBF and large firm managements concerned. In this context, a strongly individualistic entrepreneur may stand in the way of a potentially beneficial collaboration. While it is a gross oversimplification to argue that all (or most) NTBFs have rapid growth potential, it is also wrong to argue that all NTBFs are 'natural' collaborators.

In terms of innovation management, there continues to be no clear evidence of a common NTBF approach to strategy. The final papers in this section on entrepreneurship and innovation management again stress the rather anarchistic nature of the innovation process within many NTBFs. Augsdorfer in Chapter 5 reveals that a substantial proportion of early innovation development in NTBFs takes place without the formal approval of management in a 'bootleg' manner. Caird in the following Chapter 6, in her study of the UK Department of Industry SMART award winners, emphasises that, while NTBF managements experience no shortage of innovative product ideas, a major problem exists over which new invention or innovation should be selected for development to ensure commercial success, and the survival of the firm concerned.

The papers of this section on entrepreneurship and innovation management, although in some ways contradictory, bear witness to the genuinely eclectic nature of innovation strategies in NTBFs, and in the process, rather perversely deliver the valuable message that the archetypal concept of the NTBF as a highly motivated, skilfully managed, fast growing new enterprise applies in only limited geographical, sectoral and organisational contexts. This impression is further supported by evidence below on the heterogeneity of NTBFs' performance, while also providing an explanation for the failure of over simplistically optimistic assumptions on the growth potential of NTBFs discussed in the introduction to this chapter.

NTBF finance

Given the emphasis in NTBFs on the need for substantial 'front end' investment in R&D, often well before any saleable product is forthcoming, adequate investment capital is a critical ingredient to the formation and early growth process (Oakey, forthcoming). The 'funding gap' with regard to small firms has been the subject of continuous comment since the early part of this century. The important milestones represented by the reports of Macmillan (HMSO, 1931), Bolton (HMSO, 1971) and Wilson (HMSO, 1979) are more a testimony to the inability of successive governments to solve the funding problems of small firms than any lasting improvement in the availability of small firms finance. The clear link between the growth of venture capital organisations and NTBF growth in local geographical areas within the USA (e.g. Silicon Valley, Boston's Route 128) at the end of the 1970s led to the growth of similar provision in the UK in the early 1980s as one of the assumed necessary conditions for the replication of NTBF growth on this side of the Atlantic Ocean. However, both the general arguments made in the introduction to this chapter, and the detailed evidence below suggests that such provision continues to exhibit serious shortcomings, to the extent that it might soon be appropriate to initiate another Royal Commission on small firm finance, in keeping with a long established tradition!

Apart from the previously observed general flight of venture capital firms from the funding of NTBFs as the 1980s progressed noted above, a number of fundamental problems associated with the involvements that did occur surfaced as the 1980s progressed. An early shortcoming of those charged with decisions on the extension of investment capital to NTBFs was their predominant accountancy skills, and their consequent inability to judge the technical merits of a proposed venture, which was exacerbated by an insistence on the security of physical assets as a basis for capital investment (Oakey, 1984). The continuation of this trend at the end of the 1980s is noted by Philpott in Chapter 7 where it is observed that the emphasis of venture capital investors on physical assets continues to be a particular problem for NTBFs, in cases where technological potential may be the only asset that the new entrepreneur (or entrepreneurs) possess with which to convince accountancy oriented decision makers. In terms of international comparisons, Lumme, Kauranen and Autio in Chapter 8 generally find that the extent of venture capital provision in the UK is superior to provision in Finland. However, a study by Deakins and Philpott in Chapter 9 of the quality of European venture capital provision, represented by the attitudes of venture capitalists in Germany and Holland, suggests that the above noted UK preoccupation with physical assets may be a particularly British problem, since German and Dutch venture capital organisations are found to be far more likely to consider the technical basis of a proposed NTBF venture. An increasingly unfavourable impression created by UK venture capital provision is further confirmed by the work of Mason and Harrison in Chapter 10, where it is observed that the impact of both venture capital organisations and 'Business Angels' in the USA are proportionately much greater than in the UK. The general impression created by both mainland European and US material is that a truer spirit of venture capital provision is adhered to, whereas the British 'venture capitalists' are becoming increasingly more risk averse, particularly where NTBFs are concerned. This problem with the risk capital funding of NTBFs in the UK must partly explain why high technology small firm growth was disappointing during the 1980s.

Intellectual property problems

Technical entrepreneurs as founders of NTBFs are frequently the possessors of intellectual property at the time of (or even prior to) the formation of the firm. While, in ideal circumstances, such entrepreneurs may be able to fully exploit their new product ideas without a loss of intellectual property ownership, in many cases a proportion of the intellectual property must be sold in exchange for investment capital. However, assuming that there is external interest in the proposed technology, a major decision for the entrepreneur is the amount of intellectual property control to be surrendered for much needed investment capital. Interestingly, this observation links with the above discussion of funding in that it has been noted that a problem with UK investment decision makers in venture capital organisations is their lack of technical knowledge when assessing product ideas that NTBFs propose as the basis for a new business venture. In the UK, the relative ignorance of venture capital institutions on technical matters, may force NTBF technical entrepreneurs 'into the arms' of larger actual or potential competitor manufacturing firms who do have a clear understanding of the technical merits of the NTBF's product, but may wish to acquire such technical assets at a unfair price. The detailed case study provided by Garnsey and Wilkinson in Chapter 11 gives an appropriate illustration of the problems NTBFs face when seeking to expand while retaining ownership of their original product idea.

Although many of the new ideas that form the basis for intellectual property originate from public sector institutions, there has been little evidence of any co-ordinated attempt to promote and ease the 'incubation' of such new ideas in universities in order to benefit the individual originators of the idea and/or the host institutions that are part owners of the intellectual property concerned. In a study of the intellectual property policies of 9 British universities, Harvey in Chapter 12 clearly indicates that the policy responses of these institutions to the challenges posed by the need to exploit intellectual property have been piece meal and uncoordinated. In many cases, the general commitment to an exploitative approach to intellectual property, high in the apex of the organisational pyramid, is contradicted by other detailed rules and regulations at its base that inhibit the researcher or lecturer who develops the new ideas.

The final paper in this section on intellectual property represents a refreshing antidote to the above evidence of a rather negative Anglo-Saxon approach to the Intellectual Property debate. Jong-Tsong Chiang in Chapter 13 presents an intriguing view of the way in which intellectual property issues can be seen in terms of opportunities for NTBF exploitation in 'follower firm' contexts. Since not all NTBF 'follower firms' exist in developing countries, there are many insights in this paper from Taiwan that will interest entrepreneurs and policy makers in the west. It is argued that, with favourable private and public institutions, intellectual property protection legislation can be turned to the advantage of new small firms, since, as discussed above, it is not always the inventor firm that fully exploits new technologies. For follower firms employing a SWOT analysis to intellectual property issues, there should be more emphasis on the 'O' for opportunities than the 'T' for threats, since such worries are clearly only a problem for the first mover. Indeed, this issue re-evokes the discussion of the exploitation of basic science in the United Kingdom where it might be argued, with some force, that the UK needs more 'second mover' firms to exploit new inventions and innovations originally put into the public domain by first mover firms that do not fully exploit the technology that they have created.

Policy issues

The 1980s have provided a decade of experience that has enabled researchers concerned with NTBF formation and growth to formulate both general and specific views on the policy framework in which NTBFs should exist and be encouraged. The contributions in this final section do not represent conclusions on the issues raised in earlier chapters of this book, but comprise policy issues raised at the conference of relevance in UK and international contexts. This section begins with a wide-ranging direct consideration of the broad framework for policy by Metcalfe (Chapter 14) who, in a paper concerned with the broad context in which NTBFs operate, calls for policies that stimulate and support the complete national system of innovation from which NTBFs emerge, and to which they contribute. At a more specific level, Laranja in Chapter 15 considers the development of NTBFs in Portugal and, in keeping with the earlier assertions of Bower and Whittaker (Chapter 4) argues, with the aid of Portuguese evidence, that NTBFs might be used in a regional policy context to act as a catalyst between public institutions and large private firms. This argument carries an important ethical message that policy may well be best directed at encouraging 'natural' trends that exist in an unassisted state, but may be enhanced by the successful removal, through appropriate government policies, of logistical bottlenecks to greater growth.

Although prudently calling for more corroborative evidence in support of his findings, Hauschildt in Chapter 16 cites the results of his research in Germany to claim that science park locations in this particular national context have stimulated a better performance among NTBFs, when compared with similar firms not benefiting from such a location. This work is an illustration of how empirical work can not only be used to initially suggest policy, but also may act as a test of policies that have already been initiated. Other international work by Manimala in Chapter 17 provides welcome evidence of NTBF innovation in a developing country. He interestingly calls for new Indian policies to remove protection from NTBFs in order to create a more dynamic interactive innovation environment between NTBFs and incoming internationally-based large firms. Manimala also argues that the Indian education system should be less formal in order to stimulate more divergent thinking. These suggestions might be seen as an attempt to 'fine tune' the Indian system to achieve an optimal balance between the protection of emergent industries and the ossification that over protection can inadvertently cause if short term protective measures become institutionalised.

The policy section is concluded by Keeble in Chapter 18 where he argues, with the aid of relevant empirical evidence, that the agglomerative model of NTBF development as represented by Silicon Valley is not the only vehicle for NTBF growth. Indeed, he argues that some forms of NTBF growth can take place in less-favoured regional economies, and that such relatively deprived industrial environments may disproportionately benefit from NTBF growth. This is a valuable contribution to policy, since it balances the view held by many UK businessmen and politicians that, where NTBFs are concerned, it is virtually impossible to establish and grow a business outside the South East of England. The increasing 'natural' trend for NTBFs to select more peripheral locations for a number of technical and personal reasons is a tendency that national government might further exploit in a regional development context.

While it would be presumptuous in the extreme for academics to expect governments to follow their policy prescriptions without question, it is reasonable to expect governments to take note of clearly identified problems with the current environment for NTBFs. The purpose of this book, and the annual conference from which it has emanated, is to provide government with a continuing and evolving focus on both the problems faced by NTBFs, and suggestions for their amelioration. The 1980s have provided us with enough accumulated evidence of the needs of NTBFs to allow better informed policies that will help ensure that the 1990s will not repeat the lost opportunities of the previous decade.

REFERENCES

BIRCH, D. L. (1979) The Job Generation Process, Working Paper, MIT Program on Neighbourhood and Regional Change, Cambridge, Mass.

FLECK, V. and GARNSEY, E. (1987) Strategy and Internal Constraints in a High-Technology Firm: The Management of Growth at Acorn Computers, Research Paper No. 2/87, University of Cambridge, Cambridge.

FOTHERGILL, S. and GUDGIN, G. (1979) The Job Generation Process in Britain, Centre for Environmental Studies Research Series No. 32, London, CES.

FREEMAN, C. (1982) The Economics of Industrial Innovation, Frances Pinter, London.

KEEBLE, D. E. and KELLY, T. (1988) Regional distribution of NTBFs in Britain, in New Technology Based Firms in Britain and Germany, Anglo-German Foundation, London.

HMSO (1931) Report of the Committee on Finance and Industry, Cmnd. 3897, London (The Macmillan Report).

HMSO (1971) Report of the Enquiry on Small Firms, Cmnd. 4811., London (The Bolton Report).

HMSO (1979) Interim Report on the Financing of Small Firms, Cmnd. 7503, London (The Wilson Report).

MORSE, R. S. (1976) The Role of New Technical Enterprises in the US Economy, Report of the Technical Advisory Board to the Secretary of Commerce, Washington DC, January.

OAKEY, R. P. (1984) Finance and innovation in small independent firms, *Omega, International Journal of Management Science*, Vol. 12, 2, pp. 113-24.

OAKEY, R. P. (1991) High technology small firms: their potential for rapid industrial growth, *International Small Business Journal*, Vol. 9, 4, pp. 30-42.

OAKEY, R. P. (1995) *High-Technology New Firms: Variable Barriers to Growth* Paul Chapman, London.

OAKEY, R. P., Faulkner, W., Cooper, S. Y. and Walsh, V. (1990) *New firms in the Biotechnology Industry*, Frances Pinter, London.

ROTHWELL, R. and ZEGVELD, W. (1982) *Innovation and the Small and Medium Sized Firm*, Frances Pinter, London.

WILSON, H. I. M. (1993) An inter-regional analysis of venture capital and technology funding in the United Kingdom, *Technovation*, Vol.13, 7, Oct/Nov. 1993.

PART II Entrepreneurship and Innovation Management

CHAPTER 2

The Changing Nature of the Innovation Process: Implications for SMEs

ROY ROTHWELL

INTRODUCTION

Interest in the role that SMEs in general, and NTBFs in particular, play in industrial innovation has been high amongst academics and public policy makers alike during the past twenty years or so. This interest has been based largely on a belief that there are certain features of SMEs that make them inherently more innovative than their larger counterparts; and that NTBFs play a crucial role in the emergence of new technology-based sectors and have potential for growth to national and sometimes international status.

In the case of SMEs' role in innovation, comprehensive and systematic data are still, perhaps surprisingly, relatively sparse. At least two detailed studies have, however, shed some light on this issue. The first of these, an analysis of 4,500 significant innovations introduced by UK companies between 1945 and 1984, showed that the innovation share of SMEs (firms employing between 1 and 499) averaged about 24% in the period 1945-69; reached about 30% in 1975-79; and increased to 38% in 1980-83 (Townsend and Pavitt, 1981). SMEs' increased innovation share was gained almost entirely at the expense of firms in the 1,000-9,999 size category. The study also indicated strong sectoral specificities: it was in sectors where capital and R&D entry costs were relatively modest and where market segmentation was high (e.g. specialist machinery, scientific instruments) that SMEs made their major innovatory contribution (Rothwell, 1986). The data also showed that SME innovation share could vary over the industry cycle.

The second study was based on a sectoral level analysis of some 8,000 innovations introduced in the USA in 1982 (Acs and Audretsch, 1988a). Small firms (employment below 500) enjoyed a higher 'innovation rate' (number of innovations divided by total employment) in industries with lower capital/output ratios and in highly innovative industries where skilled labour is relatively important. Examples of sectors in which small firms' innovation rate was relatively high in comparison with large firms are scales and balances, computing equipment, control instruments and scientific instruments. Several studies have also indicated that SMEs can be more 'R&D efficient' than their larger counterparts (Acs and Audretsch, 1988b; Wyatt, 1984).

Turning to NTBFs, there is considerable evidence to suggest that whilst they have generally played an important role in the US economy during the post war era, their role in Europe, at least up to the 1980s, was to say the least, modest. NTBFs have been especially important in the emergence in the USA of several major new technology-based industry sectors including semiconductors (Dosi, 1984), computer-aided design

(Kaplinski, 1982) and, latterly, biotechnology (Orsenigo, 1989; Office of Technology Assessment, 1984). During the 1980s the situation in Europe appears to have changed and evidence (from the UK and Germany) suggests that since the late 1970s NTBF formation has increased significantly (Segal Quince and Wicksteed, 1986; and Garnsey and Cannon-Brookes, 1993). In both the USA and Europe there has been marked NTBF 'clustering' (Roberts, 1991; Segal Quince and Partners, 1985; Oakey, Rothwell and Cooper, 1988).

Some of the reasons underlying the increased rate of NTBF formation in Europe are:

- a rapid growth in venture capital;
- more favourable attitudes towards industrial production and wealth creation; infrastructure development (science parks, innovation centres) (Rothwell, Dodgson and Lowe, 1989; Massey, Quintas and Wield, 1992);
- emergence of generic technologies, most notably information technology, that are knowledge intensive rather than capital and labour intensive and which have opened up many new market niches; and
- a plethora of government SME innovation support schemes.

Today SMEs and NTBFs are faced with a turbulent economic environment and intensifying competition. Technology is seen as an at least partial means by which firms can strive to adapt to the requirements of this difficult and uncertain environment. However, technological change – its rapidity and complexity – is itself part of the difficulty.

Table 2.1 *Corporate Strategy Evaluation*

PERIOD 1: 1950s-MID 1960s
Period characterized by post-war recovery, the growth of new technology-based sectors and the technology-led regeneration of existing sectors. Introduction and rapid diffusion of major new product ranges. Demand exceeds production capacity. Corporate strategic emphasis on R&D and on manufacturing build-up.

PERIOD 2: MID 1960s-EARLY 1970s
Period of general prosperity, emphasis on corporate growth, both organic and acquired. Growing level of corporate diversification. Conglomerates formed through acquisition and merger. Capacity and demand more or less in balance. During the latter part of the period, intensifying competition. Growing strategic emphasis on marketing.

PERIOD 3: MID 1970s-EARLY 1980s
Period of high inflation and demand saturation (crisis of 'stagflagation'). Supply capacity exceeds demand. Strategies of consolidation and rationalization with emphasis on scale and experience curve benefits. Some de-diversification. Growing strategic concern with accountancy and financing issues (cost focus).

PERIOD 4: EARLY 1980s-1990
Period of economic recovery. Concentration on core businesses and core technologies. Growing awareness of the strategic importance of emerging generic technologies with increased strategic emphasis on technological accumulation (technology strategy). Growing emphasis on manufacturing (manufacturing strategy). Growth in strategic alliances, strategic acquisition and internationalisation in ownership and production. Global strategies. Technology fusion.
Major impact of new technologies. High rates of technological change. Intense competition. Rapid product cycles with growing strategic emphasis on time-based strategies. Increased intra-firm and inter-firm integration (networking). Integrated technology and manufacturing strategies. Emphasis on flexibility and product diversity and quality. Continued emphasis on technological accumulation. Environmental issues of growing strategic concern.

These factors are causing firms to forge new horizontal and vertical alliances and to seek greater organizational flexibility, development speed and efficiency to enable them to cope with the dynamically changing demands being imposed upon them. This is shifting some leading edge innovators towards the adoption of a new style of innovation – the fifth generation (5G) innovation process – which is discussed below.

TOWARDS THE 5G INNOVATION PROCESS

The external environment faced by companies has varied considerably during the post World War II era, as have the strategies they have adopted in order to cope. This is briefly illustrated in Table 2.1 (Rothwell, 1991a).

During the same period both perceptions of, and the practice of, what constitutes 'best practice' innovation have varied considerably also. This is illustrated in Table 2.2, which lists 5 generations of the innovation process. (It is important to note at the outset that this does not imply a sequential substitution process, and today all 5 generations of innovation process co-exist in various pure or hybrid forms. There are also marked sectoral specificities.

Two of the most important watersheds in the debate on the nature of the innovation process have been:

- a shift from the technology-push (1G) versus the need-pull (2G) argument to the acknowledgement of innovation as a techno-market coupling process (3G) (Mowery and Rosenburg, 1978; Rothwell and Zegveld, 1985); and

Table 2.2 *The Fifth Generation Innovation Process*

FIRST GENERATION: (1950s to second half of the 1960s)
Technology push: Simple linear sequential process. Emphasis on R&D. The market is a receptacle for the fruits of R&D.

SECOND GENERATION: (Second half of the 1960s to first half of the 1970s)
Need-pull: Simple linear sequential process. Emphasis on marketing. The market is the source of ideas for directing R&D. R&D has a reactive role.

THIRD GENERATION: (Mid-1970s to Mid-1980s)
Coupling model: Sequential, but with feedback loops. Push or pull or push/pull combinations. R&D and marketing more in balance. Emphasis on integration at the R&D/marketing interface.

FOURTH GENERATION: (Mid-1980s to date)
Integrated model: Parallel development with integrated development teams. Strong upstream supplier linkages. Close coupling with leading edge customers. Emphasis on integration between R&D and manufacturing (design for makeability). Horizontal collaboration (joint ventures, etc.)

FIFTH GENERATION: (Early 1990s- ?)
Systems integration and networking model (SIN): Fully integrated parallel development. Use of expert systems and simulation modelling in R&D. Strong linkages with leading edge customers ('customer focus' at the forefront of strategy). Strategic integration with primary suppliers including co-development of new products and linked CAD systems. Horizontal linkages: joint ventures; collaborative research groupings; collaborative marketing arrangements, etc. Emphasis on corporate flexibility and speed of development (time-based strategy). Increased focus on quality and other non-price factors.

Source: R. Rothwell (1991) Successful industrial innovation: critical factors for the 1990s, *R&D Management*, Vol. 22, no. 3, pp. 221–39.

- a shift in perception of innovation as a sequential process to innovation as a markedly parallel process (4G) (Imai, Nonaka and Takeuchi, 1985).

There exists considerable evidence to suggest that during the past decade industrial innovation has become significantly more of a networking process: during the 1980s the number of horizontal strategic alliances and collaborative R&D consortia increased considerably (Contractor and Lorange, 1988; Hagedoorn, 1990; Dodgson, 1993; Haklisch, Fusfeld and Levinson, 1986); vertical relationships, especially at the supplier interface, have become more intimate and strategic in nature (Maier, 1988; Lamming 1992; Rothwell, 1993a); and innovative SMEs are forging a variety of external relationships with both large and small firms (Rothwell, 1989a; Rothwell, 1991b). During the same period pressures to become a fast innovator increased, causing companies to adopt time-based product development strategies. Concurrent with these changes there have occurred developments in information technology which have provided companies with a sophisticated electronic toolkit (e.g. 3D-CAD, CAD/CAE, simulation modelling, expert systems, EDI) that are enhancing the speed and efficiency of product development across the complete system of innovation (in-house functions, suppliers, customers, collaborators). These developments are shifting leading-edge innovators towards the 5G innovation process, which is one of systems integration and networking. 5G essentially is a development of 4G in which the technology of technological change is itself chang-

Table 2.3 *The Fifth Generation Innovation Process: Systems Integration and Networking (SIN)*

UNDERLYING STRATEGY ELEMENTS

- Time-based strategy (faster, more efficient product development)
- Development focus on quality and other non-price factors
- Emphasis on corporate flexibility and responsiveness
- Customer focus at the forefront of strategy
- Strategic integration with primary suppliers
- Strategies for horizontal technological collaboration
- Electronic data processing strategies
- Policy of total quality control

PRIMARY ENABLING FEATURES

- Greater overall organizational and systems integration:
  - parallel and integrated (cross-functional) development process
  - early supplier involvement in product development
  - involvement of leading-edge users in product development
  - establishing horizontal technological collaboration where appropriate
- Flatter, more flexible organizational structures for rapid and effective decision making:
  - greater empowerment of managers at lower levels
  - empowered product champions/project leaders/shusas
- Fully developed internal databases:
  - effective data sharing systems
  - product development metrics, computer-based heuristics, expert systems
  - electronically assisted product development using 3D-CAD systems and simulation modelling
  - linked CAD/CAE systems to enhance product development flexibility and product manufacturability
- Effective external data links:
  - co-development with suppliers using linked CAD systems
  - use of CAD at the customer interface
  - effective data links with R&D collaborators

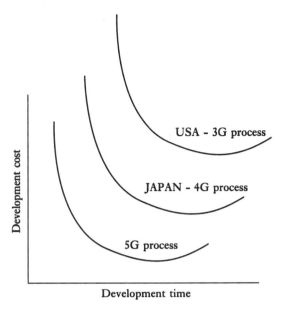

Figure 2.1
Product development time/cost relationships for the 3G, 4G and 5G innovation processes

ing. The underlying strategy elements and the primary enabling features of 5G are outlined in Table 2.3 (Rothwell, 1993b). The key features of the process are:

- Integration
- Flexibility
- Networking
- Parallel (real time) information processing

It has been argued elsewhere (Doz, 1988) that 4G innovation is characteristically a Japanese process and its parallel and integrated nature has afforded Japanese firms the measured time and cost advantages they have frequently enjoyed over their western (USA) counterparts (Stalk and Hout, 1990; Clark and Fujimoto, 1989; Mansfield, 1988). Best practice in most western companies, at least up to the second half of the 1980s, is probably best characterized by a modified (partial functional overlap) 3G process. It was also argued that 5G, because of its more powerful and real-time information processing capability, is an inherently more efficient process than its predecessors, especially in those sectors for which overall systems integration and parallel processing are important, i.e. assembly sectors, systems integrators (e.g. computers, electrical equipment, automobiles, aircraft). This is illustrated graphically in Figure 2.1 (Doz, 1988). In other words, 5G is a lean innovation process.

ADVANTAGES AND DISADVANTAGES OF SMEs IN INNOVATION

Before attempting in the final section of the paper to speculate on the significance of 5G for innovation in SMEs, a brief summary is presented of the main advantages and disadvantages of SMEs and of large firms in innovation. These are listed in Tables 2.4 and 2.5 respectively and suggest that:

Table 2.4 *Advantages And Disadvantages Of Small Firms In Innovation*

ADVANTAGES	DISADVANTAGES
MANAGEMENT • Little bureaucracy; entrepreneurial management; rapid decision-making; risk-taking; organic style.	• Entrepreneurial managers often lack formal management skills.
COMMUNICATION • Rapid and effective *internal* communication; informal networks.	• Lack of time and resources to forge suitable *external* S&T networks.
MARKETING • Fast reaction to changing market requirements; can dominate narrow market niches.	• Market start-up abroad can be prohibitively costly.
TECHNICAL MANPOWER • Technical personnel well plugged-in to other departments.	• Often lack high-level technical skills. Full-time R&D can be too costly. (Need technical specialists for external links.) Can suffer diseconomies of scope in R&D.
FINANCE • Innovation can be less costly in SMEs: SMEs can be more 'R&D efficient'.	• Innovation represents a large financial risk; inability to spread risk; accessing external capital for innovation can be a problem. Cost of capital can be relatively high.
GROWTH • Potential for growth through 'niche strategy' Techno/market leadership (differentiation strategy).	• Problems in accessing external capital for growth; entrepreneurs often unable to manage growth.
REGULATIONS • Regulations sometimes applied less stringently to SMEs.	• Often cannot cope with complex regulations; unit costs of compliance can be high; often unable to cope with patenting system; high opportunity costs in defending patents.
GOVERNMENT SCHEMES • Many schemes have been established to assist innovation in SMEs.	• Accessing government schemes can be difficult: high opportunity costs. Lack of awareness of available schemes. Difficulty in coping with collaborative schemes.

Innovatory advantage is unequivocally associated with neither large nor small firms;

• Innovatory advantages of large firms are associated with greater financial and technological resources;
• Innovatory advantages of small firms are those of flexibility, dynamism and responsiveness;
• In short, the advantages of large firms are mainly material while the advantages of small firms are mainly behavioural;
• Large firms that can combine material and behavioural advantages are in a very strong position in terms of techno/market dynamism; and
• Large/small firm combinations can assist in overcoming disadvantages and provide complementary benefits (Rothwell, 1989b).

Table 2.5 *Advantages And Disadvantages Of Large Firms In Innovation*

ADVANTAGES	DISADVANTAGES
MANAGEMENT • Professional managers able to control complex organisations and establish corporate technology strategies.	• Often controlled by risk-averse accountants; managers become bureaucrats and lack dynamism; mechanistic organisations.
COMMUNICATION • Able to establish comprehensive external S&T networks.	• Internal communication can be cumbersome; long decision chains result in slow reaction times.
MARKETING • Comprehensive distribution and servicing facilities; high market power with existing products.	• Can ignore emerging market niches with growth potential; see new technology as a threat to existing products and not as an opportunity in the marketplace
TECHNICAL MANPOWER • Ability to attract highly skilled specialists; can support the establishment of a large R&D laboratory: Economies of scale and scope in R&D.	• Technical manpower can become isolated from other corporate functions.
FINANCE • Ability to borrow; can spread risk over a portfolio of products; better able to fund diversification.	• Shareholder pressures can force a focus on short-term profits. Can access external capital on favourable terms.
GROWTH • Ability to obtain scale and learning curve economies through investment in production; can fund growth via acquisition; can gain price leadership.	
REGULATIONS • Ability to cope with government regulations; can fund R&D necessary for compliance; able to defend patents.	• Regulations often applied more stringently to large companies.
GOVERNMENT SCHEMES • Can employ specialist to assist in accessing government schemes. Able to manage collaborative schemes.	• Increasingly government innovation support has focused on SMEs.

One of the more important areas of potential disadvantage for SMEs is that of external communication. In terms of external technical communication, lack of in-house technical specialists can inhibit SMEs' ability to access external technology and related know-how in the first place, and limit their capacity to assimilate and further develop technology that has been successfully acquired from external sources. Engaging in external networking in general is a demanding and time-consuming activity that can carry with it considerable opportunity costs for SMEs possessing limited resources. Adequate interactions with overseas customers can present particularly severe problems to innovative and dynamic SMEs.

5G: IMPLICATIONS FOR SMEs

If the advantages of SMEs in innovation are mapped against the primary enabling features of 5G listed in Table 2.3, then it is clear that they match well in the areas of internal integration, organizational flexibility and rapid decision making. Innovative SMEs should enjoy good contacts with leading-edge customers, although where these are geographically distant this can present problems. The same is true of key suppliers. It is, perhaps, in the area of horizontal technological collaboration that SMEs face most difficulties because of the stringent requirements on management for properly engaging in such a demanding activity (IRDAC, 1987). For NTBFs in particular, establishing effective linkages with external sources of manufacturing capacity can be problematical.

It seems, then, reasonable to suggest that the adoption of the electronic toolkit outlined in Table 2.3 should go some way towards enabling SMEs to overcome a number of the innovation-related disadvantages associated with external networking. If, as appears to be the case, networking has become an increasingly key feature of industrial technological change, this might act to increase SMEs' innovatory capabilities and NTBFs' growth potential. At the same time, any action that increases the overall efficiency of innovation ought to act to the advantage of resource-constrained SMEs.

Some of the uses in which IT linkages have potential for providing benefit to SMEs are:

- establishing up-to-date database on new component availability and characteristics; (this can help to reduce produce development cycle times);
- using innovator/supplier linked CAD systems for co-development;
- establishing close innovator/customer CAD linkages to capture early stage customer inputs to product development; ability to interact with geographically distant customers;
- employing CAD linkages for co-development with large and small firm collaborators in horizontal ventures;
- creating CAD/CAE linkages with manufacturing contractors; design for manufacturability; improved quality; reduced cycle times;
- generally obtaining greater overall information processing efficiency across the innovation system;
- enabling the use of fast prototyping techniques.

The use of CAD and simulation modelling should enhance the in-house efficiency of SMEs' product development activities. CAD has considerable 'built-in' power to display, manipulate and alter 3-D images – in turn empowering the developmental activities of the user – and simulation models can become powerful heuristics leading to more effective product development and higher product quality. In areas where the technology is well understood, expert systems can contribute to overall innovation efficiency (e.g. in designing printed circuit boards for manufacturability).

The effective use of 3D CAD in product development by one medium sized European company is outlined in the Appendix. However, the use of IT systems does carry with it dangers for SMEs as well as opportunities, especially where lack of industry-wide EDI operating standards locks small suppliers or dealers exclusively into a particular large company's network:

Palpac Industries, a plastic moulder for packaging materials located in Ottawa, Ohio, was earlier a supplier to General Motors. In order to work for General Motors it had to plug into the Corporation's telecommunications network. Palpac is now stuck with equipment that is incompatible with other systems. Overall, there are a growing number of suppliers who fail to work with dealers who do not have online capabilities. (Sawhney, 1993, p. 146).

For firms of all sizes, there will be considerable entry costs to the 5G-systems integration and networking-innovation process. These include equipment costs, training costs and learning costs. It is a case of 'pay now, SIN later'. Perhaps because of these entry costs, to date it appears to be mainly large firms that are the prime movers in shifting towards 5G, at least judging by the available literature. If this continues to be the case, perhaps the advantages of speed and flexibility inherent in 5G, and especially its capacity for information integration and efficiency, will enable large firms to capitalize on their material advantages whilst at the same time gaining some of the 'organic' advantages generally associated with SMEs. Whatever the case, it seems likely that it is those companies, large and small, that move to master the essential features of 5G today who will become the leading innovators of tomorrow.

REFERENCES

ACS, Z. J. and AUDRETSCH, D. B. (1988a) Innovation in large and small firms, *American Economic Review*, Vol. 78, pp. 678-90.

ACS, Z. J. and AUDRETSCH, D. B. (1988b) Innovation in large and small firms, *Technovation*, Vol. 7, pp. 197-210.

CLARK, K. B. and FUJIMOTO, T. (1989) Lead time in automobile product development: exploring the Japanese advantage, *Journal of Engineering and Technology Management*, Vol. 6, pp. 25-58.

CONTRACTOR, F. J. and LORANGE, P. (1988) *Cooperative Strategies in International Business*, Lexington Books, Lexington, Mass.

DODGSON, M. (1993) *Technological Collaboration in Industry*, Routledge, London.

DOSI, G. (1984) *Technical Change and Industrial Transformation*, Macmillan, London.

DOZ, Y. L. (1988) Technology partnerships between larger and smaller firms, in Contractor and Lorange (1988). Lexington Books.

GARNSEY, E. and CANNON-BROOKES, A. (1993) The Cambridge Phenomenon revisited, *Entrepreneurship and Regional Development*, Vol. 5, no. 2, pp. 179-297.

HAGEDOORN, J. (1990) Organizational needs of inter-firm cooperation and technology transfer, *Technovation*, Vol. 10, no. 1, pp. 17-30.

HAKLISCH, C. S., FUSFELD, H. I. and LEVINSON, A. D. (1986) *Trends in Collective Industrial Research*, Centre for Science and Technology Policy, Graduate School of Business Administration, New York University.

IMAI, K., NONAKA, I. and TAKEUCHI, H. (1985) Managing the new product development, in K. Clark and R. Hayes, *The Uneasy Alliance*, HBS Press, Boston.

IRDAC (1987) *SMEs and Their Role in New Technologies*, IRDAC Working Party 3, EC, Brussels.

KAPLINSKI, R. (1982) *The Impact of Technological Change on the International Division of Labour*, Frances Pinter, London.

LAMMING, R. (1992) *Supplier Strategies in the Automotive Components Industry: Development Towards Lean Production*, D.Phil Thesis, SPRU, University of Sussex, Brighton, BN1 9RF, UK.

MAIER, H. (1988) Partnerships between small and large firms: current trends and prospects, Conference on Partnerships Between Small and Large Firms, EC, Brussels, 13-14 June.

MANSFIELD. (1988) The speed and cost of industrial innovation in Japan and the United States: external vs. internal technology, *Management Science*, Vol. 34, no. 19, pp. 1157-68.

MASSEY, D., QUINTAS, P. and WIELD, D. (1992) *High Tech Fantasies*, Routledge, London.

MOWERY, D. C. and ROSENBURG, N. (1978) The influence of market demand upon innovation, *Research Policy*, Vol. 8, April.

OAKEY, R., ROTHWELL, R. and COOPER, S. (1988) *Management of Innovation in High Technology Small Firms*, Frances Pinter, London.

OFFICE OF TECHNOLOGY ASSESSMENT (1984) *Commercial Biotechnology*, Congress of the United States, Washington D.C.

ORSENIGO, L. (1989) *The Emergence of Biotechnology*, Frances Pinter, London.

ROBERTS, E. B. (1991) *Entrepreneurs in High Technology*, Oxford University Press, Oxford.

ROTHWELL, R. (1986) Innovation and the smaller firm, in W. Brown and R. Rothwell (eds.), *Entrepreneurship and Technology*, Longman, Harlow UK.

ROTHWELL, R. (1989a) SMFs, inter-firm relationships and technological change, *Entrepreneurship and Regional Development*, Vol. 1, pp. 275-91.

ROTHWELL, R. (1989b) Small firms, innovation and industrial change, *Small Business Economics*, Vol. 1, no. 1.

ROTHWELL, R. (1991a) Successful industrial innovation: critical factors for the 1990s, *R&D Management*, Vol. 22, no.3, pp. 221-39.

ROTHWELL, R. (1991b) External networking and innovation in small and medium-sized manufacturing firms in Europe, *Technovation*, Vol. 11, no. 2, pp. 93-112.

ROTHWELL, R. (1993a) User-producer interactions in the innovation process, Presented at 6 Countries Programme Conference, Espoo, Finland, 26-27 November 1992. Forthcoming, *International Journal of Technology Management*.

ROTHWELL, R., (1993b) Systems integration and networking: the Fifth Generation innovation process, Conference '93. V. 28, Chaire Hydro-Québec, Université de Québec à Montreal (Mimeo), Science Policy Research Unit, University of Sussex, UK.

ROTHWELL, R., DODGSON, M. and LOWE, S. (1989) *Technology Transfer Mechanisms in the UK and Leading Competitor Nations*, NEDC, London.

ROTHWELL, R., and ZEGVELD, W. (1985) *Reindustrialization and Technology*, Frances Pinter, London.

SAWHNEY, H. S. (1993) Rural telephony, small business and regional development, *Entrepreneurship and Regional Development*, Vol. 5, no. 2, pp. 141-54.

SEGAL QUINCE and WICKSTEED AND ISI (1986) *New Technology-Based Firms*, (Mimeo), Segal Quince and Wicksteed, Cambridge.

SEGAL QUINCE and PARTNERS (1985) *The Cambridge Phenomenon*, Segal Quince and Partners, Cambridge.

STALK, G. and HOUT, T. M. (1990) Competing against time, *Research Technology Management*, March-April, pp. 19-24 .

TOWNSEND, J. and PAVITT, K. (1981) *Innovation in Britain Since 1945*, Occasional Paper Series No. 16, SPRU, University of Sussex.

WYATT, S. (1984) The role of small firms in innovative activity (Mimeo), SPRU, University of Sussex.

APPENDIX

IBEROMOLDES: Using 3D-CAD to enhance user interaction, product development efficiency, product quality and product development speed

Simultaneous Engineering Technology: SET

AIMS OF SET
- Reducing mould construction times
- Eliminating design and engineering errors that require mould remakes through the construction of high quality engineering prototypes.
- Involving customers at all stages of the design process to attain enhanced user satisfaction

PROBLEMS ADDRESSED BY SET
- Insufficient or inadequate specifications from customers. Often not apparent until two-dimensional designs are transformed into solid 3-D mould forms.
- Poor intra-firm and inter-firm communication
- Frequent need to remake or alter moulds after the production of first samples
- Longer-than-necessary development cycles.

Note: Iberomoldes is a Portuguese mould manufacturer employing about 750 people. This Appendix is based on material contained in *SET NEWS No. 1*, published by Iberomoldes, Mariaha Grande, Codex, Portugal and on an interview with Mr H. Neto, a founder and director of the company.

The chart on the right compares the traditional and new methods, for mould product development and its interface with toolmaking. It clearly points out the time gain using SET, both in tool construction and through the reduction of time needed for mould rework after first samples are produced.

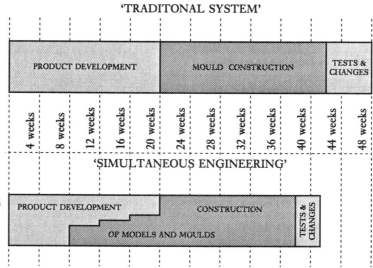

HOW SET WORKS

- Clients conceive their new products in three-dimensions. SET can provide assistance if the customer does not have the facilties for three-dimensional design.
- From this three-dimensional model, SET uses information technology to produce individual three-dimensional designs of the product.
- Solid marketing and engineering prototypes are then produced that use components rigorously identical to the parts that will be later produced from moulds.
- These protoypes are produced using CNC machining, stero-lithography and mouldmaking techniques – but without the need for producing a mould. Prototypes can be produced in several different materials, the most common being ABS.
- Simultaneously with this process, SET carries out the necessary studies to guarantee that high quality moulds can be produced first time without the need for remakes or alterations. This stage includes simulation analysis of plastic flow and cooling.
- This process enables mould production to begin three to six weeks before engineering prototypes are completed. This makes it possible for alterations to be made in the design of the product based on tests made with the prototypes – before moulds have been produced.
- In general, SET enhances producer/user interactions throughout the mould development process. It creates an iterative user/producer design interface with effective and frequent information exchange. It assists Iberomoldes to interact with geographically distant customers.

CHAPTER 3

New Technology-Based Firms (NTBFs) and Interorganisation Networks: Developing a Conceptual Framework

GARY J. STOCKPORT AND ANDREW P. KAKABADSE

INTRODUCTION

The importance of interorganisation networks in the entrepreneurial process is being given increasing attention in the small business literature (Aldrich and Zimmer, 1986). Nevertheless, previous research has rarely considered the contents of a relationship or the development of relations between organisations. Furthermore, our understanding of the entrepreneurial process has seldom been advanced through the development of conceptual frameworks. This may be partly due to the lack of in-depth grounded data on this topic area (Bygrave, 1989). The purpose of this paper is to aid our understanding of the entrepreneurial process through the construction of a conceptual framework which illustrates the development of the contents of a relationship between organisations.

NTBFs and Science Parks

Any study of interorganisation networks should begin from the perspective that organisations are open systems. This means that organisations must interact with their environment in order to obtain resources (Pfeffer and Salancik, 1978). NTBFs provide a useful subject of study of interorganisation relations as they operate within an environment characterised by information uncertainty and resource dependency. In this increasingly turbulent environment, continual innovation and quickly growing and declining product life cycles are commonplace. Product and process innovation depends upon an interactive process between suppliers, manufacturers and customers (Oakey, 1984). The new ventures that exist within this setting may lack resources such as skilled staff, finance, time etc., which are required to gather market research data about recent innovations and emerging markets. They may further lack the resources which are required to create innovations and exploit markets. All this results in entrepreneurs establishing new ventures that are distinguishable by a high risk factor.

   Science parks[1] may provide an information and resource charged environment. NTBFs may try to manipulate a science park to their own advantage by obtaining information and resources. Consequently, science parks could act as an instrument for reducing business risk. They may be viewed as a mechanism which enables interorganisation networks to occur and the process of development to be speeded up.

NETWORK LITERATURE

Definition

Networks are abstract concepts (Birley, Cromie and Myers, 1991, p. 57), and may include relationships between persons (Tichy and Fombrun, 1979, p. 924), or organisations (Aldrich and Whetten, 1981). When considering small firms it may prove difficult trying to differentiate between persons (typically the owner managers) and organisations. Nevertheless, a weakness of Kamm and Aldrich (1991) is their failure to consider the outside contacts of other persons within the organisation which may be of benefit to it. The importance of any person for communication flow within high technology organisations has been considered by Allen (1970) and Allen and Meyer (1982) in their discussion of technological gatekeepers. These are typically a small number of key staff (such as engineers or scientists) upon whom other staff rely for information and who effectively couple an organisation to the outside world through, for example, their readership of professional journals and from maintaining wider ranging and longer term relationships with engineers and scientists outside their organisation.

Process

A weakness of previous entrepreneur network research (Aldrich, Rosen and Woodward, 1987; Birley, Cromie and Myers, 1989; Birley, Cromie and Myers, 1991; Cromie and Birley, 1990; Kamm and Aldrich, 1991) is that it does not consider the contents of a relationship within a network, and more specifically, the development process from awareness, acquaintance, information exchange, resource exchange, joint ventures and mergers. The failure to clearly distinguish and discuss the contents of a relationship has led to confusion in some research. As correctly pointed out by Blackburn, Curran and Jarvis (1990), Szarka (1990, p11) incorrectly refers to Mitchell (1973) by discussing communication networks and exchange networks when reference should have been made to communication content and exchange content. It appears Szarka (1990) is suggesting that communication and exchange networks are the same as what Birley, Cromie and Myers (1989) describe as professional networks. As a consequence of this limited research it can be argued there is a great need for some new data about the development processes of networks.

Boundaries

Networks are loosely coupled (Weick, 1976), and have fuzzy boundaries (Johannisson, 1986), and this may cause difficulties in research, particularly where networks overlap (Blackburn, Curran and Jarvis, 1990). In order to overcome these difficulties Mitchell (1973) suggests that a particular problem or theme should be highlighted and discussed. Curran, Jarvis, Blackburn and Black (1991) developed this approach by considering critical incidents. They argue that critical incidents may temporarily destabilise the business or may even threaten its survival and give the examples of an organisation gaining or losing a partner or Director and acquiring a major asset. This chapter investigates the development of interorganisational networks through studying (as they happen) the problems (or themes) organisations face. These problems (or themes) are conceptualised as competing forces contributing towards (+) or detracting from (-) interorganisation relations.

METHODOLOGY

Data was collected by using ethnography. Ethnography has its origins within the Chicago School of Sociology (Faris, 1970), and involves the researcher becoming a part of the research setting. This methodology collects data by observing and recording events as they happen (Stockport, 1990), and these events may be later revisited through interviews with the participants (Stockport and Kakabadse, 1992). The role adopted was participant-as-observer[2] and this role was chosen in order to gain entry, acceptance and depth of data (for instance, the continual access to staff and documentation) (Stockport, 1992). Data has been gathered for over 4 years and has included Gary Stockport working for one day per week each with the Manager of the University of Durham Science Park[3] and with organisations engaged in biotechnology, computer software and microelectronics production. The many tasks undertaken included an analysis of the market for soft drinks and the target marketing of an electronic changeable information system. During the research it was possible to study all 25 organisations on the science park and every person (approximately 170) was observed. When recording data the following classification of responses was used:

- unprompt verbal (saw and heard by researcher) between organisations.
- unprompt verbal (saw and heard by researcher) within one organisation when discussing another organisation.
- unprompt written (read by researcher) between organisations.
- prompt verbal (prompted by researcher).

This study is quite unusual as quantitative analysis is used within a qualitative framework. Quantitative analysis was used, for example, to count (measure) the number of times and minutes organisations exchanged information. Such measurements helped to develop a conceptual framework.

FINDINGS

(+) and (-) Forces

This chapter asserts that there are competing problems or themes (forces) operating at the same time which are pushing ((+) forces) or pulling organisations away from ((-) forces) the formation of interorganisation relationships. These forces are in conflict, and which force wins, depends upon the relative importance of any problem (force) compared with other problems (forces) an organisation faces at a specific point in time (see figure 3.1). Forces have an important time dimension, and this has implications for any theory of interorganisation networks. The following examples show a wide variety of different forces at work:

Organisation (a) (computer software) faced the problem (theme) of being behind schedule with the development and completion of its software product. This was its over-riding (-) force and was diverting attention away from the development of interorganisation relationships. When the product suddenly had a systems crash, Ivan (owner manager) said:

I do not know exactly how long it will take to rectify the problem. I have been working on it for the last 3 days. I cannot think of anything else and I have not had a wink of sleep. It may lose me up to 3 weeks. *(unprompt verbal)*

IVAN ADDED (A WEEK LATER):
The windowing pointing facility was not working properly. It lost me about a week. I had

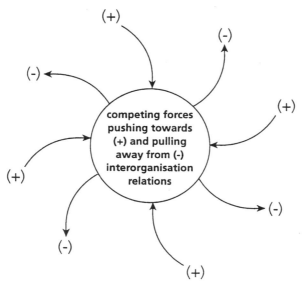

Figure 3.1
Competing Forces

to try a lot of things to find out what was wrong with the programme. It could have been a lot worse. The solution had to be first written down on paper. My plan today is to get back to the programme.   *(unprompt verbal)*

An example of a (+) force (towards interorganisation relations) was the need for Ivan to obtain information about a site licence agreement straightaway after organisation (a) had attended the Computing Training Exhibition at Olympia. Before Ivan had attended the Exhibition, he had only considered purchase agreements for his software. This information was regarded as being urgent but was not readily available as the pricing structure of site licence agreements is highly specific to software organisations. Ivan added that advice was given by organisation (b) (computer software):

Said to know the organisations you are dealing with. That is his philosophy. Single sites or multiple sites. There is a division in terms of no copying to be made or one master disk and you are allowed to make as many copies. Have a fall-back position during negotiations. Those were the salient points from the chat.   *(prompt verbal)*

A different example emanates from a microelectronics organisation which lacks in-house technical expertise. This organisation may consequently regard the necessity to develop interorganisation relations as its predominant (+) force. With a forensic science organisation, however, the over-riding (+) force may be the general need for information. Keith (owner manager) from a forensic organisation (c) said that it:

saves time and increases our earning capacity. Five minutes of their time could be seven hours of ours... It is impartial advice. They may not think they are helping us but they are. The snowpake example. Speed with which information was given. Objective opinion which is related to probability. A person was accused of using snowpake on a document. We wanted to prove there were many ways of using snowpake.

(prompt verbal)

Any particular problem may result in both (+) and (-) forces. An illustration of this occurred when organisation (d) (biotechnology) purchased manufacturing facilities in Scotland and had to increase sales. Craig (Director) said:

Sales are poor. We have too few orders. Work in progress has fallen dramatically. One of the main causes was the last managing director. When the business was going to be sold he more or less gave up. Consequently, there were no new orders put into the pipeline for some 3 to 4 months. Then there was the Monopolies and Mergers Commission Report on beer. As brewers are uncertain as to the result of the Report they have frozen their purchasing of beer processing systems.   *(prompt verbal)*

This diverted attention away from ((-) force) the possibility of intertrading with organisations within the science park as it was likely that the 3 directors would have to spend a considerable amount of time trying to generate sales. Nevertheless, it led it to subcontracting the kind of routine biotechnology analysis it usually undertook itself ((+) force). This example shows that there may be a subtle balance between competing forces.

Negative (-) forces, may include the owner managers' personal problems. Owner managers are the heart of their organisations, which could soon start to deteriorate if the heart stops functioning properly for even the shortest period of time. The following comments about Tom (director from organisation (e) (microelectronics)) show this:

Tom has had a lot of trouble from home. Please do not mention anything to him. Tom has just found out that his wife has been playing around and that she wants a quick divorce. Apparently her fella is a 30-year-old meat packer.

(unprompt verbal) (SECRETARY)

Tom is in a bad way. Business is just being put on a back burner for the time being. Telephone calls are not being returned as quickly as they should be by Tom. A lot of the time he just disappears.   *(unprompt verbal)* (SECRETARY)

This is further shown by another comment from an engineer:

That guy is falling to pieces. He keeps dropping us right in the shit! I am fed up. The trouble is Tom runs his business from his head and nothing is written down so it is difficult for anyone to pick up the tabs.   *(unprompt verbal)*

All these examples show how problems (or themes) ((+) and (-) forces) provide a useful building block upon which a conceptual framework for the study of interorganisation relations can be developed.

Network patterns

This paper argues that the development of interorganisation relations may follow 3 different patterns. These are the step, roulette wheel and catherine wheel patterns.

Step

The findings suggest that there is a step pattern in the development of the contents of a relationship between organisations. For example, from awareness, to acquaintance, to information exchange, to resource exchange (see figure 3.2). As Richard (director) from organisation (f) (microelectronics) said about its developing relations with organisation (d):

It started off by nodding to Rick (managing director) on the corridor. Over time this progressed to saying hello. Rick used to get my name wrong. My relationship with

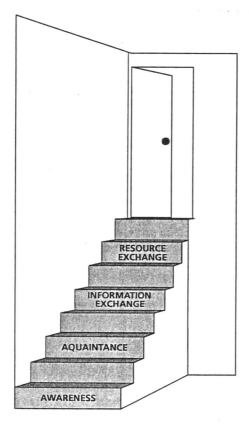

Figure 3.2
Step or Sequential Process

them began in a forelock tugging mode while I tried to curry favour. They accepted this and took on a paternalistic attitude towards us with a slight measure of arrogance just below the surface. Then we gave them help with their IBM machine and helping them find lost files. Sometimes we borrow their hoover. It may result in intertrading. We have even offered them a price for their IBM machine ... This may develop into making STE bus industrial process control systems for the Federation Brewery. It was my aim from the start.   *(prompt verbal)*

Organisation (e) said that with organisation (a) the process has been to:

firstly nod. Say hello. Who are you. What do you do. Then we discuss the possibility of trading. Business is about knowing people. The more people you know the better.
                    (prompt verbal)

Keith from organisation (c) added:

Familiarity. Just the way I am. To let them know. Who we are. Where we are. We are · here. We are pleased to meet you. It is just old fashioned courtesy. Try and meet them on the corridor and obtain a point of contact. It is something we can use at a later date. Can you help us with this. It is impartial advice.   *(prompt verbal)*

Roulette Wheel

Other findings suggest that the pattern of relations between organisations may resemble a roulette wheel (see figure 3.3). This pattern is based upon the argument that the process of interorganisation relations may depend upon the specific problem ((+) and (-) force) an organisation faces at that particular point in time. As an organisation will probably not know what the next problem will be it cannot perceive what content of a relation will be needed. For instance, an organisation which suddenly loses some important computer files would not probably foresee that this was about to happen or that it may have to urgently seek advice from other organisations. The first content of a relation between these organisations could well be the seeking of help (information exchange). Thus, this (+) force pushes the organisation to jump over preliminary relations (such as awareness, acquaintance) in order to quickly arrive at more advanced interorganisation relations (information exchange).

An analogy can be drawn with a roulette wheel. A roulette wheel spins. It spins around and around and eventually it starts to slow down. The ball comes to rest at a number on the wheel and the outcome is unknown as it depends upon chance. Similarly, an organisation does not know what content of a relation will be needed as it depends upon the particular problem ((+) and (-) force) an organisation faces at any given time. As previously mentioned, forces have an important time dimension and this has implications for any theory of interorganisation relations. A number of examples illustrate this:

For instance, between organisations (e) and (f) it concerned the design of a remote control unit for a digital cartridge player. The specific problem ((+) force) for organisation (e) was the need to have the job completed in 4 weeks and to find a subcontractor with the technical capability to do the job. The first content of the relation between these 2 organisations was resource exchange. Organisation (e) said:

The job had to be finished in 4 weeks. Other organisations we traded with could not meet this constraint. We do not have the technical capability. We were desperate to find somebody. Were urgently looking through the tenants list. Saw organisations (f) and (g) (microelectronics). We did not know them. We had not met them before. Went into the unit which they jointly share and talked with Peter from organisation (g). Peter said that he was not in a position to say whether they could do the job. Organisation (g) is owned by Senior Lecturers from the University of Northumbria. If Peter had said yes they would have got it. Richard from organisation (f) came into the unit. Said straightaway yes we can do this. And they did.   *(prompt verbal)*

Keith from organisation (c) argued that information may be so important it may push it to jump over preliminary relations:

In forensic science you may need information straightaway. Sometimes you have to walk straight into the unit. It depends upon the information you need. It may be urgent. May be too much strain to rely upon chance contacts.   *(prompt verbal)*

Another example illustrating the roulette wheel pattern occurred when organisation (h) (economics consultancy) had lost its copy of a master disk for a software programme. It had to make a first meeting:

Blunt enquiry into organisation (j) (computer software). Had to barge into their office. Excuse me. Can you help me. Have you got a copy of this programme. We need it urgently.   *(prompt verbal)*

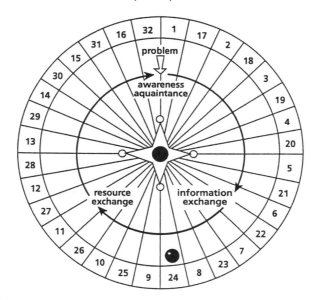

Figure 3.3
Circle or Roulette Wheel

Catherine wheel

Some of the findings suggest that the pattern of relations between organisations may develop further than a roulette wheel. This is conceptualised as a roulette wheel pattern spinning into a catherine wheel pattern (see figure 3.4). A roulette wheel at first spins slowly. Then it begins to spin faster. The roulette wheel then spins faster and faster. Eventually it spins so fast it spins into a catherine wheel. This could occur when the contents of a relation and organisations cannot be differentiated from each other. Examples include organisations which share staff and equipment, share the same unit, joint ventures and mergers. An illustration of this pattern was given by Richard from organisation (g) and concerned the sharing of staff and equipment:

Flymo are visiting tomorrow to look us over. Graham (engineer) from organisation (e) is coming here to pad the place out and work on circuitry. I am also going to borrow their oscilloscope. When British Aerospace were going to visit organisation (e) I agreed to work there. This is for credibility reasons. The more technical staff you have the more credible you are. *(prompt verbal)*

Another example of the catherine wheel analogy is between organisations (f) and (g) who moved into the same unit to jointly develop an electronic tagging system for workers on oil rigs. This system was supposed to accurately identify workers as they passed along bridges interconnecting 3 off-shore platforms. It was known as the Automatic Personnel Location System (APL). Anybody visiting the unit would find it difficult trying to differentiate between the 2 organisations as there were no partitions between them and both shared each other's equipment. A further illustration is the possibility of a merger between organisations (e) and (f). Richard from organisation (f) said to Gary Stockport on 29 November:

This may be of interest to you. You are the first person I have told. Tom from organisation (e) says that he is going to get a technical director. Said that organisation (e) is

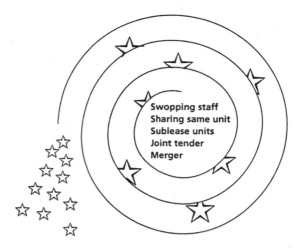

Figure 3.4
Catherine Wheel

interested in a merger with us. Tom had a board meeting with his financiers during which the subject of organisation (e)'s lack of technical expertise was discussed. Shortly before the board meeting Tom talked to me in our unit and demonstrated his habit of trying to read any visible documents on my desk. I think one of these was a particularly pessimistic cash flow I had prepared. This may have prompted another meeting during which he offered to buy organisation (f). I feel a combination of flattery and anger following this approach. The former because it was good to hear an outsider place value on something you have made. The latter because I had been careless enough to allow Tom to see confidential documents. I was not surprised at his action as we had already received an approach from another customer which we declined and it was entirely in keeping with Tom's behaviour as a commercially astute business operator. I said no thank you. It was not of any interest to us at the present time. Tom said how about it. But it was almost a threat. Tom said he did not know the buying practices of the new technical director. *(prompt verbal)*

The relationship between organisations (e) and (f) grew from the design of a remote control unit to the design of another remote control unit and an interface (which was to be used between several digital cartridge players and a control computer). During this time organisation (f) was frequently recorded within organisation (e) exchanging technical information. For example, five times for 24 minutes on 5 July and two times for 35 minutes on 27 September. Additionally, 2 times for 33 minutes on 6 December. Counting the number of times and minutes these organisations visited each other helped to prove the transition from a roulette wheel to a catherine wheel. Over this period the contents of a relation developed to the sharing of staff (prompt verbal on 11 September) and became more of a joint venture type of arrangement (prompt verbal on 27 September) before the possibility of a merger (prompt verbal on 29 November). Richard from organisation (f) said on 27 September:

We discussed a major programme to develop an integrated networked system for digital audio players based around their Series 9 machines. We gave organisation (e) a good deal of advice and I accompanied Tom on a number of visits to customers at radio stations around the country. From these visits we were able to develop a specification for the system. It became evident that the system would require a substantial investment in its development and that organisation (e) was not in a position to provide this. They had invested in the Series 9 machine and they had built up a high stock level. The level of interaction that we had achieved led us to talk about a venture whereby organisation (f) developed the system in return for a share in the sales of the system. This was an attractive proposition from our point of view. The largest part of the development costs were in staff time and the added value to be achieved in selling the Series 9 machines in a system solution gave substantially increased margins. Organisation (f)'s psychological position was therefore becoming more of a joint venture arrangement with organisation (e) rather than a straightforward customer supplier relationship. This would increase their dependence on us. We continued to discuss the networking project and I felt that there was more equality in my relationship with Tom although I was always guarded when we spoke. I made it clear that for organisation (f) to invest such a substantial amount I would need to see detailed assessments of the market with satisfactory financial data. This was always promised but never materialised.   *(prompt verbal)*

A different example of a catherine wheel pattern is the merger between organisations (d) and (k) (biotechnology). Organisation (k) was never recorded during the first 14 days of participant observation within organisation (d). Staff were firstly recorded for two minutes on 4 September and four times for 90 minutes on 11 September using technical equipment. Additionally, seven times for 55 minutes on 9 October and 12 times for 143 minutes on 16 October. Moreover, two times for 42 minutes on 23 October. Using the roulette wheel analogy, the wheel was at first spinning very slowly. Then it began to spin faster and faster. Eventually it was spinning so fast it spun into a catherine wheel (merger). A representative of organisation (d) said on 12 December:

Merger with organisation (k). We converted the laboratories into a self-contained unit. One of their staff (Mick) is paid by us. Works here most of the time. We have access to Mick whenever we want. The merger has given us more time and access to skilled staff.
           (prompt verbal)

Changing and ending relations

The findings suggest that there may be changing and ending patterns of relations. For instance, step or roulette wheel patterns may end. An example occurred when organisation (l) (secretarial services and employment agency) had a bad debtor within the science park and was forced to take legal action in order to recover the money owed. It may be further possible for catherine wheel patterns to revert back to roulette wheel patterns (see figure 3.5). This could occur when the contents of a relation change from being a joint venture to infrequently exchanging information.

Catherine wheel patterns may cease (figure 3.5). Examples include a merger which finally results in the de-coupling of the organisations or organisations which once shared the same unit and developed a product as a joint venture but are now competitors. As Richard from organisation (f) said about their deteriorating relationship with organisation (g):

There have been some technical problems on their side. They are doing other design work. Being run by academics. The guy who works there full-time... He interrupts me in my work. When people visit he always interrupts our conversation. You have to be careful what you say. We are now competitors. My company is progressing far better than theirs.   *(unprompt verbal)*

RICHARD ADDED:
They are so secretive. They keep everything so close to their chest. We moved in to work together to share equipment and marketing research. The whole thing is just ridiculous. They tried to copy our work... One of their part-time Directors used to visit. He was either a research assistant or research fellow from the University of Northumbria and they used to whisper. It was stupid.   *(unprompt verbal)*

CONCLUSIONS

This paper has attempted to aid our understanding of the entrepreneurial process by developing a conceptual framework of the development of the contents of a relation between NTBFs on a science park. Theory generation should start from the premise that as interorganisation networks are loosely coupled and have fuzzy boundaries the best way to investigate them is to consider particular problems or themes. This chapter suggests that there are competing forces pushing towards (+) or pulling away from (-) interorganisation relations. Forces have an important time dimension and this has implications for network theory. The chapter argues that the development of the contents of a relation may follow step, roulette wheel and catherine wheel patterns. The findings suggest that there may be changing and ending patterns of relations. Data was collected by using ethnography (participant-as-observer) research and this methodology enables in-depth data to be gathered by observing and recording events as they occur. This study is quite unusual as quantitative analysis is used within a qualitative framework.

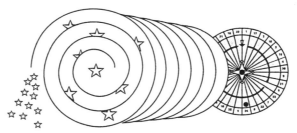

(a) a catherine wheel may turn into a roulette wheel

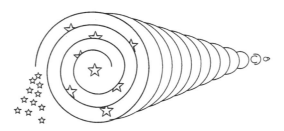

(b) a catherine wheel may end

Figure 3.5
What happens to a Catherine Wheel

There is a need for more research investigating how interorganisation relationships develop (with further conceptual frameworks of this process). Additional research could study how artificially created environments (such as science park buildings) enable interorganisation networks to occur and the process of development to be speeded up. Generally, there is a need for research investigating interorganisation relations which involve a larger sample size and cover a wider range of industries. Furthermore, there is a requirement for studies investigating the relationship between large and small firms. Other investigations could study the development of the contents of a relation at any gathering of similar organisations. For example, at business clubs or during (and after) training courses such as Firmstart or the Business Growth Programme. Combined with all this further research is a need to collect data by using ethnography. The requirement for grounded data is widely acknowledged in the study of entrepreneurship. The success of ethnography depends predominantly upon the social skills of the researcher and it is very different and far riskier compared with a purely quantitative approach. Consequently, additional research could address the various methodological considerations whilst in the field.

NOTES

1. The United Kingdom Science Park Association (UKSPA) defines a science park as 'a property based initiative which:

   - has formal operational links with a University or other higher educational or research institution;
   - is designed to encourage the formation and growth of knowledge based businesses and other organisations normally resident on site;
   - has a management function which is actively engaged in the transfer of technology and business skills to the organisations on site.

   The term science park is used to include initiatives called by other names eg. research park, innovation centre, high technology development etc., where they meet all the essential criteria set out above'.

2. There are 4 ethnographer roles. These are:

   (a) the complete observer is entirely removed from those under observation. An example is observation through a one-way mirror.
   (b) the complete participant operates under conditions of secret observation and full participation. This is referred to as covert research.
   (c) the observer-as-participant is a role intermediate between the first 2 where the identity of the researcher is known but he or she remains a relative stranger.
   (d) the participant-as-observer characterises situations in which the researcher becomes more closely involved and identified with those under observation.

3. The University of Durham Science Park was officially opened by the then Chancellor of the University of Durham, Dame Margot Fonteyn de Arias, in July 1986. The amount of constructed buildings totals 40,000 sq ft of which 33,700 sq ft (84%) is lettable. The building comprises 3 blocks and is shaped like a propeller. Its units range upwards from 400 sq ft. The 25 organisations housed within the science park cover a wide variety of activities including computing (software), electrical (microelectronics and instrumentation), chemical and biotechnology.

REFERENCES

ALDRICH, H. E., ROSEN, B. and WOODWARD, W. (1987) The impact of social networks on business foundings and profit. A longitudinal study, *Frontiers of Entrepreneurship Research*, Babson College.

ALDRICH, H. E. and WHETTEN, D. A. (1981) Organisation sets, action sets and networks. Making the most of simplicity, in P. C. Nystrom and W. H. Starbuck, (eds.) *Handbook of Organisational Design*, Oxford University Press, New York.

ALDRICH, H. E. and ZIMMER, C. (1986) Entrepreneurship through social networks, in D. L. Sexton and W. Smilor (eds.) *The Art and Science of Entrepreneurship*, Ballinger, Mass.

ALLEN, T. J. (1970) Communication networks in Research and Development Laboratories, *Research and Development Management*, Vol. 1, pp. 14-21.

ALLEN, T. J. and MEYER, A. (1982) Technical communication among scientists and engineers in four organisations in Sweden: Results of a Pilot Study, *Alfred P. Sloan School of Management Working Paper*, Massachusetts Institute of Technology.

BIRLEY, S., CROMIE, S. and MYERS, A. (1989) Entrepreneurial networks: some concepts and empirical evidence, *Proceedings of the 12th National UK Small Firms Policy and Research Conference*, Thames Polytechnic, November.

BIRLEY, S., CROMIE, S. and MYERS, A. (1991) Entrepreneurial networks: their emergence in Ireland and overseas, *International Small Business Journal*, Vol. 9, no. 4, July-September, pp. 56-74.

BLACKBURN, R. A., CURRAN, J. and JARVIS, R. (1990) Small firms and local networks: some theoretical and conceptual explorations, *Proceedings of the 13th National UK Small Firms Policy and Research Conference*, Leeds Polytechnic, November.

BYGRAVE, W. D. (1989) The entrepreneurship paradigm (1): A philosophical look at its research methodologies, *Entrepreneurship Theory and Practice*, Vol. 14, no. 1, Fall, pp. 7-26.

CROMIE, S. and BIRLEY, S. (1990) Personal networking: an invaluable asset for female entrepreneurs, *Proceedings of the 13th National UK Small Firms Policy and Research Conference*, Leeds Polytechnic, November.

CURRAN, J., JARVIS, R., BLACKBURN, R. and BLACK, S. (1991) Small firms and networks: constructs, methodological strategies and some preliminary findings, *Proceedings of the 14th National UK Small Firms Policy and Research Conference*, Manchester Business School, November.

FARIS, R. E. L. (1970) *Chicago Sociology 1920-1932*, University of Chicago, Chicago.

JOHANNISSON, B. (1986) Network strategies: management technology for entrepreneurship and change, *International Small Business Journal*, Vol. 5, no. 1, Autumn, pp. 19-30.

JUNKER, B. (1960) *Field Work*, University of Chicago, Chicago.

KAMM, J. B. and ALDRICH, H. E. (1991) Differences in network activity between entrepreneurial individuals and teams, Paper presented at the *11th Annual Babson Entrepreneurship Research Conference*, University of Pittsburg, April.

MITCHELL, J. C. (1973) Networks, norms and institutions, in J. Boissevain and J. C. Mitchell (eds.) *Network Analysis Studies in Human Interaction*, Mouton, Paris.

OAKEY, R. P. (1984) *High Technology Small Firms. Regional Development in Britain and the United States*, Frances Pinter, London.

PFEFFER, J. and SALANCIK, G. E. (1978) *The External Control of Organisations. A Resource Dependence Perspective*, Harper and Row, New York.

ROSEN, M. (1991) Coming to terms with the field: understanding and doing organisational ethnography, *Journal of Management Studies*, Vol. 28, no. 1, January, pp. 1-24.

STOCKPORT, G. J. (1990) Ethnography - getting in, staying in, getting out and getting back, *Proceedings of the British Academy of Management Workshop: The Economics and Management of Small Firms*, Manchester Business School, April.

STOCKPORT, G. J. (1992) *Developing Interorganisational Relations within an Incubator on a Science Park - an Ethnographic Study*, Cranfield Institute of Technology, unpublished Ph.D thesis.

STOCKPORT, G. J. and KAKABADSE, A. P. (1992) Using ethnography in small firms research, in K. Caley, E. Chell, F. Chittenden and C. Mason (eds.) *Small Enterprise Development. Policy and Practice in Action*, pp. 178-91, Paul Chapman, London.

SZARKA, J. (1990) Networking and small firms, *International Small Business Journal*, Vol. 8, no. 2, January-March, pp. 10-22.

TICHY, N. M. and FOMBRUN, C. (1979) Network analysis in organisational settings, *Human Relations*, Vol. 32, no. 11, pp. 923-65.

WEICK, K. E. (1976) Educational organisations as loosely coupled systems, *Administrative Science Quarterly*, Vol. 21, no. 1, pp. 1-19.

CHAPTER 4

Client Communication and Innovative Efficiency in US and UK Biotechnology Companies

D. JANE BOWER AND ERICA WHITTAKER

INTRODUCTION

Major scientific breakthroughs in genetic manipulation and monoclonal antibody construction (Cohen et al, 1973; Köhler and Milstein, 1975) have led to the formation of a large number of new firms, the biotechnology companies (Kenney, 1986). The earliest of these firms were founded in the USA, where they are still most numerous, but a growing number are now developing in other countries (Bower and Whittaker, 1993). Most of these firms have been founded to develop these novel, bioscience-based technologies into products and manufacturing processes for the pharmaceutical and other industries. They have evolved a distinctive development strategy and pattern of financing. The financing approach has included a venture funded start as an R&D company, with a specific area of technical expertise in contract research. This is followed by finance from joint development projects with large companies seeking access to new technology to which the smaller company has proprietary rights, then a public quotation attracting substantial investment by independent institutional investors. A distinguishing strategic characteristic of this group of companies is their carefully maintained relationship with the science base. The majority of the biotechnology companies have spun out of universities or research institutes, with which they retain close links. A minority have been set up on the initiative of venture capitalists or other groups but virtually all have sought to forge strong relationships with basic science groups with special expertise in research on biological systems which could offer exploitation possibilities.

Firms founded recently by bioscientists, exploiting technologies other than the two which are cited above (i.e. genetic manipulation and monoclonal antibody technology), but following a similar strategy, are usually classified as part of this 'biotechnology industry', as are a number of others which are primarily suppliers of highly specialised reagents and instruments to the core group.

This varied group of new companies known as the 'biotechnology industry' has attracted considerable interest. The core subgroup which has expensive and lengthy development projects has created a model path for the transfer of new technology from the basic science laboratory into social and economic usefulness, in industries which exhibit very high barriers to the entry of new members. These companies have persuaded a heterogeneous group of supporters to provide them with the finance and complementary expertise to take risky projects through many years' development and major regulatory hurdles to the market.

The 'biotechnology industry' was founded in the USA partly because there was already a local tradition of high technology company creation based on microelectronics technology, and a well-developed venture capital market to support it. However, the phenomenon was by no means localised to the USA. It was underpinned from the earliest stages by large company sponsorship from Europe as well as the USA, and more recently by large Japanese companies as well. In addition, much of the scientific expertise and inventions being exploited originated at least partly outside the USA, usually in universities or other public sector laboratories.

Outstanding scientists in these other countries are part of the same international network as the American scientists who first decided to commercialise their technological expertise. Both they and their American colleagues continue to generate ideas with commercial potential. Not surprisingly, scientific entrepreneurs in other countries, encouraged by government, are attempting to adapt the pattern of commercialisation which has been successful in the USA to models which can operate in other business environments.

US biotechnology industry characteristics

In a detailed survey of the US industry, including suppliers and instrumentation companies, Burrill (1989) found that of the total of 1095 companies which fall within his definition of biotechnology companies in mid-1989, 68% were privately held, 17% (186) were publicly quoted and 15% were subsidiaries. Another survey (Papadopoulos, 1992) considered only those US companies which were founded to develop novel products using bioscience technology, which were publicly-quoted. It excluded wholly-owned subsidiaries and also companies which were purely suppliers of reagents and instruments. It found that by 1991 there were 52 publicly-quoted companies with a market capitalisation in excess of $100m, of which 7 had market capitalisation in excess of $1bn. A more recent survey (KPMG, 1993) of 500 leading US biotechnology companies (34% response rate of which 49% public) found that 56% of its respondents were developing novel therapeutic products. Profits records of companies developing these technologies have been less discussed since few, and none of Papadopoulos' (1992) 7 most highly valued companies, had yet reached breakeven in 1991.

The industry outside the USA

'Biotechnology companies' are even less precisely defined in Europe than in the USA, and directories purporting to list them sometimes include companies which do not choose to describe themselves as 'biotechnology companies'. Because of these definitional problems, and the variable utility of directories, the number of 'biotechnology companies' in Europe which are reasonably comparable to the subsets within the American group is difficult to determine. However, it would appear that the number of those which have been formed to undertake expensive, long-term development projects is as yet only a fraction of the number in the USA. Most are located in Britain, and they are relatively younger than the American group.

UK biotechnology firms have experienced initial financing difficulties, and their founders have operated in a less sophisticated support environment for new technology-based firms (NTBFs) than their American counterparts (Oakey et al, 1990). In spite of these barriers an increasing number are managing to grow through building an international investor base and an equally international contract and R&D partnership client base (Bower & Whittaker, 1993).

The importance of strategic alliances

The crucial role of strategic alliances with large companies, mainly in the pharmaceutical or agrochemical industries, in the development of this group of biotechnology companies has attracted attention (see, for example, Hull and Slowinski, 1990; KPMG, 1993; Bower and Whittaker, 1993). For the smaller company the alliance is not only a source of cash but also of wider industry know-how, expertise and contacts. For the larger partner the small company offers access to risky new technology with less commitment than would be required for a full, in-house development. There may also be an informal flow of other benefits to the partners. This situation is not peculiar to the biotechnology sector. A study comparing small firm/large firm technology partnerships in the electronics and biotechnology industries in the USA found that in both industries, in addition to the formal contributions that the partners make there is an informal exchange of resources between them (Hull and Slowinski, 1990). These resources consist of knowledge and skills in development, management, manufacturing and marketing. In the smaller firm, these skills centre around the core technological expertise which the large company is accessing through the partnership. The large firms bring a wider range of resources including industry-specific knowledge and expertise.

The informal exchange not only facilitates the successful completion of the contractual project, it also alters the competitive advantage of both partners in the longer term (Hull and Slowinski, 1990). This is because it is less an exchange than a pooling of resources. While both partners gain some expertise from the other, neither actually loses through this formal exchange, where cash or property rights pass from one to the other. From the perspective of the small firm, this is an important opportunity to acquire a better understanding and skills in operating within the wider industry, which will enhance its ability to develop its won products independently and retain more of the eventual returns. For the large firm, the period of the joint project is also a continuing learning experience during which the smaller firm's novel technological expertise is transferred in part or even entirely. The impact on the industry as a whole, where many or most large firms are engaging in such partnerships, is to raise the whole industry to a higher plane of technical sophistication.

Since in addition to substantial amounts of cash the R&D partnerships provide important non-financial resources for the development of the US biotechnology firms, effective management of these relationships is likely also to be a significant factor for success of British-based firms. This paper reports the results of a comparative survey of UK and US biotechnology companies investigating aspects of the management process of R&D partnerships which permit the informal exchange of resources between the partners which contribute to development of the small firm's knowledge of how to operate effectively within the industry. The patterns of communication between biotechnology firms and their large clients and the relationship between these and perceived satisfactory project management were investigated.

METHODOLOGY

'Strategic alliance' is usually used to denote an R&D partnership which is of strategic importance to both partners (Burrill, 1989). Since in this survey the views of only one of the partners was sought, the more general term 'R&D partnership' is used. Thus while all such partnerships involve substantial commitments from the smaller partner, the degree of commitment by the larger partner can be assumed to be variable.

Since in both the UK and the USA, directories and other industry sources include a rather heterogeneous collection of companies (see above), the sample frames of UK and US companies were compiled from these sources by restricting frames to the subsets of

Table 4.1: *Respondent firms*

	USA		UK	
No. respondent firms	49		15	
Private*	5	10%	11	73%
Public*	42	86%	3	20%
No. employees (median)	98		50	

* 2 US and 1 UK firms were in the process of their initial public share offering and were not included in either public or private.

companies who included among their activities the development of production processes or therapeutic products for human healthcare markets. Thus any conclusions drawn may not apply to those companies operating only within the extensive but different regulatory regimes of the agrichemical and food industries.

Sources used to identify companies and their activities included the Genetic Engineering News Directory, other biotechnology directories, and healthcare and financial industry publications, all current at the end of 1991. The UK sample included the 17 companies in the UK sample frame, from which 15 (88%) companies responded. The US sample consisted of the 175 USA-based firms which fulfilled the selection criteria, of which 49 (28.7%) responded.

Postal survey

A postal questionnaire survey was carried out in September 1992. Results are presented below. Since this was part of a wider research project in which top management of most of the respondent UK and several of the US companies were interviewed (detailed results to be presented elsewhere), some points are taken from the interviews to clarify the findings of the postal survey.

The USA respondent sample (see Table 4.1) included 10 of the top 20 publicly-quoted biotechnology firms, in terms of market capitalisation. Since the overall response rate from the USA was 28.7%, this implies that the US respondent group is biassed towards the more successful and longer-established firms. The UK respondents appeared to show a similar bias, since all of the three publicly-quoted companies responded. Thus the responses represent management practice in the industry's more successful firms.

The median number of employees at US firms was 98 compared with 50 at UK firms. This may have been a function of their shorter average lifespan, but may also reflect lower growth rates in the UK.

Most of the UK firms in the sample were privately held. In addition, of the three UK firms which were publicly-quoted one was quoted on the Australian Stock Exchange, one had just obtained quotations simultaneously in the USA, on NASDAQ (the largest American screen-based market, operated by the National Association of Securities Dealers) and London, and the third had just achieved quotation solely on NASDAQ. This reflected the different rules governing quotations on the two countries' stockmarkets. Most UK firms without a profits record were debarred by Stock Exchange regulations from quotation until 1992. Limited exceptions can now be made for biotechnology companies developing healthcare products.

The respondent firms were founded between 1961 and 1992 with a peak in 1981 for US firms, and a peak in 1988 for UK firms. Burrill's (1989) universe of US biotechnology companies also had a peak year for company creation in 1981. The US respondent firms in the KPMG (1993) survey were slightly younger than the sample presented here but had approximately the same number of employees, reflecting the later date of the KPMG survey.

Table 4.2: *Firm's primary long-term business or products*

	USA		UK	
	f	%	f	%
Biopharmaceuticals	36/49	73.5	12/15	80.0
Drug delivery	13/49	26.5	2/15	13.3
Diagnostics	4/49	8.2	5/15	33.3
Miscellaneous	7/49	14.3	4/15	26.7
Reagents supply, etc.	3/49	6.1	3/15	20.0
Contract research	3/49	6.1	1/15	6.7

Note: f = frequency

The UK and US groups' perceptions of their firms' main long-term business (see Table 4.2) were quite similar. The stronger focus on diagnostics in the UK was probably due to the relatively low amounts of capital required to get into this low-margin business.

The relative importance of current sources of income also reflected differences in companies' sources of capital. US companies, which raise large tranches of capital in public offerings, invest this in securities and report the interest as revenue. UK companies which lack this source of cash generate more earnings through the production and sale of diagnostics and reagents, which do not require substantial capital outlay, but are often peripheral to the main business of the company. Firms in both countries earned more through contract research than through any other category of activity (USA – 40.3%; UK – 33.3%).

A major source of funds for the firms' R&D projects came from R&D partnerships. These are the expensive, long-term projects involving development of the biotechnology company's proprietary products to which it generally retains some of the rights, and from which it expects eventually to generate its main earnings stream. The external partner takes most rights in the eventual product in exchange for providing a substantial part of the finance for the project, and may also formally contribute some marketing and other expertise to the deal.

Contract research also provided some support. For the UK firms, probably because they were younger on average, this was an important source of R&D finance for 40% of respondents, compared with only 22% of US firms (see Table 4.3).

Other differences are highlighted by the methods the companies used for financing their R&D activities. For example, a greater proportion of UK firms used venture capital finance than did US firms (see Table 4.3). Both US and UK companies funded a large proportion of R&D through partnerships. Limited partnerships were until recently a tax-effective vehicle for investment in USA companies, usually in specific projects.

Table 4.3: *Methods for financing R&D activities*

	USA		UK	
	f	%	f	%
R&D partnership	37/49	75.5	12/15	80.0
Public share offering	39/49	79.6	4/15	26.7
Venture capital	16/49	32.7	9/15	60.0
Product sales	13/49	26.5	5/15	33.3
Contract work	11/49	22.4	6/15	40.0
Limited partnerships	12/49	24.5	0/15	0.0
Private shares	5/49	10.2	2/15	13.3

Although now less fiscally-favoured, they are still an attractive vehicle for external investment in risky projects. The limited partners contribute only finance, while the general partner (the biotechnology company) contributes the technological or other expertise and carries out the project. The general partner has the option to buy back full rights for a preset price at a later date. These independent sources of finance not only increase the total amount available for R&D, they also restrict the potential of large company partners to control the smaller partner, by reducing their proportionate importance to the financial viability of the small company.

Ninety per cent of all the respondent firms reported that they were seeking R&D partnerships. The same proportion at the time of the survey, or previous to it, had had experience of R&D partnerships, and 82% had had experience with established pharmaceutical and/or chemical companies. Most of the firms' partnerships were with established drug companies and university groups, but there was also a strong tendency towards partnering with other biotechnology firms and research institutes (see Table 4.4). The results were reasonably comparable for both US and UK companies, except that UK companies appeared to have substantially more partnerships with other biotechnology firms. The firms were also asked to quantify their partnerships, and the median value for the number of partners was also similar. For example, biotechnology companies generally had two partnerships with established drug companies, and agreements with about four different university groups.

The establishment and management of partnerships

When asked to list what resources firms used to identify potential partners, all of the firms surveyed relied on the personal knowledge of people in their own organisation. A similar question in the KPMG (1993) survey also found that personal networking was the most important method. The firms ranked these internal resources as the most helpful in identifying partners. Also highly ranked was attendance at conferences and other meetings. Firms who had used outside consultant and on-line services judged these resources to be of the least use to firms looking for potential corporate partners. Overall, personal contact was seen as the most effective method for initiation of R&D partnership agreements.

Table 4.4: *Biotech firms' types of partners in R&D collaborations*

	USA	UK
Drug companies	81.8%	92.9%
(frequency)	(36/44)	(13/14)
Median no. of partners	2	3
Universities	70.5%	78.6%
(frequency)	(31/44)	(11/14)
Median no. of partners	4	4
Biotech firms	50.0%	71.4%
(frequency)	(22/44)	(10/14)
Median no. of partners	1	2
Research institutes	47.7%	35.7%
(frequency)	(21/44)	(5/14)
Median no. of partners	2	2

Table 4.5: *Management problems in R&D partnerships*

	USA		UK	
	f	%	f	%
Different time scales	31/40	77.5	7/13	53.8
Different priorities	28/40	70.0	6/13	46.2
Poor communication	16/40	40.0	9/13	69.2
Geographical distance	14/40	35.0	9/13	69.2
Lack of feedback	14/40	35.0	6/13	46.2
Contract problems	11/40	27.5	6/13	46.2
Changes over time	11/40	27.5	8/13	61.5
e.g. Stategic changes	2/40	5.0	3/13	23.1
e.g. Personnel changes	3/40	7.5	2/13	15.4

In the day-to-day management of R&D collaborations, the most frequently encountered difficulties were those of different time scales and different priorities between the two partner organisations (see Table 4.5). A number of firms wrote that personnel changes in the large partner organisation were particularly disruptive to management of the partnership. Once again, this stresses the importance of personal communication in the management of these strategic alliances, also a finding of the KPMG study. It also underlines the point that effective communication between different organisations cooperating in complex projects is mediated by individual relationships, developed over a period of time. Contract problems figured more with the UK than the US firms, perhaps due to their lesser experience. The KPMG (1993) survey indicated that detailed coverage of management issues and responsibilities in the original agreement was a key to successful partnership.

Almost all of the firms surveyed stated that they rely on both frequent contact between the partners and also the designation of a special management team in order to help make the partnership work (see Table 4.6).

In both the USA and the UK, 'frequent contact' was similarly defined: the majority of American and British firms had weekly telephone contact and quarterly meetings with their corporate partners (see Tables 4.7 and 4.8).

Internal correlation of responses showed that firms that indicated 'lack of feedback' as a common problem in the management of R&D partnerships had less frequent telephone contact with partners than did firms who did not find lack of feedback a problem. Table 4.7 shows that in the total sample of respondent firms, weekly telephone contact was most common (54.2%), with about 40% of the firms making bi-monthly telephone calls to partner firms. Of those firms that indicated they had a problem with lack of feedback, 40% made weekly calls and 59.1% made bi-monthly calls. Of the firms who did not

Table 4.6: *How biotech firms' partnerships work*

	USA		UK	
	f	%	f	%
Frequent contact	37/40	92.5	13/13	100.0
Special mgmnt team	34/40	85.0	11/13	84.6
Maintain informal links	27/40	67.5	10/13	76.9
Keep own personnel informed	17/40	42.5	8/13	61.5
Financial resources	10/40	25.0	5/13	38.5

Table 4.7: *Frequency of telephone contact between partners*

	USA		UK	
	f	%	f	%
Weekly	20/40	50.0	8/13	61.5
Bi-monthly	18/40	45.0	4/13	30.8
Daily	3/40	7.5	2/13	15.4
Varies	1/40	2.5	1/13	7.7

Table 4.8: *Frequency of meetings between partners*

	USA		UK	
	f	%	f	%
Quarterly	29/40	72.5	8/13	61.5
Monthly	9/40	22.5	3/13	23.1
Varies	2/40	5.0	2/13	15.4
Yearly	2/40	5.0	0/13	0.0

indicate lack of feedback as a problem, 62.2% made weekly calls and 29.7% made bi-monthly calls. Thus if telephone contact is more frequent (weekly rather than bi-monthly), lack of feedback may be less likely to be a problem.

Channels of communication

Contact between the biotechnology firm and the larger partner took place across a broad interface which routinely involved most groups within the smaller firm, and several within the project team of the larger firm, as well as some contact with senior management (see Tables 9 and 10). This breadth of contact was also found to be important by the KPMG study.

CONCLUSIONS

The US respondent companies, in terms of age, proportion publicly-quoted and number of employees corresponded to the larger and longer-established companies in Burrill's (1989) study. Since few of them have reached profitability yet, they are consequently among the more successful companies in the industry in their ability to inspire

Table 4.9: *Telephone contact and meetings: participants from the biotech firm*

	USA		UK	
	f	%	f	%
Senior management	35/40	87.5	13/13	100.0
Project leaders	38/40	95.0	13/13	100.0
Staff scientists	30/40	75.0	8/13	61.5
Technicians	13/40	32.5	5/13	38.5
Marketing	8/40	20.0	4/13	30.8

Table 4.10: *Telephone contact and meetings: participants from the pharmaceutical company*

	USA		UK	
	f	%	f	%
Senior management	26/40	65.0	11/13	84.6
Project leaders	39/40	97.5	13/13	100.0
Staff scientists	33/40	82.5	10/13	76.9
Technicians	10/40	25.0	4/13	30.8
Marketing	9/40	22.5	3/13	23.1

confidence, since they have obtained correspondingly more finance from their corporate partners and investors. For most companies in this sector which are undertaking major long-term product developments, this ability is still the only measure by which their success can be judged. However, since inspiring confidence in R&D partners is an essential prerequisite for success by any other criteria, it is of considerable significance.

The UK respondent companies showed the expected differences from US companies. The peak year for new company creation was six years later than in the USA, they had about half as many employees, and they were more dependent on minor product sales and contract work to generate revenue, in the absence of an easily accessible public equity market.

Apart from these characteristics however, they are surprisingly similar to the US respondents. The criterion of selection, that they were developing therapeutics, ensures that most regarded this as their main, long-term business, and R&D partnerships are essential in both countries for these lengthy and expensive projects. However, the similarity in numbers of corporate and academic partners in the two groups indicates a high degree of similarity in the way they (have been able to) structure their development.

Personal contact

In terms of their approaches to setting up and managing partnerships, they were also very similar. A very strong emphasis was placed on the importance of personal contact and individual relationships. This confirms data collected from biotechnology companies in the UK and USA in in-depth interviews carried out by the authors (in preparation) and was mirrored in the views expressed by large pharmaceutical company R&D managers in the same study. It also echoes the findings of Hull and Slowinski (1990) for both large and small company partners in the US biotechnology and electronics industries.

Continuity was an important feature, with changes in the communicating personnel constituting a problem. This implies that individual relationships are important, with all that this signifies – the time taken to establish common ground and trust, shared language, knowledge of the other's concerns, personal commitment to the project. It implies that the success of communication depends not just on the understanding of the other corporation's aims, but on the shared membership of a project team of individuals from both, who have created a team identity of their own. Hull and Slowinski (1990) report that the average size of their small firms was 74 employees of which 32% were dedicated to the partnership. They interacted with a subunit of the large firm which had 54 people on average, of whom 17% were dedicated to the project. Thus there was a fair degree of symmetry in terms of the human commitment to the projects they studied. As with the current study, there was a broad interface between the firms, with communication involving most individuals although with varying frequency.

Frequency of communication

In the current study UK and US biotechnology companies showed similar patterns of communication in terms of breadth and frequency. Interestingly, both used the word 'frequent' with the same meaning in real time. This was unexpected – that two such different national work cultures should give rise to a similar definition. It suggests that the nature of the task is driving the perception. Hull and Slowinski showed that US large firms also rated frequent multifunctional communication highly, especially when they had a high rate of internal interfunctional communication, usually weekly. However, the current study also showed that more than half of the management problems in the partnership were ascribed to 'different timescales' (see Table 4.5). This suggests that the difference may be created not so much by differences in perception of appropriate rates of individual response between the interacting units in the two firms, but rather by the unit in the large firm having to deal with many other layers in its organisation.

While the analysis of the data collected in this survey indicates that higher levels of contact between partners are associated with a lower level of project problems, the numbers are not great enough nor were the questions phrased in a way which would clarify whether the optimal levels of contact were reached. Would greater satisfaction have been achieved with more daily contact? Studies of project management in other industries indicate that informal daily contact between organisations was beneficial, although only between a few key individuals (Kezsbom et al, 1989). It is not clear here whether different types of project determine the optimal frequency, or whether we are dealing with a fundamental characteristic of human communication. If the latter, we would expect that the optimal frequency of contact for any complex project would be the same.

The purpose of communication

Doheny-Farina (1992) has argued that technology transfer processes are highly rhetorical – 'individuals and groups negotiate their visions of technologies and their applications'. This description applies rather well to the process of negotiating and managing an R&D partnership in biotechnology. At the start the small company must convey to the large company potential partner a vision of what a little-understood and risky technology can achieve, in terms of products and processes. Since at present there are few products on the market using technologies in this category, and individual small companies have very limited track records, there is little apart from this vision to capture the interest of the large company.

After the partnership is set up, the smaller partner must continue to communicate how progress towards this vision is being achieved and to maintain credibility and interest through the ups and downs of the development process. Even where there is a contractual commitment to fund the process to completion, it is important that the large partner is able to take the novel technology in-house at this point, and this requires that the preparations have been made in adequate knowledge of the technology. Thus the continuing communication between the partners serves not only to communicate specific bits of information about progress, but also transfers fundamental knowledge of the developing technology – what it can do, its limitations, conditions which affect performance, the wider basis of these conclusions in previous empirical and theoretical work, and so on – a whole context of knowledge and expertise. Not least, it must maintain the ongoing commitment and interest of the larger partner. This is needed if the large partner is to make preparations to share in the ultimate marketing of the technology. Thus the process of transferring the technology is very much a phenomenon of communication (Ginn & Rubinstein, 1986), not just the dispatch of a test tube or package containing the completed construct or product. The large firm must receive a coherent body of knowledge and insight into the processes leading to the production of the subject of the collaboration, which gives it a wider body of skills and understanding to use itself.

What does the smaller firm receive? Hull and Slowinski report that in US partnerships both partners perceive that partnerships in which both firms contribute actively to many aspects of the project are more successful than those in which the large partner is either overdominant or very uninvolved. As individuals in both firms struggle to find a common language sufficient for such a wide purpose, they have to mutually communicate much of their own industrial and scientific experience, values etc. For any individual, precise meaning of a statement is dependent on past experience, and to communicate this meaning some of the context of past experience must also be transmitted to the recipient. Each communication between the partners will have a specific, project-related content which it is the overt objective of the contact to transmit. However, this datum must be embedded in the context of 'common language' developed by the individuals from the two organisations and their joint project management group to ensure correct interpretation. Consequently much other knowledge must be transmitted informally with it. Thus both parties internalise a great deal of knowledge about the other which can be drawn on in the future. Both learn empirically how, from their own position, to communicate effectively with members of the other type of organisation, and how to become more like the other where desirable.

The role of the small company as interpreter

This leads on to a wider question. What exactly does the small company contribute which could not be more cheaply carried out through a direct collaboration between the university scientists who initially developed the technology and the large company? Communication problems may be the key to understanding this apparent anomaly. The rhetorical core of technology transfer (Doheny-Farina, 1992) requires a volume and sophistication of communication which could only take place between partners which share a sufficient degree of common experience and language from the start, and strong motives to increase it. University-based science groups and conventional companies notoriously each have difficulties in achieving an adequate understanding of the priorities and values of the other party (reviewed in Bower, 1992). There are some regions where there is common ground. One is where company scientists want to keep in touch with advances in their field through seminar contact or other general contact. This is, in effect, a continuing professional training function. Another is where a specific piece of scientific investigation is needed by the company, and a university scientist has special expertise in this area.

University laboratories are not, however, a good environment for developing products or processes to the marketplace. The academics' roles as basic scientists and communicators are incompatible with the demands for total commitment to the application of research and to confidentiality in commercial development. When a company requires very novel technology and there is no in-house expertise, a corporate development partner with the necessary expertise is a more practical choice. Indeed, when asked during an interview, a senior R&D manager of a Swiss pharmaceutical company which has many major R&D collaborations stated that for his firm, academic collaborations were only possible when there was corresponding in-house expertise, whereas if there was no in-house skill in a desired technology, a small company partner was sought (Bower and Whittaker, 1993).

But if companies and basic science are incompatible, how is it feasible for the small company to relate to the basic science lab? In the case of the biotechnology companies, some proprietary knowledge and expertise resides in the small company, but the technology is usually so close to the basic science bench that development needs some continuing input from the science base. The spinout biotechnology company is an intermediary organisation, whose technology is still close to the basic science, but whose mission and organisation is commercial. It retains close personal and professional links with university scientists who may often have retained some rights to the technology, and non-executive positions in the company. It has, therefore, an established relationship with the academic scientists whose input is still necessary for the successful completion of the innovation. On the other hand, it is a company, evolving away from an academic perspective and eventually drawing managers from a large company background. Its full-time personnel are totally committed to its projects, unlike its academic consultants and non-executive directors whose prior commitments to, for example, taking a class in half an hour, or publishing research results as quickly as possible, may take precedence over a demand for help from a company. As a commercial organisation the biotechnology company shares the large company's desire to get products to market and generate revenue. It lies between the university and the large company, at a distance from both but close enough to communicate effectively with either, and thus to act as an interpreter which can transform and transmit knowledge relatively easily.

The small company with intimate links to the science base and managers from industry is conversant with the different languages of the groups which are essential to the invention and marketing of new technology. It can bridge the communication gap between the science base and the large company during the crucial period of product innovation. It has other important roles – as risk-sharer who must communicate effectively with independent investors, carry out much of the development work, and play the lead role of project manager. However, its unique role, shared with spinout companies in other industries, may be that of interpreter. As an intermediary it generates transaction costs for the other participants in innovation. But in the absence of this transforming and interpreting function which allows technology to be transferred across a cultural communication gap, no transaction is likely to take place which will lead to a successful innovative outcome.

ACKNOWLEDGMENTS

Thanks are due to Professor Ken Murray of Edinburgh University and Biogen NV, for invaluable advice and discussions, to Dr Ken Lyall of Walter Scott and Partners for company information, to the managers of biotechnology firms for completing questionnaires, and to the Leverhulme Trust of Great Britain which funded this study.

REFERENCES

BOWER, D. J. (1992) Company and Campus Partnership, *Supporting Technology Transfer*, Routledge, London.

BOWER, D. J. and WHITTAKER, E. (1993) The Golden Triangle: Strategic trends in pharmaceutical product development, *European Business and Economic Development*, Vol. 2, pp. 20-4.

BURRILL, G. S. WITH THE ERNST & YOUNG HIGH TECHNOLOGY GROUP (1989) *Biotech 90: into the Next Decade*, Mary Ann Liebert, Inc., New York.

COHEN, S. N., CHANG, A. C. Y., BOYER, H. W., and HELLING, R. B. (1973) Construction of biologically-functional plasmids in vitro, *Proceedings of the National Academy of Sciences of the USA*, Vol. 70, pp. 3240-61.

DOHENY-FARINA, S. (1989) A case-study of an adult writing in academic and non-academic settings, in C. Matalene (ed.) *Worlds of Writing: teaching and learning in discourse communities at work*, Random House, New York.

DOHENY-FARINA, S. (1992) *Rhetoric, Innovation and Technology, Case Studies of Technical Communication in Technology Transfers*, MIT Press, Cambridge, Mass.

GENETIC ENGINEERING NEWS (1991) *Guide to Biotechnology Companies*, Mary Ann Liebert, Inc, New York.

GINN, M. E. and RUBINSTEIN, A. H. (1986) The R&D/production interface: a case study of new product commercialisation, *Journal of Product Innovation Management*, Vol. 3, pp. 158-70.

HULL, F. and SLOWINSKI, E. (1990) Partnering with technology entrepreneurs, *Research – Technology Management*, November/December, pp. 16-20.

KENNEY, M. (1986) *Biotechnology: the University/Industrial Complex*, Yale University Press, New Haven and London.

KEZSBOM, D. S., SCHILLING, D. L. and EDWARD, K. A. (1989) *Dynamic Project Management*, Wiley, New York.

KÖHLER, G. and MILSTEIN, C. (1975) Continuous cultures of fused cells secreting antibody predetermined specificity, *Nature*, Vol. 256, pp. 495-97.

KPMG (1993) *Corporate Alliances: Strategies in Biotechnology*, KPMG Peat Marwick Health and Life Sciences Practice, New York.

OAKEY, R., FAULKNER, W., COOPER, S. and WALSH, V. (1990) *New Firms in the Biotechnology Industry*, Frances Pinter, London.

PAPADOPOULOS, S. (1992) *Biotechnology: an Industry Review*, July, PaineWebber Inc., New York.

CHAPTER 5

Taxonomy of Management Attitudes towards Bootlegging, Uncertainty

PETER AUGSDORFER

THE ILLUSION OF MANAGEABILITY

This paper discusses the phenomenon of bootlegging in industrial firms through the attitude of management towards innovation. The traditional assumption in the literature is, that innovation is under the direct control of management within a company (Lewin, 1951; Peters and Waterman, 1982). Their ability to instigate, plan and direct all forms of innovation has been taken for granted, creating a present-day misinterpretation appropriately termed 'the illusion of manageability' which implies that innovation is capable of being directly influenced by those possessing organisational authority (Anderson, 1992).

Bootlegging is a special type of the 'bottom-up' innovation because it is covert research and certainly not under the direct control of management. Our research showed that in over 75% of the investigated laboratories in new technology-based firms, bootlegging is being carried out.

Surprisingly it has never received much attention in existing innovation literature, although well known as a phenomenon in new product innovation. The phenomenon of bootlegging can be investigated from several different points of view. The most important ones are the organisational, the management, and the researcher. The organisational point of view considers the availability of resources for innovation. The researcher's point of view includes the incentives for carrying out bootlegging that reflect his personal nature. However, in this article, stress is placed on the managerial decision process concerning the acceptance of an innovative idea, and its influences on bootlegging, well knowing that all the above factors are not completely separable from each other.

In the first section, we will briefly define innovation, the function of research and bootlegging in industrial firms. In the second section we will describe the methodology used to obtain data. The third section discusses the results obtained with regard to the phenomenon of bootlegging. The fourth section explains the decision process with regard to innovation uncertainties, and by using these insights, in the fifth section we develop a taxonomy of management attitudes towards bootlegging and uncertainty.

DEFINITION OF BOOTLEGGING[1]

The existing literature defines innovation using terms that differ widely. This paper adopts an approach which envisages innovation as an emergent process in work settings in accordance with Anderson:

Innovation is the emergence, import or imposition of new ideas which are pursued towards implementation.

This definition points out two major functions of innovation research (Anderson, 1993).

In reaction to environmental changes R&D has to propose innovations to management. In a highly dynamic technology, where product life cycles are getting shorter and shorter, R&D has to monitor technology and react quickly. This enables the 'survival' of the company in volatile environmental conditions.

R&D has to solve the technical problems of an innovation, thus reducing the technological uncertainty of an innovation process.

Our definition of bootlegging is based on the existing literature (Knight, 1967; Shepard, 1967; Gleicher, 1967; Burgelman, 1986; Owen, 1990; Roussel et al., 1992) and incorporates the dimension of formal secrecy.[2] Although, quite often, the majority of members of a company may informally know of its existence, formal recognition of bootlegging projects is lacking. It is research in which motivated individuals secretly organise the innovation process. In other words, such activities do not appear on project sheets drawn up by the management of firms. In this sense, every innovative action taken by a researcher outside the formal budgetary planning of the firm, or every abuse of budgets allocated to other projects, is considered to be bootlegging. Our definition of bootlegging might be criticised because it considers also pre-production stages of products. In fact, quite a number of bootleg projects have their origins in pre-production small experiments, and the time of revealing them depends on intra-company circumstances which include the motivation of the researcher, availability of slack, and the relationship with the boss.

CASE STUDY APPROACH

With the help of case studies in 24 British new technology-based firms we tried to establish a number of contingencies between the decision to bootleg and factors influencing it. To obtain detailed information on bootleg activities, confidence between the researcher and the interviewer had to be established. Therefore we chose a qualitative approach which permitted us to obtain information about the structural situation and about non-factual subjects, like feelings and attitudes.

Interviews were conducted in most of the cases on two levels: the R&D management and researcher levels. The reason for this was less a cross check of information than additional information and deeper insights of the two actors and their universe. Special attention was paid to the time lapse between the date of the case and interview. General information about frequency of bootlegging over time according to the experience of the interviewee was obtained. In addition, relevant general information like annual reports etc. was collected to complete information about organisational concerns like level of hierarchy or strategy. As an interview method, we used a semi-structured questionnaire to have both sufficient liberty and the assurance not to leave out any important factors. We were interested in the main influencing factors. New information found in interviews was added to the questionnaire.

The companies were selected according to the following main criteria:

- We looked for research intensive companies, because the assumption was that greater levels of research activity would be associated with the phenomenon.
- The company should have a high degree of separation of functions in terms of organisational structure. For example, if the owner and researcher is the same person then, by definition, bootlegging is not possible. The assumption was that a highly structured organisation favours the phenomenon; thus larger new technology-based companies were preferred.

- To show contingencies between bootlegging and differing technologies, the sample contained companies active in different fields (e.g. software, telecommunication, electronics, chemicals, engineering). Different technologies are related to different technological and market uncertainty, resource investment, product size, and research methods, which can cause bootlegging for different reasons.

THE PHENOMENON OF BOOTLEGGING

Importance of bootlegging

In 19 of the 24 cases we found bootlegging carried out in laboratories. Of these 19 cases, in one case bootlegging was formally organised, we were introduced to 10 bootleg-products, and 8 laboratories confirmed its existence without naming a product. In 5 cases we could not find confirmation of bootlegging, but it may have existed.

On average between 5 and 10% of the researchers in a laboratory were carrying out bootlegging, whilst in one case the proportion was 50%. The hyper-creative people, who bring the majority of the bottom-up ideas, are the bootleg researchers. They spend on average between 5 and 20% of their time bootlegging, although in some cases this can be 100% for short periods. In most of the cases bootlegging is carried out during a short intensive period and not for a regular percentage of each day. Bootlegging was mainly funded with slack resources, which accounted for 20% of bootlegging time, or it was carried out in the worker's own time. The importance of slack in equipment and material resources in this bootlegging process is negligible because the amount of physical assets required is not very high, and can usually be obtained through other channels that cannot be controlled (e.g. free materials from suppliers).

Purpose of bootleg-innovation

Table 5.1 shows the extent to which bootlegging meets the research needs of a firm, and in how many laboratories it was found. The classification considers different intentions and activities of the researcher.

A quick experiment is defined as verification that an idea works or fails in practice. A preparation of a proposal is bootlegging to show levels of technology and market uncertainty, with some forecasts of cost/benefit, return on investment, etc. The novel product is defined as a prototype of a future product. However, no case was found where bootlegging had reached the production stage. Pre-research for objectives is carried out to verify in advance that objectives can be met at the end of the planning period. In 16% of cases, the bootleg activity had only scientific use. However, the distinctions between these classifications are not rigid, because they are often interrelated. But as our results show, the general purpose of bootleg-innovation is the same for researcher and company. It is clearly directed towards new product innovation. 'A

Table 5.1: *Importance of purpose*

PURPOSE OF BOOTLEG PRODUCT	NUMBER OF LABORATORIES (%)
Quick experiment to show feasibility	100%
Preparation of proposal	95%
Prototype	53%
Pre-research/objectives	53%
Only scientific use	16%

researcher wants to see his ideas realised, the company offers the possibilities for doing it,' as one researcher described the situation. The value of scientific experiments is dependant upon the company's attitude towards learning. Concordance between researcher and manager about the purpose of a specific innovation has to be decided from case to case.

As product innovation is important for the future of a company, and following the definition by Mintzberg (Mintzberg et al, 1976), the decision for it to take place is even regarded as strategic, we want to examine more closely the origin of this dual rationality. According to our findings, the inherent uncertainty in the innovation process is a key variable with regard to the different attitudes of management and researcher in new product innovation.

UNCERTAINTY AND DECISION PROCESS

Every innovation process is connected with uncertainty. The sources of uncertainty in innovation are widely discussed in the literature (Freeman,1982; Gleicher, 1967; Schon, 1967; Roussel, et al., 1992; Archambault, 1992). It includes the overall uncertainty of profit or general business activity, which is the uncertainty associated with how to react to environmental change, and the specific uncertainty of innovation which is the uncertainty of feasibility of technological development expressed in the unpredictability of development costs and outcomes and the uncertainty of market success.

To investigate this uncertainty we adopted the classification developed by Pearson (Pearson, 1990). The criteria used by him to classify uncertainty are the ability to define technology and market as well as the ability to specify technical or market parameters and identification of new applications.

According to our findings, most bootleg activities were carried out to reduce technological uncertainties. 'We put a handle on the core functions of the innovation' one researcher stated. Uncertainty is difficult to measure, but one of our assumptions was that bootleg products should be 'obviously' more radical and therefore more uncertain than 'normal research projects'. In other words a higher uncertainty was seen as a likely rejection reason. Surprisingly, such a striking difference of uncertainty in comparison with 'normal' projects could not be found. Therefore we infer that the technological uncertainty is perceived in relation to the available budget. A budget consists of commitments to current developments according to the planning and some resources for new ('bottom-up') product development. When the budget is already planned for other commitments, a proposed bootleg innovation has to fit with its uncertainty within the remaining available formal budget for other activities. In other words, the tighter the budget, the higher the perceived technological uncertainty for bootlegging. There is rarely unallocated budget because 'money has to work', as a manager explained, 'We have to squeeze it in somehow.' This means that the higher the chances that budget flexibility leaves space for a new product, the lower the uncertainty with regard to the bootlegging process.

It has to be accepted that, naturally, every innovation in its early stage contains a higher uncertainty than innovations in full development. The definitions of 'low' or 'high' uncertainty are not rigorous. Each is determined by the specifics of company culture, strategies, environment and product design.

Another interesting finding was that in the early innovation process, market uncertainty is less important as a decision criteria to start bootlegging. In other words, the researcher would not stop innovating simply because he could not see a prior market for his product. Three reasons for this behaviour are likely. Firstly, it is not possible to predict a future market success accurately. Secondly, most bootleg projects are within the technological trajectory of the firm and incremental in nature. Thirdly, uncertainty is a function of investment. The more invested in a research project, the higher the inherent uncertainty. Bootlegging, in general, is very low budget research. The formal investment equals zero, 'Therefore we could give it a try, we can't lose!' as one researcher expressed it.

We can conclude, therefore, that firstly management is generally averse to risk and prefers incremental innovations. Secondly, a tightly planned annual budget leaves only limited flexibility to integrate non-programmed innovation proposals. Both facts lead to an increased chance of accepting incremental instead of radical proposals.

Due to their experience, researchers have a relatively clear idea about the 'acceptance threshold' for research budgets for innovation proposals. Therefore they reduce the costs by proceeding under cover until the project fits into the annual budget. Freeman (1982) states that 'Uncertainty can be greatly reduced through experimental development and trial production stages.' In other words by innovating. Thus, bootlegging is anticipating management behaviour. But how does management react when it finds out?

TAXONOMY OF MANAGEMENT ATTITUDES

According to our findings, the attitude of management towards bootlegging is mainly dependent on our understanding of the bootleg innovation process and its perceived uncertainty. It is well known that we can find two main levels of organisation in a company: the formal organisation and the informal organisation. The attitudes can be classified into five different types: four types according to the formal and informal acceptance of bootlegging and one additional type characterised through indecisiveness towards it.

Formal and informal rejection of bootlegging (i)

Managers are in favour of the transparent organisation where researchers immediately declare findings or ideas. The desired process of early innovation takes place in a 'Cartesian' way (Sfez, 1981): the researcher has an idea (mental), he discusses it with his boss, the boss or a decision committee takes a decision and then follows the execution of the research or innovation project (materialisation).

The uncertainties of the process are easy to control by management, because it is a linear process, the transparency avoids unwanted changes of priorities, and a decision system is established to foster good ideas. No positive value of bootlegging is recognised. Bootlegging is believed to waste resources and synergy effects cannot be integrated from the early beginning. Especially in recent management literature bootlegging is criticised very negatively (Roussel et al., 1992).

Formal rejection, but informal acceptance of bootlegging (ii)

Management is characterised by a formal rejection of bootlegging, but on an informal level the responsible manager either actively encourages it or ignores it intentionally by

Table 5.2: *Management attitudes towards bootlegging*

	FORMAL REJECTION	FORMAL ACCEPTANCE
Informal rejection	(i)	(iv)
Informal acceptance	(ii)	(iii)
and indecisivness		
(v)		

'closing his eyes'. In over 50% of the laboratories we found this 'schizophrenic' attitude. The formal organisation is adequate for management of the majority of innovation cases and the exceptions are allowed in the form of bootlegging.

Within the bootleg process, management control is not directly possible, but is controlled by mutual trust. The positive value of bootlegging is informally recognised. It is a solution to the innovation dilemma and the decision process. The dual rationality is wanted as a source for new ideas un-filtered by company constraints. The uncertainty of bootlegging is controlled because it is considered as an exception.

Formal and informal acceptance (iii)

We have to distinguish between three different cases: (a) in companies which have formally established bootlegging (permitted bootlegging) to a certain percentage (10-15%), (b) in free research and (c) as a quick experiment.

(a) In these companies, within certain limits, the manager does not want to control the early innovation process directly. The researcher can reduce technological uncertainty and a different rationality is regarded as a source for innovation. The possibility of winning support for the idea in a formal way selects ideas in a 'Darwinistic' manner. Only the best ideas get support by the company. Management relies on the company's values and culture as a way of control. We find a strong identification with the company and the company's culture and strategy which aims to create a mental funnel for new innovations, in other words a pre-selection of the innovative direction by the researcher himself. However, it has to be pointed out that there is strong psychological pressure to 'come up' with a successful product once a researcher starts permitted bootlegging. If the innovation fails, the researcher feels guilty at having wasted time (maybe not if it is the first time, but certainly if it happens more often).

An additional uncertainty is that, according to my findings, only 10-20% of the researchers are carrying out covert research even when they have the possibility. For equality reasons everybody has the right to take permitted bootlegging time. The company accepts that people using the time may not be innovating, but going to conferences and engaging in further education.

(b) The researcher determines to a large extent the content of the innovation process. Management controls the uncertainty in the following way: only persons who have already been successful are chosen for free research. The researcher, because he has got a track-record of very good innovations, is permitted to follow up other interests. This stresses the individual person. The probability of continuing success is assumed.

(c) Quick experiments can be carried out without declaring them to management. 'It is part of the job,' as a manager explained. Uncertainty is accepted within the frame of a quick experiment. The extent to which the company allows quick experiments to be carried out is dependent on the understanding of a quick experiment. This is often a blurred area because it is not and it can not be formulated in directives. This is dependent on the firm's culture and the borders are movable according to who is doing it and what kind of innovation is carried out.

Formal acceptance and informal rejection (iv)

In these companies we find bootlegging formally accepted but not realised. Officially, the manager encourages bootlegging. At the same time he reduces the uncertainty by giving the researcher more work and objectives than he can meet. So if a researcher has new ideas he has to carry out research in his spare time. At the same time it is recommended that overtime be worked. As a result of this pressure, the researcher has no choice. Proposals cannot be pursued under cover, but only within the formal planning. Choice is a farce, especially as the situation is often backed up by an incentive scheme (in the form of a reward) to meet the formal objectives. The manager is, therefore, pretending to accept bootlegging.

Formal and informal indecisiveness (v)

The manager as well as the organisation has no opinion for or against bootlegging. On the one side they know about the uncertainties, on the other they know about the positive output and the necessity for researchers 'to spread their wings' as a manager expressed it. By being philosophical about it they remove themselves from taking responsibility for it. These managers are on the one hand frightened to destroy a good idea, and on the other hand frightened to act against the existing organisation. They hope that the uncertainties do not become too great and that there is at least some positive output. 'They don't want to know what is going on,' as a researcher said. Therefore they run no risk from their directors if something goes wrong. They accept no personal responsibility. But also the organisation gives no directives. Sometimes bootlegging is damned, sometimes the bootleg-researcher makes a successful career. Researchers are either frustrated because they feel insecure or happy because they can do bootlegging and realise their ideas.

CONCLUSION

To summarise, bootlegging exists as a phenomenon in a large number of companies. It is an outcome of a selection process that chooses 'less uncertain' bottom-up ideas. For the researcher bootlegging is a way by which he can realise his new ideas and also reduce the technological uncertainty associated with it through a demonstration. The attitudes of management towards bootlegging is determined by its contribution as a source for valuable innovation and control of uncertainty. An innovative corporate culture encourages bootlegging as a valuable source for competence building.

NOTES

1. 'Skunk work' is often misunderstood as bootlegging (especially with regard to the characteristic 'knowledge of management'). Peters (1988) used this notion in his book *Thriving on Chaos*, p. 205: skunk work was originated by C. L. Johnson at Lockheed in 1943. He defines it as a sort of élite, working on a project beside the formal organisation, but with the support of management, to solve problems more efficiently.
2. When we talk about bootlegging, we mean real covert bootlegging. Companies like 3M and Hewlett Packard allow researchers to carry out 'permitted bootlegging' which means they can spend 10% or 15% of their time for own product related interests.

REFERENCES

ANDERSON, N. (1993) Innovation in organisations, *International Review of Industrial and Organisational Psychology*, Vol. 8, edited by C. L. Cooper and I. T. Robertson, John Wiley, New York.

ANDERSON, N. (1992) *Organizational Change and Innovation*, Routledge, London.

ARCHAMBAULT, E. (1992) Small is beautiful, large is powerful: manufacturing semiconductors in South Korea, SPRU, unpublished MSc dissertation.

BURGELMAN, R. A (1986) *Inside Corporate Innovation*, Free Press, New York.

FREEMAN, C. (1982), *The Economics of Industrial Innovation*, p. 149, Pinter, London.

GLEICHER, D. (1967) in R. Hainer, D. Arthur and C. Little, *Uncertainty in Research Management and New Product Development*, Reinhold Publishing, New York.

KNIGHT, K. E. (1967) A descriptive model of the intra-firm innovation process, *The Journal of Business*, Vol. 40, p. 485.

LEWIN, K. (1951) *Field Theory in Social Science*, Harper and Row, New York.

MINTZBERG, H. *et al.* (1976) The structure of 'unstructured' decision processes, *Administrative Science Quarterly*, Vol. 21, pp. 246-75.

OWEN, H. (1990) *Leaders*, Abott Publishing, USA.

PEARSON, A. W. (1990) Innovation strategy, *Technovation*, Vol. 10, no. 3, Elsevier.

PETERS, T. J. and WATERMAN, R. H. (1982) *In Search of Excellence*, Harper and Row, New York.

PETERS, T. J. (1988) *Thriving on Chaos*, p. 205, Macmillan, London.

ROUSSEL, P. A. *et al.* (1992) *Third Generation of R&D*, Harvard Business School Press, Boston.

SCHON, D. (1967) Fears of innovation, *Research Management and New Product Development*, Reinhold Publishing, USA.

SFEZ, L. (1981) *Critique de la Décision*, Presses de la Fondation Nationale des Sciences Politiques.

SHEPARD, H. A. (1967) Innovation-resisting and innovation-producing organizations, *The Journal of Business*, Vol. 40.

ZALTMAN, G., DUNCAN, R. and HOLBEK, J. (1973) *Innovations and Organizations*, p. 10, John Wiley, New York.

CHAPTER 6

Sources of Technological Innovative Ideas and their Significance for Commerical Outcomes in Small Companies

SALLY CAIRD

INTRODUCTION

There is surprisingly little research on how innovators in small high-technological companies produce their innovative ideas. This paper is based on the results of both
qualitative and quantitative interviews which were conducted with twenty four winners
of the U.K. Government sponsored Small Firms Merit Award for Research and Technology (SMART) scheme. This research explored the perceptions of SMART winners
on the nature of invention and innovation as a creative process; the sources of innovative ideas, including their importance for commercial outcomes; and the conditions
responsible for the commercial success of innovative projects.

Although there is a considerable literature available in psychology and sociology on
creativity, many of the issues raised are only indirectly relevant to understanding innovation as a creative process within the company. For example, arguments that creativity is
associated with heredity, neurosis or well being offer few insights into technological innovation and how it may be fostered within the small-medium sized enterprise (SME). The
need to understand innovation in the context of entrepreneurship and the smaller firm is
evident from the importance attributed, by the economist Schumpeter, to innovation as
the primary entrepreneurial function (Schumpeter, 1950). This paper provides some
insight on the following concerns, of importance to the high tech SME associated with:

- understanding innovation as a creative activity within the SME;
- identifying sources of innovative ideas and the process of coming up with ideas;
- understanding the significance of innovative ideas for the commercial success of
  product innovation.

The main aim of this study was to explore innovators' perceptions of how they came up
with innovative ideas and how important innovative ideas are for commercial success
within the SME context. There have been previous attempts to address these issues.
Von Hippel's work on sources of innovative ideas shows that many innovative ideas
come from the user, the supplier or manufacturer, because these groups establish the
needs for ideas (Von Hippel, 1988). Drucker (1991) examined internal sources and
external organisational sources of innovation. The Open University's Design course
team classifies innovative ideas, according to their technological and conceptual source
and applications (Open University course T264, 1992).

Furthermore, there have been previous studies which have helped to establish the main factors for the commercial success of technological innovation (for example, Langrish et al., 1972; Freeman, 1986) and the innovative capacity of small, medium and large enterprises (Rothwell and Zegveld, 1982). However, there has been little research which encourages innovators to introspectively consider their perceptions of how they develop innovative ideas.

BACKGROUND TO THE SMART COMPETITION

The Small Firms Merit Award for Research and Technology (SMART) is a British competition supported by the Department of Trade and Industry (DTI). The SMART award is open to firms, with fewer than fifty employees, which are having difficulty in attracting funding for innovation. This scheme recognises the failure of market forces to support high-technology innovation as a result of the potential failure risks associated with innovation. It aims to encourage the formation of scientific and technological firms and help them to grow to a point where they are likely to attract financial support.

Twenty four SMART (Small firms Merit Award for Research and Technology) winners were interviewed in 1991. This represented a subset of thirty two Scottish SMART award winners for 1989 and 1990. Interviews were conducted with the collaboration of the Scottish Office, Industry Department. Structured interviewing was employed in this investigation, using both telephone and face-to-face approaches. The 24 innovators, representing companies with SMART awards could be described as follows:

NATIONALITY	23 British, 1 Australian
AGE	between 30–40 years, 12 participants
	between 40–50 years, 11 participants
	50+ years, 1 participant
GENDER	23 Male: 1 Female
EDUCATIONAL BACKGROUND	23 had experience of higher education:
	1 had GCSE qualification equivalent
STATUS IN THE COMPANY	18 owner managers: 5 managing directors:
	1 technical manager
PREVIOUS EXPERIENCE OF INNOVATION	All participants

Table 6.1: *Type of innovative projects*

TYPE OF INNOVATIVE PROJECT:	N	Rank
Computer software	4	3
Industrial and commercial products	4	3
High technological products	6	2
Medical/health care	7	1
Energy/natural resources	2	5
Property/construction	1	6
TOTAL	24	

N = number of participants

THE CONCEPTS OF INVENTION AND INNOVATION

The views of innovators in this study reflect recognised difficulties associated with defining and distinguishing between invention, creativity and innovation. Henry and Walker (1991, p.3) say: 'Creativity on its own is only a beginning. Human beings are relentlessly creative. Having ideas is relatively easy – having good ideas is slightly more difficult – but the real challenge lies in carrying ideas through into some practical result'. Rogers describes creativity as the emergence of a novel product through actions, emerging from the uniqueness of the individual and the materials, events, people or circumstances of their life (Rogers, 1954). In this way, creativity may describe a person, a process or a product. Invention is a similar concept, which may be defined as the conception of an idea (Twiss, 1992). However, invention as a description of the person, process or product is usually used in a more narrow way to apply to the conception of technical ideas: creativity is more broadly associated with music, painting, writing, thinking, being, relating and so on, and is not necessarily associated with things or products.

The term innovation is used in many ways, varying with the level of analysis used in research, so that the more macro the approach taken, the more the use of the term becomes varied and amorphous (West and Farr, 1990). However, effectiveness in communication is damaged if a term has several accepted meanings within a single topic of enquiry (Rickards et al., 1992). In the business organisational context, Kanter (1983, p.20) defines innovation as the '...process of bringing any new problem-solving idea into use.' Drucker (1991) maintains that innovation is the specific function of entrepreneurship because it is the means by which the entrepreneur either creates new wealth or endows existing resources with an enhanced wealth-creating potential.

The multiple definitions of creativity, invention and innovation suggest differing perspectives taken by academics as well as rather subtle distinctions between these concepts. A useful means of clarifying the situation lies in establishing how a group of people, in this case SMART innovators, who have won prizes for their innovative practices regard the processes and understand their own experiences. When participants were questioned about what the terms innovation and invention meant to them, it became evident that the concepts were difficult to define and were often substituted for each other. Clearly, the concepts of invention and innovation have similarities in their meaning as both involve novel developments. However, 50% of the participants found it difficult to distinguish between the concepts of invention and innovation and wondered if they are distinct processes or part of the same process.

However, most of the participants attempted to distinguish between invention and innovation. Descriptions of invention suggest that it is an original, technical and patentable process with no necessary commercial application (See Table 6.2). This accords with the description of invention by the Chartered Institute of Patents Agents as 'simply something new, something which has not been thought of before and which is not obvious'.

Table 6.2: *Description of invention*

CRITERIA	N
Originality	11 (46%)
Patentable process	3 (13%)
No necessary commercial application	2 (8%)
Technical	1 (4%)

N = number of participants

Table 6.3: *Description of invention*

CRITERIA	N
A development process	7 (29%)
Problem driven	3 (13%)
An application	4 (17%)
Commercial gain	4 (21%)

N = number of participants

There were interesting views offered by different individuals which suggested that they did not closely identify with inventors as a group. One participant said that invention has a bad name, often having an association with 'nutters' (sic). Another participant thought that invention was more of a university endeavour which involved 'beating back the frontiers of science'. Others thought that invention was 'history book stuff', referring to fundamental breakthroughs and that there are very few 'true inventors' around.

By contrast, innovation usually involves the application of something (new or in a new way) to solve a problem usually for commercial gain (See Table 6.3).

Commercial exploitation may represent a key difference between the ways invention and innovation are perceived. When an invention is carried towards commercial exploitation or makes some impact on society, it becomes part of an innovative process: without a commercial application of some kind it remains an invention. Drucker (1991, p. 17) states 'Above all, innovation is work rather than genius'. An innovative process which incorporates invention, involves the development of a new product or process from seed and then the development of applications for commercial gain (and sometimes more altruistic reasons).

Comments from some participants in this study suggest that invention and innovation are perceived as forming part of a gradual process rather than one involving distinct boundaries. One pointed out that it is not clear where innovation starts and invention stops. The results suggest that it may be conceptually difficult to separate the inventive from the innovative steps in the innovative process because innovation is a dynamic process which is unique in every project.

However, it was pointed out that innovation does not always have to incorporate invention. One participant described innovation as good engineering but then added that it is not essential to have a technical component, and can relate to anything from engineering to management. Invention is not necessarily a sub-category of innovation. Another participant said that 'innovation happens all the time and is very commonplace unlike invention which is much rarer'. In this way, innovation and invention may either be part of the same process or distinct and separate processes.

SOURCES OF INNOVATIVE IDEAS

The first obvious step in the innovative process is having the innovative idea. However, in reality, the innovative idea may not really be a first step, but a last step, or a lateral step, or indeed simply part of an individual's or organisation's life work. This is evident from some comments made by participants. One participant was led to the innovative idea as a result of a general interest in science. For another participant, innovative ideas spring from the 'desire to be master of my own destiny...to do something meaningful ...not just the hair on the wart of the frog stuff, pursued in universities' . The idea that innovative ideas may spring from motivation and life interests may be explained by studies of entrepreneurs, who are primarily motivated by independence and achievement (See Caird, 1990).

Drucker (1991) examined internal sources and external organisational sources of innovation, associated with unexpected occurrences, incongruities, process needs, industry and market changes, demographic changes, changes in perception and new knowledge. In terms of these rather general sources of innovative ideas, most of the innovations within this sample had their origins in new knowledge. There have been further attempts to classify innovative ideas, supporting four main sources of ideas, which are rooted in technological and market opportunities (Open University course T264, 1992):

• adaptation, of an existing concept, solution or technology to a new application;
• transfer of expertise from one application to another;
• analogy, that is an innovative solution is suggested by a similar situation;
• and combination of existing ideas/technologies to provide something new.

Although this classification assumes the existence of expertise, from which innovations may emerge, it helps to answer the question of how innovative ideas may emerge. Some of the innovators' experiences of developing innovative ideas may be explained by this classification. For example, one innovator came up with an idea at the dentist, when the possibility of transferring technical concepts associated with dentistry to another medical context was perceived. A further 21% of the innovators claimed that their ideas were evolutions of their work, which suggests that the source of the innovation could be explained as the adaptation of an existing concept or combinations of existing ideas/technologies to new applications.

The SMART winners' perceptions of the main sources of innovative ideas are presented in Table 6.4.

A majority 71% of the participants claim that their innovative ideas originated in clarifying problems and finding solutions. One participant emphasised the importance of understanding a problem because 'once you understand a problem the technology should follow'. This suggests a view that finding the technology is not a difficulty, the issue is to understand what you want to do with it. The key issue is to identify the problem which leads to the innovative idea and there will be a technological fix for problems.

However, understanding the problem is not always sufficient for innovation because solutions for a problem are limited by the capabilities of technology. To quote another participant 'You have to understand the technology to understand what is achievable'. These comments show that the problem directs the application of the technology and the technology constrains the solution for the problem.

Some interesting comments on approaches to solving the problem were made. Techniques such as brain-storming, listening to problems, origami, the art of Japanese paper folding, maps and diagrams were employed. Another technique which helped to solve apparently insoluble problems was to consistently attempt to answer the question why and experiment with alternative solutions. The key to the solution may be 'the entry point to the problem and where this leads'.

Table 6.4: *Sources of innovative ideas*

SOURCES	N	%	RANK
Problem driven	17	(71%)	1
Discussions	13	(54%)	2
Market driven	10	(42%)	3
Work behaviour	8	(33%)	4
Eureka	5	(21%)	5

N = number of participants

Marginally over half (54%) of the participants mentioned that they were led to their innovative idea as a result of conversations both with colleagues or customers. Of these respondents, 42% of the participants said that they were led to their idea as a result of customer demands or market research. Finally, 33% of the participants mentioned that their innovative ideas emerged through their work behaviours, either as an extension of previous work or the result of experimenting with ideas and applying theory towards technical advancement.

Not all of these sources are qualitatively different and none of them are mutually exclusive sources of innovative ideas. This is clear since all of the participants gave a response which mentioned more than one source of innovative ideas. For example, one innovator experienced a Eureka style flash of inspiration at a fireworks display following discussions with colleagues and customers about a work-related problem, which needed a solution, but none seemed to be obvious: set ideas, such as the belief that a solution was impossible, had limited the imagination. Another innovator, claimed that the idea emerged as part of an evolution of normal work, as a result of trying to apply advanced scientific knowledge to solve a problem, which had been identified by market research.

THE PROCESS OF COMING UP WITH INNOVATIVE IDEAS

The idea that an innovation originated in a flash of inspiration was cited by only 21% of participants, of which one described the origin of the idea as a creative process where thoughts clicked into place. This participant pointed out that 'it cannot be made to happen', irrespective of whether you are looking for technical and business ideas and 'there are good and bad days'. Another described the innovative idea as an instantaneous thing, which is 'a result of intense concentration'. This participant said that you need to go through 'the hassle of deep thought' and endure the 'painful aspect of letting the problem get deep enough before you come up with the idea and the solution'.

Interestingly, 21% of the sample raised the question of whether innovation is a creative process and whether creativity plays a role in the process at all. For some participants innovation does not involve the originality implied in the 'Eureka' notion of original flashes of inspiration. Indeed, 21% of the participants were a little sceptical about the idea of innovative ideas coming in creative flashes or 'Eurekas', of which one was 'anti the Eureka nonsense'. This participant said that 'the vast majority of innovations are about improving something or novel applications'. Another believed that 'there is no such thing as an original idea ... most ideas are based on small steps and may be described in terms of pushing back frontiers rather than Eurekas'. Another said that 'there is no art to innovation, it is basically an engineering process...Hi-tech innovation is so sophisticated that developments tend to be evolution's and not Eurekas. There are no really unique Eurekas'..

The main reasons for the rejection of the creativity of innovative ideas, by these respondents appeared to stem from several assumptions. The first assumption was that if innovation is incremental rather than radical, then innovative ideas were not really creative at all. A second assumption was that the view of an innovative idea emerging as a flash of inspiration may be too simplistic and misrepresents the process of coming up with an innovative idea, as an easy, mystical or disorganised procedure, which is not rooted in real opportunities or resources. A third assumption stemmed from a preoccupation with commercial success. The 'anti-Eureka' contingent tended to rate considerations of technical expertise and commercial potential as more important contributions to the genesis of their ideas' than some less rational or creative process.

However, none of these assumptions, if true, actually implies that creativity is not widely associated with the innovation process. Instead, these views could suggest that these innovators undermine the significance of creativity for the innovation process. For example, one participant pointed out that within their organisation they have '...more ideas than could be practically implemented...the hardest thing to learn is to say no to ideas'. The big question for this company is, which ideas have market potential and are cost effective, not how you find innovative ideas.

THE CONDITIONS FOR INNOVATION SUCCESS

When the SMART winners were asked 'What do you think a successful innovation depends on?', the importance of good ideas was supported by 21%. Furthermore, 29% of the participants pointed out the importance of the innovator's contribution. The critical importance of a source of creative ideas and the commitment of one or more individuals for the commercial success of an innovation is supported by Twiss (1992).

However, the most cited condition for innovation success (ie by 54%) was that there must be a market demand for innovation. This is also supported as a critical success factor for the commercial success of an innovation by Twiss (1992). As one participant said 'the innovation has got to stop being an innovation and start being a commercial product'. Particular issues of importance included positioning the product in the market and pricing the product at a price which will sell. The need to overcome consumer resistance to new products coming from small companies was also an issue. For example, one participant commented on the horror that buyers have of new technology which together with the risk of a small business going 'bust' can create considerable consumer resistance. Table 5 presents the responses to the question of what successful innovation depends on. Some participants pointed out that it depends upon what success means. Not all participants accepted financial rewards or commercial success as an indication of innovation success. However, commercial success clearly features as some index of success. As one participant said 'it is hard to consider yourself a success if you go bust'.

Twiss (1992) also identifies organisational support for innovation as a critical success factor for innovative products and processes. However, the emphasis by this sample on the importance of benefiting the user, establishing technical viability, the patent, securing financial support and recruiting human resources, are not supported in Twiss's review of critical success factors. However, Twiss's review is of innovations in general and these issues may be of particular concern for the small businesses of the innovators in this sample.

Table 6.5: *Factors and problems influencing the progress of innovative projects*

AREA	FACTORS		PROBLEMS	
	N	%	N	%
Technical viability	8	33%	11	42%
Financial backing	5	21%	11	42%
Resources	3		1	4%
Market acceptance	5	21%	8	33%
Human resources	5	21%	12	50%
Collaboration with companies	3	13%	4	17%
Business versus innovation	3	13%	2	8%
Management problems	0	0%	3	13%
Personal problems	0	0%	2	8%

N = number of participants

Table 6.6: *General conditions for innovation success*

SUCCESS FACTORS	N	RANK	%
Good ideas	5	5	21%
Market demand	13	1	54%
Should benefit the user	2	7	8%
Company resources and support	2	7	8%
Technical viabilty	4	6	17%
Secure patent	1	9	4%
Financial support	6	3	25%
Skilled human resources	6	3	25%
The innovator's contribution	7	2	29%

N = number of participants

CONCLUSIONS

The perceptions of SMART innovators offer insights into sources of innovative ideas and the importance of innovative ideas for commercial success within the SME context. The first set of findings is on the nature of the innovation process and how it may be distinguished from invention. Though it may be difficult to distinguish concepts of innovation and invention which are often part of the same process: invention may be described as an original, technical and patentable process with no necessary commercial application; whereas innovation usually involves the application of something (new or in a new way) to solve a problem usually for commercial gain. This does not conflict with definitions given by Twiss (1992), Kanter (1983), Drucker (1991). The group of innovators interviewed see themselves as involved in both inventive and innovative activities. In other words, they were involved in the innovation process of developing a new product or process from seed initially and then the development of applications for commercial gain.

Innovation and the process of coming up with innovative ideas for innovation were not always perceived as creative acts. Though some participants experienced flashes of inspiration in unusual circumstances, others were critical of the collective view that innovation is an inspired, creative act. There is a current theory of creativity which suggests that incremental and radical innovations may be associated with different creative styles: a more adaptive creative style may lead to more incremental innovations and a more innovative creative style may lead to more challenging and radical innovations (Kirton, 1980). Perhaps differences in creative style could explain different views on the creative aspects of the innovators' work.

Alternatively, the anti-Eureka contingent may be concerned that their innovative work is not misrepresented as a simple and mystical process, when in reality it may be more perspiration than inspiration. They may be concerned that they are not perceived as 'nutters' (sic), ridiculed or pigeon holed as inventors. The vehemence of this group's antagonism, to ideas of themselves as inventors and inventive, may be associated with an anxiety to avoid being swallowed by the mythology of the 'mad inventor' and a struggle to follow the myth of the entrepreneur. The key to understanding entrepreneurial motivation is the need for achievement (McClelland, 1968) and this contingent, in typical entrepreneurial fashion, were concerned that their hard work and achievement was recognised. Nevertheless, this antagonism does not necessarily imply that this sub-group were not creative in terms understood by the literature and other award winners.

Some of the participants maintained that ideas for evolutionary or incremental innovations, rather than radical innovations may be more typical in this sophisticated high-technological climate. However, incremental innovation may be creative, ideas may still have an important role in the innovation development process, even if the idea does not become commercially successful.

Nevertheless, the importance of good ideas paled in comparison to the importance attributed to market potential by the sample as a determinant of innovation success. In the context of the conditions responsible for innovation success, the importance of good ideas was also rated less than having financial support and good human expertise. This could be due to taking good ideas for granted, since the importance of innovative ideas is well supported in innovation studies. Rather than argue over whether the market demand is more important than the innovative ideas, it is more sensible to perceive innovation as 'a coupling process' which takes place in the minds of 'imaginative people...at the ever-changing interfaces between science, technology, and the market' (Freeman, 1986, p33).

There was a strong view present that having innovative ideas is not an important high-tech SME issue. The big issue is how to select ideas which have market potential and are cost effective. The importance of selecting innovative ideas in conditions where ideas are prolific has been given some attention (Jelinek and Schoonhoven, 1990). There are always opportunity costs associated with ideas selected and rejected, not to mention the risks of commercial failure and the organisational problems associated with managing the commitment of those whose ideas are selected and rejected.

However, although managing the selection of ideas may be more important for high-technological SMEs, than finding ideas, it remains important to have ideas from which to choose, at the early pre-formal stages of innovation. High-tech SMEs always need ideas for locating opportunities, for choosing ideas, for developing ideas, for adjusting ideas to market and resource constraints and the business strategy, for developing product families, for applying new knowledge and for new applications and markets. Furthermore, the possibility that SMART winners constitute an exceptional set of individuals, for whom idea generation is unproblematic, should not be overlooked. Further work on matched groups of winners and non-winners seeking to innovate is needed to resolve this issue, especially since this has implications for policies on intervention and assistance for innovation in SMEs.

The main set of findings suggests how innovation may be nurtured within organisations. The main sources of innovative ideas mentioned, included: work behaviour; discussions with colleagues and customers; a strong focus on solving complicated problems; market demand and 'Eureka style' flashes of inspiration. There was frequently no clear beginning to the innovative work, which was often an evolution of ongoing work. However, the responses to questions about the sources of innovative ideas did not lend themselves to classification according to one model of the sources of innovative ideas. In general, the responses given suggest that different perspectives may be taken to examine sources of innovative ideas such as focusing on:

- the general motivation of innovators, underlying their work interests and approach to work;
- the specific events associated with the genesis of the idea;
- the innovation itself, in the context of how it draws on scientific and technical knowledge for particular applications and markets;
- whether the idea was the result of a 'Eureka' or an evolution;
- the process of coming up with innovative ideas and the feelings associated with that process;
- distinctions between questions about the sources of innovation associated with who was involved in the process of coming up with innovative ideas, where the idea came from, why the idea emerged, when the idea happened and in what context?

Each of these concerns could lead to different research perspectives on sources of innovative ideas and different ways of classifying these sources. Furthermore, it would interesting to attempt to relate these perspectives on sources of innovative ideas to the subsequent commercial success or failure of the innovation.

This study offers both quantitative and qualitative results, but these results cannot be conclusive because of the exploratory nature of the work and the small sample size. Furthermore, insights into the innovation process which emerge in this study are associated with perceptions and not facts about sources of innovative ideas and their significance for commercial outcomes. That these are the perceptions of innovators who have been given awards by the DTI is interesting, although perhaps some investigation of the appraisal system and the value sets of SMART adjudicators could reveal more about the nature of this sample's innovation processes.

Some interesting results emerged from this study of relevance to our understanding of innovation, sources of innovative ideas in SMEs and their significance for commercial success. While these results are not proven for SMEs in general, they help to clarify what is generally understood by innovativeness, which may help companies interested in fostering innovative ideas. However, greater attention needs to be given to the process and management of idea selection, especially in conditions where ideas are plentiful and where critical considerations are cost effectiveness and market potential.

ACKNOWLEDGEMENTS

I am grateful to Mr Gerry O'Neill and Mr Hugh Ross of The Scottish Office, Industry Department for greatly supporting this project. Dr McDonald and Mr I McFarlane of The University of Stirling were helpful with the design of this study. I would also like to acknowledge that this paper was first published in Creativity & Innovation Management Vol. 3. No.1 March 1994.

REFERENCES

CAIRD, S. (1990) What does it mean to be enterprising?, *British Journal Of Management*, Vol. 1, No. 3., pp. 137-147.

DRUCKER, P. (1991) The discipline of innovation, in Managing Innovation, Edited by J. Henry and D. Walker, Open University Press, Milton Keynes.

FREEMAN, C. (1986) *Successful industrial innovation, in Product Design And Technological Innovation*, Edited by R. Roy and D. Wield, Open University Press, Milton Keynes

JELINEK, M. and SCHOONHOVEN, C. (1990) *Innovation Marathon*, Basil Blackwell, GB.

KANTER, R. M. (1983) *The Change Masters*, Simon and Schuster, New York.

KIRTON, M. (1980) Adaptors and innovators in organisations, *Human Relations*, Vol. 33 No. 4, pp. 221-224.

LANGRISH, J., GIBBONS, M., EVANS, W. and JEVONS, F. (1972) *Wealth From Knowledge: A Study of Innovation in Industry*, Macmillan, London.

MCCLELLAND, D. C. (1968) *The Achieving Society*, Van Nostrand 2nd Edition, Princeton.

OPEN UNIVERSITY COURSE T264, (1992) *Design Principles And Practice-Block 3 Creativity And Conceptual Design*, Open University Press, Milton Keynes.

ROGERS, C. (1954) Toward a theory of creativity, *A Review of General Semantics*, Vol. 11., pp. 249-262.

ROTHWELL, R. and ZEGVELD, W. (1981) *Innovation And Small And Medium-Sized Firms*, Francis Pinter, London.

RICKARDS, T., MOGER, S., COLEMONT, P. and TASSOUL, M. (1992) Creativity and Innovation: Quality Breakthroughs, *Innovation Consulting Group TNO*, Netherlands.

SCHUMPETER, J. A. (1950) *Capitalism, Socialism and Democracy*, Harper, New York.

TWISS, B. (1992), *Managing Technological Innovation*, 4th Edition, Pitman Publishing, London.

VON HIPPEL, E. (1988) *The Sources of Innovation*, Oxford University Press, New York.

WEST, M. and FARR, J. (1990) *Innovation at work, in Innovation and Creativity at Work: Psychological and Organizational Strategies*, Edited by D. West and J. Farr, John Wiley and Sons Ltd, Chichester.

PART III Finance

CHAPTER 7

Banking and New Technology-Based Small Firms: A Study of Information Exchanges in the Financing Relationship

TOBY PHILPOTT

INTRODUCTION

Previous research on the financing of high technology or new technology-based (NTB) small firms has concentrated on two main issues:

- The types of finance used by high technology or NTB small firms (Oakey, 1984; Oakey et al., 1988), and
- The ways in which bank managers and high technology small firm entrepreneurs view each other as personalities (Vyakernam and Jacobs, 1991).

Although this literature covers significant facets of the financing of high or new technology-based small firms, they do not provide in-depth theoretical discussions of the financing relationship between providers of finance and entrepreneurs. They also do not provide any understanding of the processes involved in the financing of NTB small firms, treating the financing event as a 'black box'.

The literature on the uses of finance by high technology and NTB small firms does provide evidence to suggest that these firms are dependent upon banks as a major source of external capital (Oakey, 1984; Oakey et al., 1988). There is also empirical evidence to show that the venture capital industry has moved away from providing finance for high and new technology-based firms and has shown a preference for management buy-ins and buy-outs (Bovaird, 1991; Murray and Lott, 1992; Robbie and Murray, 1992). Therefore, the access to equity markets for such firms is extremely limited and there is strong evidence of the existence of an equity gap in the UK facing small firms (Mason and Harrison, 1990; Bannock, 1991; Stanworth and Gray, 1991). There is also evidence of an unwillingness by entrepreneurs to relinquish control to outsiders in return for equity (Myers and Majluf, 1984; Vickery, 1989; Burns, 1992). Given these circumstances, the dependence upon bank finance is often due to the firm's internal financial resources being rapidly exhausted in the initial research and development stage of the NTB small firm (Oakey, 1991). If the product or process is therefore to enter the market place, then the raising of finance from a bank will be critical (Oakey, 1991). However, limited access to equity markets will constrain the level of debt available to such firms as it is well documented that UK banks have a preference for a 1:1 debt-equity ratio (Binks et al., 1988; Deakins and Hussain, 1991; Deakins and Philpott, 1993a; Deakins and Philpott, 1993b; and this volume).

Some research on the appraisal and monitoring methods utilised by UK banks when determining whether to lend to small firms (NEDC, 1986) has treated financing as a process rather than as a simple event and this has enabled a more detailed investigation of the information flows between banks and small firms. The NEDC research was conducted from the perspective of the banks and therefore can be perceived to have only really captured banking policy, not the realities of actual lending decisions since it was not based upon the assessment of actual lending propositions.

Attempts have been made to gain a greater understanding of the appraisal criteria of UK bank managers for small firms in general (Berry et al., 1991; Deakins and Hussain, 1991). Berry et al. (1991) utilises cognitive mapping (see Eden, 1983 for an introduction to this method) as a means of describing the decision making processes of bank managers in their survey, and the ways in which they utilise information in those processes. However, the Berry et al. methodology is flawed in that the bank managers were placed in a position to choose propositions they had already made decisions upon. This would also enable the manager to hide mistakes. Deakins and Hussain (1991) took a business plan for a construction industry venture which was using CAD/CAM techniques as an important part of its service. The researchers acted on the part of the entrepreneurs and used an open-ended interview methodology to determine the criteria of bank managers through the questions that the bank manager asked. Deakins and Hussain's study can be criticised on the grounds that there is likely to be an element of artificiality. However, Deakins and Hussain subsequently argue (Deakins and Hussain, 1992) that the actual experiences of the entrepreneurs associated with the venture corresponded with theirs when attempting to raise finance in terms of the questions that were asked of them.

The flaws in both studies are that they do not consider the actual experiences of entrepreneurs in raising finance, the information that they must provide to banks, and the way in which that information was used by banks.

This paper intends to provide an initial exploration of the processes involved in the financing process in order to offer a better understanding of the risk assessment and monitoring stages of the financing process as it impacts upon NTB small firms. In doing so, we shall discuss the various theoretical issues which can be brought to bear on the financing relationship between banks and NTB small firms. Following from this we shall consider the methodology used in the survey which is designed to emphasise the perspective of NTB entrepreneurs. Finally, we shall discuss some of the initial findings of the survey and their potential implications for lending policies towards NTB small firms.

ISSUES AND CONCEPTS RELATING TO THE FINANCING PROCESS

Asymmetric information

The financing relationship at all stages of the financing process can be characterised as one of asymmetric information (Stiglitz and Weiss, 1981; de Meza and Webb, 1987; Stanworth and Gray, 1991). Typically, the information sets available to each side of the relationship are different. For various reasons it is not possible for the bank to obtain a perfect information set on the venture applying for finance. Therefore, given the existence of imperfect information the potential exists for resource misallocation by the banks when determining who will and who will not obtain finance. Information is not costless to obtain, either from the perspective of the entrepreneur who has to provide the information set, or from the perspective of the bank if the entrepreneur is unable or unwilling to provide certain information relating to their venture.

Technological uncertainty

The financing of NTB small firms also takes on an additional dimension when technological uncertainty occurs (Vyakernam and Jacobs, 1991). Technological uncertainty as a concept infers that the banks will find it difficult to assess the potential profitability of technological propositions, as they are not in the position to understand the technology (not being technological specialists, but rather generalists) and cannot therefore have a full understanding of a project's feasibility from a technical perspective. (Potential ways of overcoming this problem will be suggested below.) With technology-based ventures it is possible that the entrepreneur may be the main or even only expert in the application and knowledge of that technology (Oakey, 1984; Ang, 1991).

Two of the major UK clearing banks have made some attempts to overcome the problem of technological uncertainty by introducing technology officers who are supposed to be trained to understand the technological information associated with high technology or NTB small firm propositions. However, as will be discussed in the results section below, there is empirical evidence to suggest that such provision is far from adequate.

A lack of understanding of the technological concept behind an NTB business by the lending officer continues as a problem which can therefore create an additional barrier for entrepreneurs when attempting to raise finance. The different nature of high technology and NTB small firms as compared to their low technology counterparts has received attention (Vyakernam and Jacobs, 1991; Allen, 1992). However, there is evidence to suggest that banks have a tendency to treat small firms in a homogeneous fashion (Deakins and Hussain, 1992).

Adverse selection

Given the characteristics of asymmetric information and technological uncertainty it can be hypothesised that there is a greater risk of adverse selection (Akerlof, 1970) facing banks with regard to the allocation of financial resources to the NTB small firm sector, when compared to small firms in other sectors of the economy. Deakins and Hussain (1991) provide two typologies to describe the adverse selection problem. Type I errors (following the statistical hypothesis testing analogy) they describe as the bank rejecting propositions which would subsequently prove to be profitable and therefore successful. Type II errors are those propositions that are accepted by the lending officer which later prove to be failures or 'lemons' to use Akerlof's terminology (Akerlof, 1970).

It can also be conceived that the greater the risk aversion of the lending officer, the greater the probability that they will make Type I errors, rather than face the possibility of making a Type II error, which might have adverse consequences for their career. Therefore the presence of technological information which is not readily comprehensible may well act as a disincentive to lend. However, the use of technological experts might potentially eliminate the problem of adverse selection by reducing the impact of technological uncertainty and asymmetric information within the risk assessment process. This would benefit both banks who gain from increased profit opportunities, and the economy from the increased wealth generated by the innovations that new technology brings (Obermayer, 1983).

Moral hazard

Should the entrepreneur manage to overcome the hurdles facing them in the risk assessment process, then the bank will, according to principal-agent theory (Mirlees, 1975), wish to protect its investment and ensure that the entrepreneur is using the finance for the purposes intended in the contract between the two parties. However, the actions of the entrepreneur are not easily observable by the bank and the potential exists for moral hazard where the entrepreneur may well use the finance for other purposes which are personally more profitable. In order to ensure that this misuse of funds does not occur, the bank has three options open to it. Either the bank will simply monitor the account (usually by checking the bank balance and asking for management accounts on a regular basis); they will introduce some form of incentive structure (Gale and Hellwig, 1985) to reduce the risk of default on the loan (this usually takes the form of collateral, which will be discussed in more detail below); or a combination of both.

Collateral and signalling

In the sense denoted by Spence (1974) collateral can be used to signal commitment on the part of the entrepreneur to the success of the venture (Chan and Kanatas, 1985). The existence of collateral can be taken as a proxy also for the quality of a financial proposition (Stiglitz and Weiss, 1981).

However, within the new technology-based firm there are potential problems with respect to collateral. In particular, it has been pointed out that business assets which are normally available as collateral within most businesses are intangible when in the form of research and development outputs (Oakey, 1984). Banks are believed to find it difficult to value research and development output which is usually the major business asset of new technology-based small firms, and therefore a potential source of collateral is not available for securing debt finance. Given the high costs of developing new technology, the working capital of the NTB small firm will be used up very rapidly and therefore, if the personal collateral of the entrepreneur has already been used up the firm will face severe liquidity constraints.

There is evidence to suggest that in relation to other European countries, the UK banking sector has a strong preoccupation with collateral, and this could be a potential barrier to innovation and economic growth within the UK which will lead to our continued relative economic decline compared with our fellow EC partners (Deakins and Philpott, 1993a; Deakins and Philpott, 1993b).

Debt gaps (credit rationing)

Quite a considerable literature has been developed around the issue of credit rationing over the last 35 years. These approaches have moved from perceived market failure in the neo-classical microeconomic sense of the term (Kareken, 1957; Hodgman, 1960; Hodgman, 1962) through to later explanations which sought to introduce the concepts related to the economics of imperfect information such as adverse selection, moral hazard, asymmetric information and agency costs as potential explanations for the existence of credit rationing (Baltensperger, 1976; Jaffee and Russell, 1976). These latter concepts have also been used to argue that in certain instances there may well be an oversupply of credit (de Meza and Webb, 1987).

The weakness with these approaches to credit rationing are that they treat the decision process made by the bank official as a 'black box' and an instantaneous decision. This is clearly unrealistic and there needs to be developed a more realistic model of the decision-making process if we are to understand where potential errors are being made, and what can be done to improve the allocation of financial resources to NTB small firms.

As a consequence of the difficulties associated with collateral facing NTB small firms, the possibility exists that the firm will face a debt gap. Associated with the very limited access to equity markets, this imposes very severe liquidity constraints upon such firms, and there is at present no evidence to suggest that the informal equity market is making inroads into filling these gaps.

Hypotheses

We would hypothesise that new technology-based small firms experience difficulties in the following areas:

1. Technological information relating to the products and services provided by new technology entrepreneurs is not properly understood by bank officers undertaking risk assessment (technological uncertainty) and this can lead to a misallocation of financial resources by banks (adverse selection). By implication, if a bank officer is risk averse then it is likely that the majority of errors will be Type I (Deakins and Hussain, 1991) and therefore the banks will miss out on potentially profitable lending, and the economy will lose the benefits of the stifled technology. We can also conclude on an intuitive level that there are significant economic costs from Type I errors.

2. The different nature of new technology-based small firms in terms of potential profitability will not be understood. The sunk costs of research and development prior to the product or process being ready to come to the market will be considerable. We would therefore expect to see a negative cash flow for the first years of a new technology-based business. However, banks may not be prepared readily to support such firms where returns may be positive from other small firms. In other words, bank officers will also expect rapid returns from new technology-based small firms in line with small businesses in other sectors of the economy and will not understand that such firms are likely to experience low turnover in the initial research and development stage of their product (Oakey, 1991). This would show evidence of a lack of understanding of the business and has been used in previous studies on small firms in general (Binks et al., 1988; Burns, 1992) as an example of the characteristic of asymmetric information.

3. The new technology-based entrepreneur will experience difficulties with respect to collateral. The theory discussed above suggests that much of the personal financial resources of the entrepreneur is invested in the sunk costs associated with the research and development stage of product development. Therefore, there may well be difficulties in providing collateral for additional loan finance to get the product to market. In addition, the output from research and development in terms of prototypes will not be treated as an asset of the business by banks and therefore a potential source of collateral in terms of business assets is not available. Given the preoccupation with collateral in the UK (Deakins and Philpott, 1993a) this can lead to debt gaps facing new technology-based small firms and will leave the firm constrained in terms of its ability to grow.

METHODOLOGY

The methodology for this study involves face-to-face semi-structured interviewing. This has an advantage over structured interviews since it is possible to explore issues in more depth as they arise. The case for such qualitative approaches is well documented (Morgan and Smircich, 1980; Walker, 1985; Bryman, 1988).

Questions and interview topics were based on the hypotheses outlined above, and an interview guide was prepared. Each interview lasted for approximately one hour. The interviews were taped and then subsequently a full transcription of each was obtained. These transcripts were then coded to obtain information based upon the issues identified from the literature. Interviews were conducted with managing directors of new technology-based small firms in the West Midlands region. The firms interviewed to date have less than 200 employees and a turnover of less than £5 million. The total initial sample comprised 8 firms.[1]

The firms surveyed to date are in the following sectors:

- Research and development of materials and metals (applied materials science and metallurgy) (1 firm).
- Laser manufacturing systems production (1 firm).
- Scientific instrumentation (6 firms).

[RESULTS]

The results of the initial survey are tentative owing to the small numbers of firms interviewed to date. However, there are patterns emerging which can cast some light upon some of the issues developed above.

Dependence upon bank finance as the main external source of capital

In all cases, the firms have overdrafts and some have loans with major clearing banks. In all cases there is no other more important source of external funding for their firms. This would seem to confirm the continuation of patterns established in previous surveys on the sources of external finance used by high technology or new technology-based small firms (Oakey, 1984; Oakey et al., 1988). In one of the cases the overdraft facility comprised 50% of the financial structure of the company. This company is experiencing financing constraints as it is finding it difficult to finance growth and expansion since its collateral is now exhausted for raising additional debt finance, and it is having to seek an additional injection of new equity capital:

What has happened over the period of time to this point of time is that the overdraft has grown, and it stabilised 18 months ago. As you can imagine it is causing us cash flow problems because the bank refuses to either give us loans or overdraft. We've tried to get a loan, changing from a bank overdraft into a loan situation and increase the amount of the facility and again because we didn't have any personal assets the government's come up with an excellent scheme, the Small Firms Loan Scheme.

(MANAGING DIRECTOR OF FIRM A)

The pattern that has emerged regarding the development of many survey firms is that of increasing dependence upon bank finance to finance working capital. In another instance it was argued that:

I was looking at it (the level of the bank overdraft) the other day. It rose rapidly in the early years up to about £30,000, then slowly up to £50,000 and now we have an overdraft facility of £90,000.   (MANAGING DIRECTOR FIRM B)

In two of the cases, the firms have been able to raise long-term loans to finance the building or purchase of premises. However, none of the 8 firms were able to raise finance to fund research and development activity or manufacturing activity over a long period of time (more than 7 years). To do so they were obliged to attempt to raise finance from the Small Firms Loan Guarantee Scheme, and in only one case was the firm successful.

Information provided by entrepreneurs to obtain finance from banks

As was stated above, the financing process for new technology-based small firms can be categorised in at least two stages. At the initial appraisal stage, the firm seeks finance for the first time from a bank. Should this be successful, the process then moves on to the monitoring stage. It is then conceivable that the firm will seek additional debt finance, and therefore the firm will enter a subsequent appraisal stage. However, it can be hypothesised that the informational requirements will be qualitatively different at this subsequent appraisal stage, as information will have been collected by the bank on the venture during the monitoring stage. In other words the business will have a trading record upon which to make a risk assessment.

The initial appraisal stage

Informational requirements seem to have varied from respondent to respondent at this stage of financing. However, the common pattern would seem to be the standard business plan, which will contain cash flow projections (usually for three years in advance), profit and loss accounts, marketing strategies, and information relating to the products or services provided by the firm. (In one instance, the firm was required to submit proof of contracts with a government department. In another, the firm was in a position to provide information on patents that it had been successful in obtaining.) This would appear to be standard practice for small firms lending (Deakins and Hussain, 1992) excluding the technological information which could provide an additional set of information upon which to judge the feasibility of the business. However, as we will see below, this information would seem to cause the banks the most discomfort, owing to current practices employed in risk assessment by UK banks. In common with small firms in other sectors (Deakins and Hussain, 1991), it would also seem that the banks are more concerned with financial criteria when determining whether to lend, and not on the qualities of the entrepreneur or the feasibility of the technology. This is particularly true with respect to the ability to provide collateral (discussed in more detail below).

The monitoring stage

A previous survey of monitoring methods (NEDC, 1986) by bank officers found that the main method of monitoring by banks was through the current account or the loan account balance and the annual accounts of the firm. All the interviews conducted in this survey confirm that banks monitor their lending through the use of the information provided by the current account or loan account balance and in addition, they also request the annual accounts of each firm. One respondent when asked what was required of him in terms of information over the period of his first loan for £5,000 stated:

In the early days nothing, so long as we stayed within the £5,000.

(MANAGING DIRECTOR FIRM B)

Another respondent had similar experiences: I think they are only worried about one thing and that is above the overdraft limit or below the overdraft limit.

(MANAGING DIRECTOR FIRM C).

Additional information required for monitoring purposes from banks included quarterly cash flow projections, evidence of future contracts, and in one case a full set of monthly management accounts. In none of the cases did the firms get into difficulties with respect to the continuation of their financing. However, it is conceivable that where the firm is getting into difficulties the bank may well decide to 'shoot the messenger' and liquidate the firm to protect its lending. Therefore it is not always in the interests of the firm to be honest when providing additional information. If a bank manager also has faith in the abilities of a venture to succeed he or she may also play a role in hiding negative information from regional office. In the early stages of one of the ventures this did in fact happen:

The previous manager had a great deal of trust in the ability of us to survive through the early stages. So he would hide things from his superiors. But the present incumbent is more interested in filling in forms and waiting to see what the people upstairs think.

(MANAGING DIRECTOR FIRM D)

Subsequent appraisal stages

With the information gathered about the venture during the monitoring stages of previous rounds of loan finance, it should provide the bank with a larger set of available information with which to undertake risk assessment for new loan agreements.

In two of the cases within this survey (Firm A and Firm B), in order to obtain subsequent rounds of finance, the banks in each instance still required a business plan, containing similar information to that provided for the initial appraisal, only more up to date. The existence of a track record also enabled some of the companies to obtain long-term finance in terms of mortgages to finance the purchase or building of premises. Again, as in the initial appraisal stage of the financing process, the bank still showed discomfort with respect to the technological information contained within the business plan.

Evidence of the impact of technological uncertainty and asymmetric information

The impact of technological uncertainty and asymmetric information varies from firm to firm, and it does not seem at present to be showing itself in any set pattern except that the entrepreneurs interviewed take the view that the perceived lack of understanding of technology by banks is having an adverse impact upon the ability of their firms to grow at their full potential growth rates.

The introduction of technology managers by NatWest and Barclays was intended as a policy response to the recognised difference of new technology-based and high technology based small firms from other small firms in different sectors of the economy. However, evidence from this study suggests that actually meeting a technology manager is very much a hit and miss affair (only one of the entrepreneurs in the survey had ever met a technology specialist in a major clearing bank, all the others dealt with branch managers when going for finance), and even then the technology manager may attempt to treat the new technology business as any other type of small business, expecting continuous cash flows whereas new technolgoy firms which are dependent upon large contracts will face periods of time without income from sales (Oakey, 1991). It has been suggested elsewhere (Deakins and Philpott, 1993a) that this is due to the short period of training (2 or 3 days in one instance) that banks provide to their technology managers before putting them into post.

In one case this was of serious concern since this prevented the firm from obtaining finance for increasing its development. This evidence derives from a meeting between the entrepreneur and a technology specialist in one of the major banks:

He wanted to see money in on the following Monday or on the first of the month next month, and I was trying to explain to him that we hadn't got any for the next two to three months and he wasn't interested. And as a high technology business we are not selling cabbages and I got in return 'well with all due respect you have only got the turnover of a corner shop' which is a plain misconception of our business and that our biggest earnings in the future will be in the form of licences which will be worth millions of pounds. Now a corner shop simply never has that potential. But every growing company has to go through a period of relatively low turnover.

(MANAGING DIRECTOR FIRM A)

Another respondent also experienced initial reluctance from the bank with respect to his venture. This venture produces laser manufacturing machinery:

In general they thought it was high tech and they didn't want to touch it with a barge-pole...the name 'laser' frightened them. (MANAGING DIRECTOR FIRM C)

This would suggest that there is a degree of asymmetric information with respect to the understanding of the nature of a technology-based business. Duncan Matthews, the senior manager of National Westminster's Technology Unit, has publicly gone on record admitting that 'banks are technophobic'.

Respondents were also asked their perceptions of how the bank officers had dealt with the technological information within their business plans in terms of whether the technology had been assessed for its viability (which in theory will be important if the bank is to avoid making Type II errors). The issue of the understanding that the bank seemed to show of the technology upon which the firm was based was also addressed in these interviews.

In terms of the assessment of the technologies upon which the firms were based, there is no evidence in the study to date to suggest that banks undertake an assessment of the viability of a technology before deciding whether to lend. This contrasts very strongly with the attitudes of venture capitalists for instance, who often assess technologies before investing (Deakins and Philpott, 1993a).

It is possible for two scenarios to present themselves here. Either the bank will reject the proposition without assessing the technology and therefore may make a Type I error, or it will take the technology on trust and risk making a Type II error. Both types of error have social and economic costs since financial resources are finite and may not be put to the most beneficial use.

A near case of a Type I error was noted above with respect to the laser manufacturing systems producer. This firm has subsequently gone on to expand into other parts of the country and will cease to be a small firm in the not too distant future.

A possible Type II error could have occurred in one case due to the disinterest shown in the technological information provided. When asked whether the bank had assessed the technology to make sure that it was profitable and viable the respondent stated: 'The actual technology? They haven't got a clue!' The respondent, when asked about whether the bank had used all the information he was willing to provide them, went on to state:

Not the technical. I think that they only would have been worried. No I don't think that the bank at that period of time we are talking about would have given two hoots. They had a massive amount of money to hand out in all directions and we had a track record. They have got security. They've got the building, my house and everything if anything went wrong. But I've seen them doling out money to people who should never have been given it. (MANAGING DIRECTOR FIRM B)

The processing of technological information in the risk assessment procedure of banks can therefore have a critical impact upon the development of new technologies, their own potential profitability, and the benefits of new technologies to the economy.

The role and provision of collateral

As we can see from the example given above, the requirement of collateral from entrepreneurs can be used by banks as a means of putting the onus of self-selection by new technology-based entrepreneurs to avoid making Type II errors (Bester, 1985) and therefore in the sense of Stiglitz and Weiss (1981), collateral can signal the quality of a proposition. It also protects the banks from the risks of default.

In all of the cases, the entrepreneurs were required to put up collateral to obtain loan finance. The nature of this collateral, and the gearing ratios in each of the deals varied from firm to firm. A common stand amongst all the deals was that the gearing ratio was a maximum of 1:1. This confirms the results of previous studies on the lending criteria of bank managers (Berry et al., 1991; Deakins and Hussain, 1991) in the UK. This compares very unfavourably with the collateral requirements of other European states (Deakins and Philpott, 1993a; Deakins and Philpott, 1993b). With the possibility of increased mobility within the Single European Market in the future, it is conceivable that new technology entrepreneurs will relocate their developing technologies in other EC states where they can get more financial resources for their collateral. In one case the entrepreneurs had to provide £200,000 of collateral to secure a £30,000 overdraft. This led them to look at expansion abroad, with which they are now proceeding.

In terms of collateral provision, the use of personal guarantees is popular amongst banks. It is rare for the banks to use business assets as a means of securing lending, except in cases where there were business premises bought using mortgages from the banks. Indeed, as was suggested above, the difficulty for most new technology-based small firms is the intangibility of business assets as these are often in the form of research and development outputs.

There was often a perception amongst the entrepreneurs that the banks will seek to obtain as much personal collateral as they can to secure their lending. They seemed especially keen to obtain collateral in the form of property. This creates a very negative image of the banks:

I think the banks are looking to con as much security as they can out of the individuals. I mean, if we had property they would probably have tried to con property out of us and this annoys me a bit about the banks that as professionals we are not bought by the banks. We started with nothing and we can end up with nothing and we can get excellent jobs in this country or overseas. What worries me is that they would bully people with families and houses to put those on the line as security and that is what would annoy me. (MANAGING DIRECTOR FIRM A).

The level of security they want is unfair in as much as we know that they will make full use. My perception is that if you started to falter they will cut and run, taking what they could without worrying about whether it was fair what they were taking. I may be being unfair to them, but that is my perception. (FINANCIAL DIRECTOR FIRM C)

Perceptions of the banks' policies towards new technology-based small firms

The respondents also discussed their perceptions of overall bank policies to new technology-based small firms. A consistent theme running throughout, was the perceived lack of support of technology-based small firms by the banking sector and the conviction that this was based upon a lack of understanding of the nature of technology businesses and a lack of understanding of technology. It was felt that the relatively poor position of the UK compared to several other nations was in some part due to the lack of a technological culture. Several suggestions for improvements were made:

I think the banks want to get more educated in technology...I don't know a successful country that isn't technology based. I go to Singapore and I see all those people working flat out. You go to America and they have a technology culture. We haven't...The thing that really depressed me was that if they really understood the product, if they (the bank) became really interested in the product they would...Nobody has ever come from the bank and said 'we are the technology development officer and we're very interested in what you are doing, can't we make this company grow a little faster'. I could be a millionaire in a year or 5 years. I don't doubt that we could if we really wanted to, but it would require quite a considerable amount.

(MANAGING DIRECTOR FIRM D)

I've so given up on the banks and the banking system understanding technology and high technology companies and understanding that long-term payback is massive and also understanding that what is needed is a long-term view...Maybe putting some of their high fliers into our businesses as a secondment for 2 to 3 years might be the best way to go forwards. To actually have technology officers who have worked with a number of technology companies to understand the potential problems and the banking needs for these particular businesses is fairly unique. Technology is fairly unique in a business and banking sense. It's a long-term commitment, and it's the long-term pay-back.

(MANAGING DIRECTOR FIRM A)

I suppose if they had a venture capital arm which was prepared to back people like us rather than some of the people who I have seen the venture capital arm back, and consequently lost a lot of money on.

(MANAGING DIRECTOR FIRM E)

CONCLUSIONS

The theory that has been developed in relation to the financing of new technology-based small firms has indicated that there are potential difficulties associated with the processing of technological information with respect to the risk assessment process. It was seen from the initial results of this study that there would seem to be a pattern emerging in which banks prefer to use collateral as a means of determining project viability, rather than engaging in formal technological assessments. Given the likelihood that a new technology-based small firm is likely to have little in the way of tangible business assets, entrepreneurs will find themselves constrained as to the level of debt they can borrow against collateral, and this will restrict their potential growth rates.

It was also clear that the banks seem to have little appreciation of the nature of technology-based businesses, which have initially lower turnovers in the early stages of development due to the need to invest in research and development prior to the product or process coming to the market. The lack of patience with respect to financing these companies is resulting in the failure of banks to share fully in the very high potential profits of these companies. It has been suggested elsewhere (Deakins and Hussain, 1991; Deakins and Philpott, 1993a) that banks need to consider greater specialisation by staff in order that expertise and understanding can be acquired regarding high technology new businesses. The perceived lack of understanding of technology by banks is potentially remediable through a better and longer training programme of technology specialists. Specialisation should be rewarded within the banking career structure. The current practise of moving bank officers around frequently and therefore destroying relationships and making acquired knowledge of businesses redundant is a major factor in the failing of UK banks to cater effectively to the needs of new technology-based small firms.

The next stage of this research will develop further some of the themes touched upon in this paper, and it is hoped that a comprehensive model will be developed of the financing process as it impacts upon new technology-based small firms.

NOTES

1. The survey is now approaching 25 firms with the number of sectors included being much larger (May 1994).

ACKNOWLEDGEMENTS

The author would like to acknowledge the financial support for both the research and his attendence at the conference from the Business School at the University of Central England in Birmingham. Thanks are also due to David Deakins of the Enterprise Research Centre at the University of Central England for his comments on earlier drafts of this chapter. All remaining errors are entirely the fault of the author.

REFERENCES

AKERLOF, G. A. (1970) The market for 'Lemons': Quality uncertainty and the market mechanism, *Quarterly Journal of Economics*, Vol. 84, pp. 488-500.

ALLEN, J. C. (1992) *Starting a Technology Business*, Pitman, London.

ANG, J. S. (1991) Some speculations on the theory of finance for privately held firms, *3rd Annual International Research Symposium on Small Business Finance*, Tallahassee, USA, April.

BALTENSPERGER, E. (1976) The borrower-lender relationship, competitive equilibrium and the theory of hedonistic prices, *American Economic Review*, Vol. 66, pp. 401-5.

BANNOCK, G. (1991) *Venture Capital and the Equity Gap*, G. Bannock and Partners Ltd, London.

BERRY, A., FAULKNER, S., HUGHES, M. and JARVIS, R. (1991) *Financial Information, The Banker and the Small Business*, Occasional Paper No. 14. Brighton Polytechnic Business School, Mimeo.

BESTER, H. (1985) Screening vs. rationing in credit markets with imperfect information, *American Economic Review*, Vol. 75, no. 4, pp. 850-5.

BINKS, M., REED, G. V., and ENNEW, C. T. (1988) The survey by the Forum of Private Business on banks and small firms, in G. Bannock and V. Morgan (eds.) *Banks and Small Businesses: A Two Nation Perspective*, Forum of Private Business.

BOVAIRD, C. (1991) *Introduction to Venture Capital Finance*, Pitman, London.

BRYMAN, A. (ed) (1988) *Doing Research in Organisations*, Routledge, London.

BURNS, P. (1992) Financing SMEs in Europe: a five country study, 15th National Small Firms Policy and Research Conference, Southampton.

CHAN, Y. and KANATAS, G. (1985) Asymmetric valuations and the role of collateral in loan agreements, *Journal of Money, Credit and Banking*, Vol. 17, no. 1, pp. 84-95.

DEAKINS, D. and HUSSAIN, G. (1991) *Risk Assessment by Bank Managers*, Department of Financial Services, Birmingham Polytechnic Business School, Mimeo.

DEAKINS, D. and HUSSAIN, G. (1993) Overcoming the adverse selection problem: evidence and policy implications from a study of bank managers on the importance of different criteria used in making a lending decision, in F. Chittenden, M. Robertson and D. Watkins *Small Firms: Recession and Recovery*, Paul Chapman, London.

DEAKINS, D. and PHILPOTT, T. (1993a) *Comparative European Practices in the Finance of Small Firms*, University of Central England Business School, Mimeo.

DEAKINS, D. and PHILPOTT, T. (1993b) Comparative European practices in the finance of new technology entrepreneurs: UK, Germany and Holland, Paper presented to the *New Technology-Based Firms in the 1990s Conference*, Manchester, June.

DE MEZA, D. and WEBB, D. C. (1987) Too much investment: a problem of asymmetric information, *Quarterly Journal of Economics*, Vol. 102, pp. 281-92.

EDEN, C. (1983) *Messing About in Problems*, Pergamon Press, London.

GALE, D. and HELLWIG, M. (1985) Incentive-compatible debt contracts: the one-period problem, *Review of Economic Studies*, Vol. 52, pp. 647-63.

HODGMAN, D. R. (1960) Credit risk and credit rationing, *Quarterly Journal of Economics*, Vol. 74, pp. 258-78.

HODGMAN, D. R. (1962) Reply, *Quarterly Journal of Economics*, Vol. 76, pp.488-93.

JAFFEE, D. and RUSSELL, T. (1976) Imperfect information, uncertainty, and credit rationing, *Quarterly Journal of Economics*, Vol. 90, pp. 651-66.

KAREKEN, J. (1957) Lender's preferences, credit rationing, and the effectiveness of monetary policy, *Review of Economics and Statistics*, Vol. 39, pp. 292-302.

MASON, C. M. and HARRISON, R. T. (1990) *Informal Risk Capital: A Review and Research Agenda*, Venture Finance Research Project, Working Paper No. 1, University of Southampton Urban Policy Research Unit, Mimeo.

MIRLEES, J. A. (1975) *The Theory of Moral Hazard and Unobservable Behaviour – Part 1*, Nuffield College, Oxford, Mimeo.

MORGAN, G. and SMIRCICH, L. (1980) The case for qualitative research, *Academy of Management Review*, Vol. 5, no. 4, pp. 491-500.

MURRAY, G. and LOTT, J. (1992) Have UK venture capital firms a bias against investment in technology related companies? *Babson Entrepreneurship Research Conference*, July, 1992. INSEAD, Fontainebleau, France.

MYERS, S. and MAJLUF, N. (1984) Corporate financing and investment decisions when firms have information investors do not have, *Journal of Financial Economics*, Vol. 12, pp. 187-222.

NATIONAL ECONOMIC DEVELOPMENT COUNCIL (1986) *Lending To Small Firms: A Study of Appraisal and Monitoring Methods*.

OAKEY, R. P. (1984) *High Technology Small Firms*, Frances Pinter, London.

OAKEY, R. P. (1991) Government policy towards high technology: small firms beyond the year 2000, in J. Curran and R. A. Blackburn, R.A. (eds.) *Paths to Enterprise*, Routledge, London.

OAKEY, R. P., ROTHWELL, R. and COOPER, S. (1988) *Management of Innovation in High Technology Small Firms*, Frances Pinter, London.

OBERMAYER, J. (1983) The capital gap for technical entrepreneurs, *Frontiers of Entrepreneurship Research*, Wellesley, M.A., Babson College, pp. 307-15.

ROBBIE, K. and MURRAY, G. (1992) Venture Capital in the UK, *International Journal of Bank Marketing*, Vol. 10, no.5, pp. 32-40.

SPENSE, A. M. (1974) *Market Signalling*, Harvard University Press, Boston M.A.

STANWORTH, J. and GRAY, C. (eds.) (1991) *Bolton 20 Years On: The Small Firm in the 1990s*, Paul Chapman, London.

STIGLITZ, J. and WEISS, A. (1981) Credit rationing in markets with imperfect information, *American Economic Review*, Vol. 71, pp. 393-410.

VICKERY, L. (1989) Equity Financing in Small Firms in P. Burns and J. Dewhurst (eds.) *Small Business and Entrepreneurship*, pp. 204-36, Macmillan, London.

VYAKERNAM, S. and JACOBS, R. (1991) How do bank managers construe high technology entrepreneurs? *14th National Small Firms Policy and Research Conference*, Blackpool, November, 1991.

WALKER, R. (ed.) (1985) *Applied Qualitative Research*, Gower, Aldershot.

CHAPTER 8

The Growth and the Funding Mechanisms of New Technology-Based Firms: A Comparative Study Between the United Kingdom and Finland[1]

ANNAREETTA LUMME, ILKKA KAURANEN AND ERKKO AUTIO

INTRODUCTION

New technology-based firms and academic entrepreneurship have been the focus of numerous studies. Many of the earlier studies on new technology-based firms have been carried out in a single country. This approach has been understandable, since many of the studies have been the first of their kind. Not much is known about the similarities and differences between new technology-based firms in different countries. Thus, the limited focus of most studies often limits the generalizability of their results.

This paper seeks to increase knowledge on the similarities and the differences between new technology-based firms in the UK and in Finland. It focuses on the inter-relationships between firm growth and the funding mechanisms of new technology-based firms. This focus is chosen because funding is often a key factor affecting the growth of new, technology-based firms. Moreover, funding can also be relatively rapidly influenced through government policies.

The UK, and specifically Cambridge were chosen as the UK comparative environment for three reasons. First, Cambridge has one of the most important concentrations of new technology-based firms in Europe. In this study, Cambridge is used as an example of a well developed European environment for new technology-based firms.

Second, the entrepreneurial environments in the UK and in Finland differ quite sharply. This reality provides an interesting comparative international setting for the study. In the 1980s, the UK government actively promoted the development of a free market economy. Entrepreneurship was strongly encouraged by a supportive fiscal and legal environment. The taxation of firms in the UK was low compared with that of other European countries, while initiatives were launched to attract capital from private individuals.

In Finland, the fiscal environment of firms traditionally has favoured debt funding over equity capital. Accordingly, the accumulation of equity capital in the form of retained earnings has been hindered in Finnish firms. The Finnish government traditionally has played a relatively important role as a source of funding for small and medium-sized firms. Furthermore, the availability of private capital, especially that of venture capital, is likely to be much better for firms in the UK than for their counterparts in Finland. Within Europe, the venture capital industry is at its most mature stage in the UK. Adjusted to gross national product, the amount of venture capital available for firms in Finland is only about 7% of the amount of venture capital available in the

UK. Furthermore, about 70% of the total amount of venture capital invested annually in Finland has come from public venture capital sources whereas in the UK the respective value has been only about 1%.

Third, the research environment of the incubating organizations in both Cambridge and Finland may be characterized as typically European. In general, researchers are not encouraged to go into business. Academics often commercialize their inventions only if they find it personally challenging. In both Cambridge and Finland, the universities have a liberal policy towards the exploitation of research. This policy allows researchers to benefit personally from the results of their research.

PREVIOUS RESEARCH

Roberts has considered the growth and the funding of new technology-based firms in many of his studies. According to Roberts, the growth and the funding of a new technology-based firm evolves through a succession of stages. Roberts identifies three phases in the evolution of a new technology-based firm: start-up, initial growth, and sustained growth. Each stage of a firm's evolution strongly influences the type and amount of capital required. Roberts points out that the need for initial capital varies significantly among new technology-based firms. The need is a function of, for example, the industrial sector, the type of business, and the size of the firm's founding team (Roberts, 1990; Roberts, 1991a).

Segal et al, among others, have conducted specific studies on the growth and the funding of new technology-based firms in Cambridge. They applied the concepts of 'soft' and 'hard' firms. Firms which started as 'soft' were characterized as low-risk firms, both in technology and in funding. The funding needs of 'soft' firms were quite moderate and they were usually run on a part-time basis, while their founders retained their academic positions. The 'soft' firms often began from a consultancy base. The new technology-based firms in Cambridge gradually became 'harder' which meant that a firm's operations shifted from consulting towards production and involved management on a full-time basis. The funding needs for firms, and the financial and technological risks, were increased as the firms 'hardened' (Segal et al 1990), (Segal 1987).

Myllyniemi et al have focused in their literature review on different models for new firm growth, on determinants of growth for new firms, and on internal and external factors affecting growth, especially of new technology-based firms. They discuss funding as a key functional area in firm growth, stating that almost all new small firms are under-capitalized in the beginning (Myllyniemi et al 1990).

The role of professional financiers in funding the growth of new technology-based firms has been discussed in many studies. Freear et al found that new technology-based firms that had received external equity funding in the past tended to have higher forecast growth rates and greater international emphasis than firms that had not received external equity funding in the past (Freear et al 1991). Florida and Kenney concluded that although venture capital is not absolutely necessary to facilitate high technology entrepreneurship, well-developed venture capital networks provide tremendous incentives for entrepreneurship by lowering the difficulties of entering an industry (Florida and Kenney, 1988).

Roberts found in a case study of two venture capital firms in the Boston area that only a small proportion of technology-based firms were found initially to be financed by professional financiers (Roberts, 1991b). Harrison and Mason found that informal investors are playing an important role in venture funding in UK, by making investments typically of under £50,000 in the seed and the start-up phases, which is a scale of investment usually avoided by professional venture capitalists (Harrison and Mason, 1992; Harrison and Mason, 1990).

Dôutriaux has analyzed the growth and the funding of new technology-based firms from the viewpont of government support. He concluded that the government should subcontract to new technology-based firms rather than give direct support to them. Those firms which had started as government suppliers were more successful in increasing their value of sales than firms which had received other types of government support. Additionally, the firms supplying the government were better organized and more export-oriented than the other firms in the sample studied (Dôutriaux, 1991).

AIMS OF THE STUDY

The aims of this study are:

• To establish a more detailed understanding of the growth and the funding mechanisms of new technology-based firms in the UK and in Finland.
• To track similarities and differences of the growth and the funding mechanisms between new technology-based firms in the UK and in Finland.
• To identify factors in funding mechanisms hindering the growth of new technology-based firms in the UK and in Finland.

DESCRIPTION OF THE RESEARCH PROCESS

The findings of this comparative study are based on interviews with founders of 45 Cambridge firms and 85 Finnish firms. The interviews were conducted in Cambridge in the autumn of 1991 and in Finland in the summer of 1988. The study applies a quantitative approach. The response rate of the study was exceptionally high, namely 97% in Cambridge and 98% in Finland.

In collecting the two samples for the comparative study, the following criteria were used:

• The firms studied were entrepreneurial; they had been established by a founder or a group of founders.
• The firms were independent during their early years of existence (i.e. the firms were not part of or a subsidiary of another firm).
• The firms emerged from a university or a research institute (i.e. the business idea of a firm had been based essentially on exploiting advanced technological knowledge developed by or acquired in a university or a research institute). In addition, the founder or at least one person in a group of founders had been affiliated with a university or a research institute.

The research programme compares the basic characteristics, founders, start-up phase, growth and development, funding, technology transfer, and internationalization of new technology-based firms emerging from universities and research institutes in Cambridge, England, in the UK and in Finland. The research programme was carried out as a joint project between the Finnish National Fund for Research and Development, SITRA; and Helsinki University of Technology. The Small Business Research Centre at the University of Cambridge acted as the local cooperative partner in Cambridge, facilitating field research and linking the research programme to other research in Cambridge.

SOME BASIC CHARACTERISTICS OF THE TWO SAMPLES

Firms in both samples were quite young and small. At the time of interviews, the Cambridge firms were an average of 5.3 years old, and the Finnish firms 3.3 years old. At the time of interviews, the Cambridge firms employed a median number of 7.5 employees, and the Finnish firms 3.0 employees, respectively.

Most of the firms in the Cambridge sample had their roots in the University of Cambridge. The most frequent incubating organizations of the firms in the Finnish sample were Helsinki University of Technology and the University of Oulu.

The percentage of production firms was larger in the Cambridge sample than in the Finnish sample. This difference was not statistically significant. Figure 8.1 shows the main fields of activity for firms in the Cambridge sample and in the Finnish sample.

According to the founders in both samples, the motives for founding the firms were technology oriented, with the Cambridge founders being even more technology oriented than the Finnish founders. A lack of marketing know-how and low credibility in the eyes of the customers were common problems for both groups of firms. Negative push factors were not important as motives for founding in either sample.

The founders of the Cambridge firms had stronger university or research institute background than the founders of the Finnish firms. The founders in the Cambridge sample had been employed by a university or by a research institute for an average of 11 years prior to the founding of their firm. The respective number for the Finnish founders was 4 years.

No significant differences were identified in the frequency of the preparatory measures taken prior to the founding of the firms in the two samples. In both Cambridge and Finland, about half of the founders had prepared a business plan prior to the founding of their firm. A functioning prototype of the initial product had been developed prior to founding by a little more than half of the Cambridge firms and a little less than half of the Finnish firms.

The number of patents obtained by the firms in both samples was quite small. On the average, the Cambridge firms had acquired more patents than the Finnish firms. This difference was partly caused by the higher percentage of production firms in the Cambridge sample.

At the time of interviews, the Cambridge firms had a greater need for going international than the Finnish firms. Additionally, exports accounted for a higher percentage of

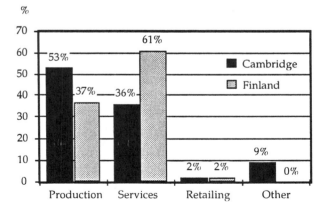

Figure 8.1
Main Fields of Activity for Firms in the Cambridge Sample and in the Finnish Sample

the value of sales in the Cambridge sample than in the Finnish sample. This difference was especially important for the service firms. The older age of the Cambridge firms partially explains their more advanced international operations.

GROWTH OF THE FIRMS

The growth of the firms is measured in this study in terms of full-time personnel and in terms of value of sales. A combination of these two indicators is preferred, since each of the two indicators alone might give an incomplete picture of firm growth. Only the number of full-time personnel is considered, because the number of part-time personnel was quite small in both samples of firms.

Since the average age of the firms in the Finnish sample was 3.3 years, versus 5.3 years for the Cambridge sample firms, comparisons of the growth rates between the two samples needed some processing of the data. In this study, the comparisons of the growth rates of firms are made by carrying out a linear extrapolation of the Finnish data and a linear interpolation of the Cambridge data. The extrapolation and interpolation procedures were carried out separately for each firm in the two samples.

Studies show that the actual growth of a firm is often a succession of stable stages and stages of change, rather than a strictly linear proces (Kazanjian, 1983). Therefore, the use of linear extrapolation and interpolation in this present study is reasoned with the following arguments:

- Linear extrapolation and interpolation characterize well the average growth rates of firms in the two samples.
- The age difference of the firms in the two samples is relatively small; in the case of small differences, a linear approximation is not likely to cause major errors.
- The analysis of differences between the two samples is systematically based on both an extrapolation of the Finnish data, on the one hand, and an interpolation of the Cambridge data, on the other hand; this way, the consistency of the results achieved using the two methods can be checked.

As the differences in the main fields of activity between the two samples were quite important, although not statistically significant, the growth as well as the funding comparisons are carried out separately for production firms and for service firms. The need for separate comparisons arises from differences in the growth and the funding needs of the firms. Production firms often need large amounts of funding to cover high costs of capital investments. Service firms often can start their operations with a small initial capital. Furthermore, a production firm most often grows through increasing its production capacity, whereas a service firm typically grows by employing more people. In this present study, the main field of activity of a firm is defined as the activity that accounts for the largest percentage of the value of sales.

All figures concerning values of sales and funding are shown in British Pounds Sterling, using the exchange rate in force in autumn of 1991, when the interviews were conducted in Cambridge. At that time, the exchange rate was 1 British Pound Sterling equal to 7.3 Finnish Marks.

Comparison of number of personnel and value of sales in production firms

During their start-up phase, the production firms in both the Cambridge sample and in the Finnish sample employed about the same number of personnel. The average number of employees was 2.3 in the Cambridge production firms and 2.5 in the Finnish production firms. At the time of interviews, the production firms had an average of 16.7 full-time employees in the Cambridge sample and 9.2 full-time employees in the Finnish sample.

The comparisons of extrapolated and interpolated numbers of personnel did not reveal statistically significant differences between the production firms of the two samples. However, the average annual growth rates of the firms differed between the two samples at significance level $p<0.05$. The average annual growth rate of the production firms was 3.7 persons in the Cambridge sample and 1.8 persons in the Finnish sample. Obviously, this difference was not yet reflected in the linear extrapolation and interpolation. Figure 8.2 shows the average number of personnel of production firms in the Cambridge sample and in the Finnish sample, with extrapolated data in the Finnish sample.

Sales data were also compared by relating extrapolated sales figures. The total value of sales that the Finnish firms would have generated at the average age of 5.3 years was extrapolated, yielding a sales value of £780,000 British Pounds Sterling at the average age of 5.3 years. The comparable average value of sales of the Cambridge production firms was £730,000 British Pounds Sterling. This difference is not statistically significant.

Comparison of number of personnel and value of sales in service firms

During the start-up phase, the number of full-time employees in the Cambridge service firms was greater than that of the Finnish service firms. The average number of full-time employees was 2.9 in the Cambridge service firms and 1.8 in the Finnish service firms. However, this difference was not statistically significant. At the time of the interviews, the service firms had an average of 14.4 full-time employees in the Cambridge sample and 5.4 full-time employees in the Finnish sample.

Growth comparisons between the service firms in the two samples were based on similar extrapolation and interpolation procedures as in the case of production firms.

First, the total number of people that the Finnish service firms would have employed at the age of 5.3 years was extrapolated. According to the extrapolation, at the age of

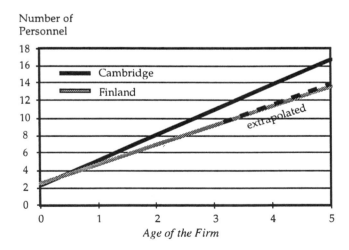

Figure 8.2
Average Number of Personnel of Production Firms in the Cambridge Sample and in the Finnish Sample, with Extrapolated Data in the Finnish Sample

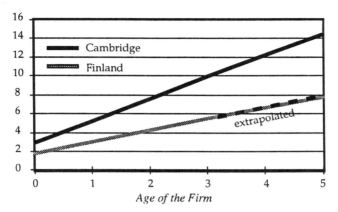

Figure 8.3
Average Number of Personnel of Service Firms in the Cambridge Sample and in the Finnish Sample, with Extrapolated Data in the Finnished Sample

5.3 years, the average Finnish service firm would have employed 8 people. At the time of the interviews, the Cambridge firms were actually employing an average of 14 people. This difference is statistically significant at significance level p<0.05.

Second, the number of people that the Cambridge service firms would have employed at the average age of 3.3 years was interpolated. According to the interpolation, an average Cambridge service firm would have employed 9 people at 3.3 years of age. At the time of the interviews, the Finnish service firms employed on the average 5 employees. This difference is statistically almost significant at significance level p<0.10. Figure 8.3 shows the average number of personnel of service firms in the Cambridge sample and in the Finnish sample, with extrapolated data in the Finnish case.

Third, the difference in the average annual growth rates of the firms was statistically significant at significance level p<0.05. The service firms increased their personnel annually by an average of 2.3 persons in the Cambridge sample and by 1.0 persons in the Finnish sample.

Fourth, the total value of sales that the Finnish firms would have generated at the average age of 5.3 years was extrapolated. The extrapolations showed that the value of sales of service firms in the Finnish sample would have averaged £190,000 British Pounds Sterling when the firms had been on the average 5.3 years of age. The comparable value of sales of the Cambridge service firms was £730,000 British Pounds Sterling. This difference is statistically significant at significance level p<0.01. Table 8.1 shows the average value of sales of service firms in the Cambridge sample and in the Finnish sample, with extrapolated data in the Finnish sample.

Table 8.1: *Average numbers of value of sales of service firms in the Cambridge sample and in the Finnish sample, with extrapolated data in the Finnish sample*

	CAMBRIDGE	FINLAND
Values of sales	£ 730,000	£ 190,000

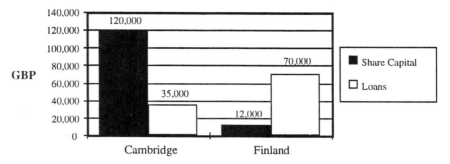

Figure 8.4
Average Amounts of Initial Share capital and Initial Loans Obtained by Production Firms in the Cambridge Sample and in the Finnish Sample

FUNDING OF THE FIRMS

Of the funding of the firms, the amounts, as well as the sources, of initial capital of the firms are studied. Characteristics of the Finnish firms and the Cambridge firms are compared. Differences found between the samples are discussed. As in the comparisons regarding the growth of firms, the funding of the firms was compared separately for production firms and for service firms.

Amounts and sources of initial capital for production firms

Differences in the funding of the Cambridge and the Finnish firms can be identified already in the start-up phase of the firms. First, the average amount of initial share capital in Cambridge production firms was £120,000 British Pounds Sterling. The corresponding Finnish production firms started with an average initial share capital of £12,000 British Pounds Sterling. This difference is statistically significant at significance level $p<0.05$. In this study, the initial capital is defined as the amount of share capital and loans that were needed for the start-up phase of a firm's operations.

Second, the amounts of the loans used to finance the start-up phase of production firms in the two samples also differed to some extent, although this difference was not statistically significant. In Cambridge, the loans averaged roughly £35,000 British Pounds

Table 8.2: *Comparison of the sources of initial capital used by production firms in the Cambridge sample and in the Finnish sample*

	CAMBRIDGE	FINLAND	SIGNIFICANCE LEVEL
Founders	71%	94%	$p < 0.05$
Relatives of founders	13%	10%	not significant
Other private individuals	8%	2%	not significant
Banks	8%	26%	not significant
Venture capital firms and corporate venturing	21%	3%	$p < 0.05$
Insurance firms	0%	0%	not significant
Other firms	4%	13%	not significant
Government	4%	33%	$p < 0.01$

Sterling. The Finnish firms started with loans averaging £70,000 British Pounds Sterling. Figure 8.4 shows the average amounts of initial share capital and initial loans obtained by production firms in the Cambridge sample and in the Finnish sample.

Third, a comparison of the frequency of sources of initial capital reveals further differences between the samples. The founders of the Finnish firms made initial investments in their own firms significantly more often than did the founders of Cambridge firms. Government funding was used more often as a source of initial capital by the firms in Finland than by those in Cambridge. Furthermore, venture capital or corporate venturing was used more often by the Cambridge firms than by the Finnish firms. These differences were statistically significant at significance levels $p<0.05$ or $p<0.01$. Table 8.2 shows the comparison of the sources of initial capital used by production firms in the Cambridge sample and in the Finnish sample. In this analysis, small investments involving negligible amounts of money were omitted.

Amount and sources of initial capital for service firms

Differences noted for production firms also can be identified in service firms. First, the average amount of initial share capital for service firms was £35,000 British Pounds Sterling in the Cambridge sample and roughly £5,000 British Pounds Sterling in the Finnish sample. This difference is statistically significant at significance level $p<0.05$. In comparisons, one outlier from both samples was excluded. In the Cambridge sample, the outlier had an initial share capital of £750,000. In the Finnish sample, the outlier had an initial share capital of £165,000.

Second, the average amount of initial loans was £20,000 for Cambridge service firms and £15,000 for Finnish service firms. This difference was not statistically significant. Again, one outlier from both samples was excluded. In the Cambridge sample, the outlier had obtained start-up loans totalling £730,000. In the Finnish sample, the outlier had obtained loans totalling £135,000. Figure 8.5 shows the average amounts of initial share capital and initial loans obtained by service firms in the Cambridge sample and in the Finnish sample.

Third, the start-up phase of the Finnish service firms was financed by banks significantly more often than that of the Cambridge service firms. In a similar way as in production firms, venture capitalists had a significantly more important role in funding service firms in Cambridge than in Finland. Government funding was more often used as a source of initial capital by the Finnish service firms than by those in the Cambridge sample. These differences were statistically significant, as shown in Table 8.3.

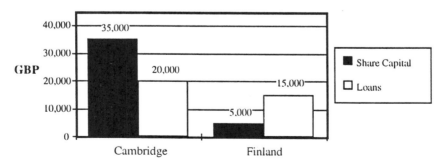

Figure 8.5
Average Amounts of Initial Share Capital and Loans Obtained by Service Firms in the Cambridge Sample and in the Finnish Sample

Table 8.3: *Comparison of the sources of initial capital used by service firms in the Cambridge sample and in the Finnish sample*

	CAMBRIDGE	FINLAND	SIGNIFICANCE LEVEL
Founders	88%	90%	not significant
Relatives of founders	0%	6%	not significant
Other private individuals	0%	2%	not significant
Banks	6%	40%	$p < 0.01$
Venture capital firms and corporate venturing	19%	0%	$p < 0.05$
Insurance firms	0%	4%	not significant
Other firms	6%	12%	not significant
Government	0%	19%	$p < 0.05$

CONCLUSIONS AND DISCUSSION

This study has sought to establish a more detailed understanding of the interrelationships between growth and funding mechanisms in new technology-based firms. For this purpose, samples of Cambridge firms and Finnish firms have been analyzed.

Comparisons between the two samples reveal that the Cambridge firms, especially the service firms, had grown more rapidly than the Finnish firms. This finding is based on the comparison of linear extrapolations and linear interpolations. The finding can be considered quite reliable because both the linear extrapolations and the linear interpolations point to the same conclusion. Additionally, the statistically significant differences in the growth rates of the firms further confirm these results.

In addition to differences in growth, statistically significant differences in the funding of the firms in the two samples could be observed. In this study, the following differences observed in the funding of the firms may at least partially explain the differing growth rates of the firms.

First, the initial funding of the firms in the Cambridge sample was healthier than the funding of those in the Finnish sample. The Cambridge firms started with a significantly larger amount of share capital and a smaller amount of loans than the Finnish firms. Growth most often is a highly capital-consuming process. Accordingly, it is clear that a healthy capital base gives a firm more freedom to invest in growth than does a heavy load of debt. A heavy load of debt limits the possibilities of a firm to obtain more debt funding and also consumes the scarce financial resources of a firm, in the form of interest payments and repayments of loan.

Second, firms in the Cambridge sample had initial venture capital inputs more often than did firms in the Finnish sample. The Finnish firms used initial funding from government sources more often than firms in the Cambridge sample. It is easy to believe that venture capital funding is much more growth oriented than is government funding. Government funding most often does not drive firms to pursue aggressive growth strategy in a similar way as venture capital funding does. Additionally, venture capital investors most often participate actively in the development of the firm, while government funding is more passive in nature.

In this present study, special attention has been paid to avoiding bias in the collection of the two samples. During the sample identification phase, several measures were taken to ensure that the samples were collected using exactly similar criteria. It is therefore the belief of the authors of this study that the differences observed between the two samples are real and not the result of a sampling error.

All of the above discussed factors point to implications for improving funding mechanisms to promote future growth of the firms. It is suggested that the better availability of private capital partially explains the healthier initial capital structure and the more rapid growth of the Cambridge firms. Therefore, the availability of private capital, that is, venture capital, corporate venturing funds, and capital from private individuals and organizations, should be made readily available to ensure growth opportunities for the firms.

In the UK, a very small amount of investments are typically made into new technology-based firms, mainly because of the high risks involved. Therefore, it is essential to ensure the availability of growth-seeking funding mechanisms for the new technology-based firms that have the potential of growing rapidly.

In Finland, a lack of adequate equity capital is a serious hindrance to the favourable development of new technology-based firms. Therefore, the availability of private capital, especially venture capital, should be increased in Finland. With growth-oriented funding mechanisms, such new technology-based firms can be nurtured that can generate considerable amounts of new wealth in a society.

Finally, it has to be pointed out that funding alone does not always determine the growth rate of a firm. The growth of a firm is affected by a combination of many different factors. These factors may include competitive new technology, well balanced and competitive management team, determination of the management team to make the firm grow, a favourable environment for the firm to grow in, sufficient funding, and, for example, growth-oriented owners and investors. However, in the case of individual firms, the effect of any one factor alone can be decisive.

NOTES

1. This paper has been published in the *Finnish Journal of Business Economics*, Vol. 43, no. 1, 1994, Helsinki, Finland.

REFERENCES

DOUTRIAUX, J. (1991) High-tech start-ups, better off with government contracts than with subsidies: new evidence in Canada, *IEEE Transactions on Engineering Management*, Vol. 38, no. 2, pp. 127-35.

FLORIDA, R. and KENNEY, M. (1988) Venture capital and high technology entrepreneurship, *Journal of Business Venturing*, Vol. 3, pp. 301-19.

FREEAR, J. F., SOHL, J. E. and WETZEL, W. E. (1991) Raising venture capital to finance growth, *Frontiers of Entrepreneurship Research 1991*, Center for Entrepreneurial Studies, Babson College, Mass.

HARRISON, R. T. and MASON, C. M. (1990) Informal risk capital in the United Kingdom, *Frontiers of Entrepreneurship Research 1990*, Massachusetts, Center for Entrepreneurial Studies, Babson College, Mass.

HARRISON, R. T. and MASON, C. M. (1992) International perspectives on the supply of informal venture capital, *Journal of Business Venturing*, Vol. 7, pp. 459-75.

KAZANJIAN, R. K. (1983) The organizational evolution of high technology new ventures: the impact of stage of growth on the nature of structure and planning process, Doctoral Dissertation, The Wharton School, University of Pennsylvania.

MYLLYNIEMI, T., KAURANEN, I., AUTIO, E. and KAILA, M. M. (1990) *The Growth of New Technology-Based Companies*, SITRA, Helsinki.

ROBERTS, E. B. (1990) Initial capital for the new technological enterprise, *IEEE Transactions for Engineering Management*, Vol. 37, no. 2, pp. 81-93.

ROBERTS, E. B. (1991a) *Entrepreneurs in High Technology, Lessons from MIT and Beyond*, Oxford University Press, New York.

ROBERTS, E. B. (1991b) High stakes for high-tech entrepreneurs: Understanding venture capital decision making, *Sloan Management Review*, Winter 1991, pp. 9-20.

SEGAL, N. (1987) Some issues in the start-up and growth of small high technology companies, 1987, *Gestion 2000*, Vol. 3, no. 6, pp.45-62.

SEGAL, QUINCE and WICKSTEED (1990) *The Cambridge Phenomenon* (3rd edition) Segal Quince Wicksteed Limited, England.

CHAPTER 9

Comparative European Practices in the Finance of New Technology Entrepreneurs: United Kingdom, Germany and Holland

Evidence from case studies of different financing arrangements in three regions: West Midlands, Baden-Württemberg and Twente

DAVID DEAKINS AND TOBY PHILPOTT

INTRODUCTION

Providers of funds to new technology entrepreneurs (NTEs) face problems that arise from the combination of small business start-ups and the uncertainty that surrounds the assessment of new technology and its proposed applications. Problems of risk assessment of new propositions are accentuated by additional factors of technological uncertainty (Vyakarnam and Jacobs, 1991) and the evaluation of R&D (Oakey, 1984). Problems in risk assessment arise because of asymmetric information. Funding providers face the twin problems of adverse selection and moral hazard (Stiglitz and Weiss, 1981; Binks, Ennew and Reed, 1988). Banks and venture capitalists have different methods and criteria which are used to assess NTEs which may reflect these problems. In recognition of some of these funding problems national and regional governments may provide alternative funding programmes designed to relieve such constraints and finance gaps for NTEs. Short term funding horizons operated by the banks will obviously conflict with the requirements of new technology business owners who have particular term maturity funding requirements, which are relatively long term due to the need for seed, development and later stage funding.

For risk assessment of NTEs it is reasonable to hypothesise that banks and venture capitalists will require a large information set from the entrepreneur on management abilities, qualifications and expertise in the application of the technology. Bank officers and venture capitalists may have little knowledge of the technology and we would hypothesise that officers concerned with risk assessment will seek outside expertise to assess the technology. Venture capitalists are known to have close working relationships with funded entrepreneurs. They will also specialise in certain sectors and activities. This involvement overcomes moral hazard. Banks, however, will find it difficult to overcome moral hazard because (for relatively small amounts of finance) it is not economic to devote resources to closely monitor ventures. Thus, in the future, banks can be expected to devote new resources to overcome the adverse selection problem. Investment in risk assessment of NTEs can pay dividends through marketing and funding opportunities as the technology is developed.

For bank decisions, the role of collateral will be significant. In theory, given asymmetric information, it can be argued that collateral signals commitment from the entrepreneur (Chan and Kanatas, 1985). Banks, therefore, can be expected to require security to secure commitment. However, it may be possible that collateral will act as a surrogate criterion in risk assessment where information is lacking, or the bank officer finds it easier to use than a subjective assessment of the entrepreneurial abilities and the potential of the new technology.

The issues that surround the provision of equity to NTEs are concerned with the dilution of equity holding (the loss of control) (Oakey, 1984), and the extent of value added provided by the investor on the management and development of the technology. The investor may seek to minimise the risk associated with an investment by taking some measure of control in the investee firm by providing management on the board. This will provide advice and investment to the entrepreneur who wishes to develop the technology and expand the business. The investor is able to monitor the performance of the company and the intention will be to add value in the management of the enterprise (Mason and Harrison, 1992; Sapienza, Manigart and Herron, 1992; Murray and Lott, 1992). This paper is concerned with comparative risk assessment criteria and funding arrangements in 3 European regions: West Midlands in the UK, Baden-Württemberg in Germany and Twente in Holland.

RESEARCH METHODOLOGY AND DATA SOURCES

This study utilises a variety of data sources. Firstly, the findings from the first stage research interviews with 30 UK bank officers from the West Midlands region. Secondly, four further face-to-face interviews were carried out with some participating banks at higher management levels in the UK concerning policy towards new technology firms. Thirdly, we were able to arrange interviews with 6 respondents in Germany and a further 4 respondents in Holland. We were able to compare risk assessment practices through case study material of UK and German bank officers when dealing with new technology firms. In addition we have interview material with venture capitalists and support agencies in both Holland and Germany.

All the interviews were tape recorded and fully transcribed. Research involving cross country analysis may suffer from problems of interpretation and translation. Some of the interviews were conducted in German, but we were fortunate to secure an interpreter (see acknowledgements) who was able to provide the interpretation both of our questions and of the respondents' replies. In each case we were able to see the person directly concerned with decision-making and in dealing with small firm propositions. We were fortunate in having good links with the Fachhochschule in Pforzheim, who through their participation in the region and their links were able to secure agreement for us with appropriate people at each participating institution (see acknowledgements). These sources combined represent an in-depth case study of financing arrangements and banking practices in the three regions.

In the UK, we took on the role of entrepreneurs who were applying new technology to the construction industry. It involved the application of new CAD/CAM techniques and programming to provide a completely integrated QS service involving design, build and maintenance. We were seeking a funding decision from bank officers in the West Midlands region of the UK for this start-up proposition. A significant feature of the proposition was the reliance of the business on an Automisation Director who was responsible for the application and development of the new technology. A detailed business plan was provided for the UK bank officers in which the role and application of the new technology was explained. In addition, the business was closely tied to a revolutionary housing product again involving a separate application of new technology controlled by the Automisation Director, in respect of which, patents had been applied for.

In Germany, bank officers took us through a case study of a new technology start-up firm. This was especially prepared for our visit by the local Sparkasse Bank. The bank officers explained the criteria which would be important for the assessment of the concern. Using this information we were able to make direct comparisons with the risk assessment practices of the UK banks. The results are reported in more detail in our research reports (Deakins and Hussain, 1991; Deakins and Philpott, 1993).

COMPARATIVE BANKING PRACTICES

Table 9.1 shows that important technical, managerial and strategic information was used only by a small minority of UK bank officers. This indicated a bias in approach, when assessing applications from new technology-based firms or those applying new technology. Information associated with the application of the new technology was either ignored or was unimportant for risk assessment. For example, the extent to which the venture was dependent on the role of the Automisation Director, and the relationship between him and the other entrepreneurs, was pursued in detail by only one manager. Yet the business was dependent upon his role for the application of new technology and the future growth of the business was closely tied to the development of the new technology. This may have reflected a lack of experience in dealing with applications that involve new technology. Some managers expressed an opinion that it was 'above my head' and were quite open in admitting that they knew little about the technology involved. Only one of our 30 managers in this first stage study was familiar with the terminology that concerned the new technology applications in the construction industry.

In the UK, there is very limited specialisation, a reluctance to appreciate the benefits of specialisation and a distinct lack of involvement by outside experts, who may be able to assess the application of the new technology. There was little in the way of specific strategies for NTEs. The two banks with the largest market share in the UK, Barclays and NatWest do employ some 'technology specialists'. However, this specialism is not highly developed. For example, the National Westminster Bank has a 'Technology Unit' with some 50+ 'Technology Managers'. These managers specialise in assessing new and high technology applications. If an NTE applies to the Bank, the Technology Manager may make an initial assessment. If the manager wishes to proceed with the application, outside consultants then may be brought in to make a risk assessment. This policy was found to suffer from a number of drawbacks. For example, there is no requirement for any individual manager to refer an NTE to a Technology Manager and the amount of specific technology training received by such managers was only '2-3 days'. In addition it was admitted that the process was rather 'a hit and miss affair' since whether an NTE saw a Technology Manager depended upon which branch manager was approached.

Combining the UK results with the interview material from Germany and Holland reveals some key differences in risk assessment practices of NTEs. These are summarised under the headings of gearing, collateral, technical and managerial information, monitoring and term maturity.

Gearing

Table 9.1 shows a preoccupation with the gearing for our proposition by UK officers. This concern arose because the proposition was relatively highly-geared at 2:1. This created considerable difficulty for the UK bank officers who would have preferred a standard 1:1 ratio. This contrasts with attitudes to gearing in German and Dutch banks,

Table 9.1: *UK criteria on the applied new technology proposition*

INFORMATION	PERCENTAGE OF MANAGERS
Gearing	83%
Entrepreneurs' financial position	73%
Forecasted B/S and P/L account	66%
Entrepeneurs' drawings	63%
Entrepreneurs' industry contacts	60%
Timing of income payments	60%
Contingency plans	57%
Entrepreneurs' personal collateral	50%
Market research	50%
Entrepreneurs' qualifications/careers	43%
Cash flow assumptions	40%
Entrepreneurs' starting separately	37%
Role of IT consultant	33%
IT development costs	27%
Business/managerial strategy	13%
Enterprise and small business experience	10%
Technical expertise and knowledge	3%

where there was less of a concern with high gearing ratios. Cases of gearing ratios of 5:1 were not uncommon. In general we can say that high gearing ratios are more acceptable in German banks than in UK banks. In Holland, gearing ratios of around 2:1 were considered normal. For example we were told that: 'If, let's say, the entrepreneur puts in 11,000 guilders, then most of the time, the bank puts in 20,000 guilders.'

An interview with one new technology entrepreneur in Twente revealed a high gearing ratio, where the entrepreneur's equity only accounted for less than 10% of his long-term capital (although this was partly accounted for by alternative funding sources).

Collateral

The concern with gearing ratios in the UK is also connected to requirements that entrepreneurs should provide security. Table 9.1 shows that 50% of UK bank officers were concerned to establish the level of collateral (personal security in property) that the entrepreneurs could provide. The importance of security is noticeably different in Baden-Württemberg and Twente. It was stated by a number of bank officers in Germany that security was either of minor importance or not required if the technology was perceived to be good enough. In Holland, although security may be required by banks, it was of less importance than the knowledge and expertise of the NTE in their product. In Germany it was felt that security might be awkward to manage and the bank would prefer to lend without security if the proposition was sufficiently strong. This could be because security is often taken on business assets which will depreciate. For example one comment was made that: 'The nicest loans are those without collateral.'

Personal guarantees seemed to be more important than they would be in the UK. For example, one officer from the Sparkasse bank commented that: 'They like to have a personal guarantee from the owner to motivate him.'

These contrasts in approach may well reflect other differences in society. For example, in the UK there is a high degree of home ownership which may lead the UK banks to expect that there will be some personal collateral available in property. These contrasts also reflect differences in other criteria which are given different importance.

These differences in social and economic infrastructure could be both a cause and a consequence of concerns with collateral.

Technical and managerial information

We were able to examine a case study of a proposition from a new technology-based firm by officers from the local Sparkasse bank. At the top of the list of criteria examined were personal characteristics and experience of the entrepreneur, together with technical expertise. Criteria included the extent of education and training, a requirement for at least 11 years experience, qualifications, details of career and concern with technical, managerial and commercial abilities. Thus, human capital attributes were regarded as crucial in risk assessment. Comments included:

> The founder is the most important thing for us...In our experience most reasons that firms go broke is due to management experience...More important (than security) is to see the personality of the founder, experience is very important and that is the reason why he is successful or not.

The family name could also affect the decision. Local knowledge of past dealings with the family was found to have an effect. In Germany there seem to be closer links with the local community and any knowledge of the family history of the entrepreneur affected the lending decision. This emphasis on the personal qualities of the entrepreneur was also regarded as vital by the local Industrie-und-Handelskammer (IHK) (Chamber of Commerce). The Director responsible for the development of new technology orientated firms considered that:

> The personal qualities of the entrepreneur are very important and the entrepreneur must be a good businessman. They must know their product and be convincing.

A greater emphasis on personal attributes was also apparent in Holland. If a technology-based entrepreneur applies for a loan then they will be required to acquire management qualifications. This will be a condition of the loan if the bank feel that there is a gap in management ability or knowledge. For example the following comment is illustrative:

> In the Netherlands we have a completely different system from the one that you have in the UK. When you want to start a business here you need to have education...If you are not qualified they will not lend.

Market research was regarded as essential by our respondents in Germany. If the NTE does not possess this knowledge then he/she will be required to obtain consultancy and advice from either the local IHK or Fachhochschule (technical college). It was noticeable, in Germany, that the local network between banks, the IHK and the technical educational institutions was much more advanced than in the UK. Also, there was a willingness to share information. Often, in Germany more than one bank would be involved in financing and assessing a proposition. If one bank had a network of contacts or a specialist in the area then information could be shared.

One of the implications of these differences in risk assessment is that it can be more difficult for an NTE to establish a business than in the UK. It is also noticeable that much of UK support has been targeted at start-ups (Stanworth and Gray, 1991; Storey, 1992). In the UK the small firms sector has seen the most growth although mainly in micro firms (employing less than 10 employees), but this growth has also been accompanied by much volatility, due to record numbers of bankruptcies (Daly et al., 1991). In Germany, for example, it is more difficult to establish new technology businesses. Even the Sparkasse Bank which concentrates on helping small businesses, with 80% of their business clients having a turnover of less than 2m DM, stated that only 3 out of 10 start-up proposals were successful on average.

Monitoring

In the UK we found that bank officers generally required monthly monitoring accounts from a new proposition. We also know that in the UK, banks, in general, adopt a non-interventist policy once a proposition has been accepted (Forum of Private Business, 1993). Although this approach may suit some NTEs, it can limit the effectiveness of some technology-based entrepreneurs who may benefit from advice, while it also means that the information set used for control by the bank is also limited.

Other writers have pointed out that German banks have a more interventionist policy (Vittas, 1986). This was confirmed by our respondents but the extent of intervention can vary depending on the type of finance provided. The local Sparkassen banks use their network to provide information which can be used to compare the performance of existing clients. An intelligence network provided a database which could be used to provide financial information on profitability, turnover, labour costs, productivity and exporting. Respondents in Germany stated that they were willing to intervene to provide advice and help with sales/marketing where this was possible. The intervention included help with sales and getting orders. There is a closer working relationship between the bank and its NTE than would be the case in the UK. Concern was expressed in helping the client through the early years of trading. For example the following comments come from a Deutsche Bank respondent:

> We try to support the small firm through the first three years to try to give it the best chance of survival, with advice...We consider that the profits come from a long-term relationship.

In the case study of the new technology company, the bank was willing to provide the three stages of seed, development and later stage finance. During the development stage the bank stated that it required monthly analysis of the business but also other information, including information on potential customers, on potential competition, on technical development, on a review of financing requirements and on comparisons of current financial performance with those that were planned. This indicated the importance that the German bank attached to monitoring and also to developing a close working relationship with its NTE.

Our evidence from Holland is that banks require the monitoring of accounts, but do not get involved in the business to the same extent as German banks. The opinion of one respondent was that the banks 'do not get involved at all'. However, evidence from an NTE suggested that there can be a close relationship, but as in the UK, the relationship depended on the personality and motives of the bank officer. For example, one NTE commented:

> He looked at it as his baby and wanted to get involved, and he gave me room when I needed it. But he moved last year and the new people are more laid back. Clearly monitoring by UK and Dutch banks may be little different.

Term maturity

In the UK the emphasis was short term. Our proposition sought a £60,000 advance for 2 years and provided a cash flow forecast and strategy for 4 years. UK bank officers were concerned only with forecasts for 12 months. All the bank officers that were prepared to proceed with this proposition wanted the financing arranged as an overdraft. The concern with overdrafts may have reflected the financing arrangements that are commonly used in the UK. This bias towards short-term financing instruments has been confirmed by other evidence (Burns and Clements, 1992). Significantly, German respondents indicated that short-term borrowing through overdrafts was discouraged and term loans are used rather than overdrafts. It was stated that overdrafts are used where a firm may have liquidity problems. For example one bank mentioned that out of a total credit figure of 2,600m DM with small firms, only 150m DM of this (5.8%) was in the form of credit lines (overdrafts).

In Germany a variety of term loans were available to meet the different needs of NTEs. Term loans of 5 years were regarded as typical and term loans of 10 years regarded as 'quite normal'. The Technology Director from the IHK considered that: 'Banks are willing to provide as a rule loans at fixed interest rates of 6 to 12 years for technology firms.'

In the case study that was discussed with us the bank was prepared to wait 4 years for a return. The needs of NTEs for a relatively long development period before the product reaches the market seemed to be appreciated and, to some extent, catered for.

There was some evidence that Dutch banks were prepared to lend long term, but for new technology firms they preferred to have some support from alternative financing arrangements (say from a regional scheme). However, it was also stated that overdrafts were used as well. It seems that if finance is secured under alternative means then Dutch banks will be willing to provide more long-term capital.

COMPARATIVE PRACTICES IN VENTURE CAPITAL

Writers have observed that in the UK the venture capital sector has rapidly expanded. For example, prior to 1979 there were fewer than 20 venture capital firms, but by 1993 the number of firms had grown to over 150 and the value of the total funds has been placed at over £1,000m (Murray and Robbie, 1992; Mason and Harrison, 1991). However, the significance of this for the NTE is limited. Recent research has shown that the majority of venture capital funds have focused on supporting MBOs and MBIs. For example, in 1988 62% of all venture capital in the UK went into MBOs and MBIs (Pratt, 1990).

In addition, of course, venture capitalists will have minimum requirements which are often £250,000 plus. In the early 1980s, the venture capitalist industry did provide a significant proportion of funds for NTEs, but the proportion of funds going to these applications has declined dramatically. By 1988, only 7% of funds went into start-up and early stage financing (Pratt, 1990). Studies of funding requirements of NTEs in the Cambridge area (associated with the so-called Cambridge phenomenon) have confirmed that there has been a retreat by venture capitalists from new technology-based firms (Garnsey and Cannon-Brookes, 1993).

It has been well documented that there is a high rejection rate by venture capitalists of propositions. For example, research conducted in 1989 indicated that two-thirds of venture capitalists invested in less than 5% of the proposals that they received. In total, only an average of 3.4% of proposals receive investment capital (Cary, 1991; Dixon, 1991).

Some writers have indicated that the venture capital industry is not as well developed in Germany as in the UK (Bovaird, 1990; Bannock, 1991). However, our findings indicate that venture capital is certainly available in the Baden-Württemberg region and may not suffer from the same drawbacks as most venture capital funds in the UK. In Germany, Federal States have considerable independence and power to introduce their own schemes. We found, for example, in Baden-Württemberg that the Land had been able to set up a venture capital fund to supply long-term risk capital to NTEs. Compared to the UK, amounts invested would be small; for new technology-based propositions the amounts may be 300,000 DM (£120,000). One of our respondents considered that: 'There are a lot of (technology) companies that use venture capital.'

As with Germany, writers have indicated that the total available funds from venture capital sources is considerably less in the Netherlands. For example, the total venture capital pool in Holland was estimated at only 55% of that available in the UK in 1987 (Bannock, 1991). The Dutch venture capital industry is similar to the original UK venture capital industry where most of the funds were targeted at high-tech ventures. Data from interviews with Atlas Venture who specialise in new technology revealed that 50% of Atlas Venture's funds go into NTEs and approximately 50% of their business is in the Netherlands. In European terms only 6.1% of their income came from investments in the UK, whereas 35% of income came from investments in Germany. They were looking for international applications to invest in NTEs. For example, one respondent considered that:

> As far as (new) technology is concerned it should be technology that is applicable in an international way. In the past we have dealt with companies that have a very limited geographical potential. Now it should be of international potential.

Research with venture capitalists in the UK has indicated that the important criteria in assessing ventures are the management team's experience, the market sector and marketing skills (Dixon, 1991). Important criteria for Atlas were the management team and the type and the extent to which technology was unique or advanced. For example, one of our respondents stated that:

> It is an old joke that within the venture capital market the value of real estate is location, location, location. We also have the main thing which is management, management, management. And we are interested in how advanced the product is, not necessarily the patent situation.

For NTEs it was important for the technology to be unique. If this was the case, the venture capital company could help the NTE to develop the technology so that it had global applications and could help it to establish global patents. Minimum stakes were similar to those which we would expect in the UK. Minimum investments were 500,000 guilders (£160–180,000) and average stakes were 1.5m guilders (£600,000) in new technology companies.

The issues of added value through intervention and the reluctance of the entrepreneur to lose control have been mentioned in the introduction. Atlas considered that their main strength was their ability to bring in specialists and to use their network to help with strategic management decisions. It was considered important to monitor the development of the technology. The rate of progress in the development of the technology was as important as the development of the business. On the issue of the dilution of equity, European entrepreneurs generally were considered too conservative. The growth of companies was often limited because the entrepreneur did not want to lose a 51% stake. The USA was considered to be different:

> In the USA they supply $10m up front if there is good technology and a good management team. We are dealing with an immature infrastructure in Europe.

In summary, we would stress that although the UK would appear to have a more developed venture capital industry than both Holland and Germany, as some writers have claimed, this can give a misleading impression of the importance of venture capital to NTEs. A comment by one of our Dutch respondents is illustrative:

> I went to BVCA[1] 2 months ago. They are in management finance which they do with huge MBOs; and they call themselves venture capitalists. This is ridiculous!

ALTERNATIVE SOURCES OF FUNDING

In the UK the alternative funding schemes have focused on perceived difficulties that NTEs face in securing finance. For example, the Small Firms Loan Guarantee Scheme (SFLGS) is designed for NTEs that have limited equity. Our first stage report found that bank officers rated it as only of nominal importance. Obviously the scheme can only apply when equity has been exhausted and applications are controlled through bank nominations. The Business Expansion Scheme was aimed at relieving the equity gap, but following low take up rates and funding going to property firms, the scheme was withdrawn in 1993. The Enterprise Allowance Scheme is, of course, aimed at encouraging business start-up. However, our first stage study indicated that UK bank managers perceived it to be only of marginal importance when making an assessment decision. Of course there may be a range of other funding schemes depending on location. There may be more specific support for NTEs through special awards such as SMART and SPUR.

Both in Twente and Baden-Württemberg there were a range of alternative financing schemes provided by authorities at different administrative levels. However, there are a number of significant differences in the way these schemes are promoted and administered. This, we believe, is the key difference. For example, in Baden-Württemberg, much more importance is placed on promoting alternative funding schemes and assistance by the local Chamber of Commerce. An example of this is contrasts in the take-up of similar loan guarantee schemes in the UK and Germany where take-up rates in Germany are 10 times those of the UK.[2]

In Baden-Württemberg, a range of schemes existed targeted at NTEs designed to provide the different stages of funding, seed, start-up, developmental and later consolidation stages. As in the UK the ability to qualify for schemes depended on geographical location. Baden-Württemberg had special incentives for new technology SME firms and may not have been typical. In Pforzheim, the municipal authority had its own schemes for innovative technologies and for founder firms. In addition there were further state schemes. For example, in 1984 the Bonn Government set aside 6 regions for special assistance for innovation. The Pforzheim-Karlsruhe area was one such designated area. Under this state scheme, NTEs could qualify for a first stage subsidy of 6,000 DM, a development stage grant of 75% of costs and further finance in the third stage funding. Each of the 6 areas selected had a high degree of autonomy to implement the scheme according to their own needs. The aim of the project was to encourage technology transfer and to promote the development of new technology.

Some of the state schemes have been withdrawn as Germany grapples with the problems of re-unification. For example some of the state support has now shifted to the East. However, the Regional Governments (Länder) retain a powerful base, which means they are able to set up and implement a wide range of their own schemes. There is little doubt that there is far more independence from central state control and much greater devolution of power than in the UK. In Germany the regional Länder can identify needs, and have the power to implement schemes. In the UK (and Holland) there is no such equivalent tier of regional government. In addition local authorities have seen some of their powers and independence stripped away. In most cases the authorities are too small to act strategically to provide a coherent policy. Where power has been devolved, for example, to Training and Enterprise Councils (TECs), the body or authority is often too small to make a significant impact. For example, in the West Midlands region alone there are 10 TECs. With budgets of around £20m they can only make a limited impact on the state of UK enterprise and training.

CONCLUSIONS

The financing arrangements and practices are more conducive in helping NTEs in Germany and Holland than in the UK. In risk assessment, German bank officers would accept higher gearing ratios, lower levels of collateral and place greater emphasis on management information than their UK counterparts. In the UK, the approach of bank officers is biased towards a narrow range of financial criteria. In both Germany and Holland the information required by the banks from NTEs will be larger and more complete than that required by UK banks. It is more likely that the NTE will be required to obtain additional information and qualifications in Holland and Germany. It is more likely that specialists or consultants will be brought in by bank officers in Germany and Holland.

In Germany, the IHK has a pivotal role in providing contacts and information. Networking between the banks and other institutions is more advanced than in the UK. We see this successful networking as a crucial factor in determining the success of applications and in facilitating the take-up of alternative sources of finance by NTEs. The levels of co-operation between institutions was also higher in Holland than in the UK. A university course in management was regarded as essential before start-up for NTEs. In Germany bank officers are more likely to intervene and take a less 'hands-off' approach.

We agree with writers that claim we suffer from short-termism in the UK. Certainly UK bank financing instruments that are actually taken up by NTEs are more short term than in Holland or Germany. There is an emphasis on financing through overdrafts in the UK. More important, however, is that banks are prepared, certainly, in Germany to take a longer term view and are more patient than their UK counterparts.

The beginning of strategies to deal with specific industry sector groups, such as NTEs, by having specialised training for staff are to be welcomed in the UK banks. However, these practices are more developed in German banks.

There was more variability in the scope and types of alternative funding schemes due to the greater independence of regional governments (e.g. the Länder), but the crucial difference was in the way such schemes are promoted. If Baden-Württemberg is typical, then it is likely that the take-up and awareness of schemes designed to help specific types of entrepreneurs, such as NTEs, are greater in Germany.

NOTES

1. BVCA is the British Venture Capital Association.
2. Charles Batchelor, *Financial Times*, 23 March 1993.

ACKNOWLEDGEMENTS

The authors are grateful for the help and assistance provided by Dr John Page from UCE who acted as interpreter and translator in Baden-Württemberg. We are also grateful for the assistance of staff at the Fachhochschule in Pforzheim who arranged the interviews with German bank officers and the local Chamber of Commerce.

REFERENCES

BANNOCK, G. (1991) *Venture Capital and the Equity Gap*, National Westminster Bank, London.
BINKS, M., ENNEW, R. C. and REED, G. (1988) The survey by the Forum of Private Business on banks and small firms in G. Bannock and V. Morgan (eds.) *Banks and Small Businesses: A Two Nation Perspective*, Forum of Private Business, Knutsford, Cheshire.
BOVAIRD, C. (1990) *Introduction to Venture Capital Finance*, Pitman, London.
BURNS, P. and CLEMENTS A., (1992) German SMEs and their relationship with the bank: myth or

reality? *15th National Small Firms' Policy and Research Conference*, Southampton, November.

CARY, L. (1991) *The Venture Capital Report Guide to Venture Capital in the UK*, Pitman, London.

CHAN, Y. and KANATAS, G. (1985) Asymmetric valuations and the role of collateral in loan agreements, *Journal of Money Credit and Banking*, Vol. 17, no. 1, pp. 84-95.

DALY, M., CAMPBELL, M., ROBSON, G. and GALLAGHER, C. (1991) Job creation 1987-89: the contributions of small and large firms, *Employment Gazette*, November, pp. 589-94.

DEAKINS, D. and HUSSAIN, G. (1991) *Risk Assessment By Bank Managers*, Birmingham Polytechnic, Birmingham.

DEAKINS, D. and PHILPOTT, T. (1993) *Comparative European Practices in the Finance of Small Firms*, University of Central England, Birmingham.

DIXON, R. (1991) Venture capitalists and the appraisal of investments, *Omega*, Vol. 19, no. 5, pp. 333-44.

FORUM OF PRIVATE BUSINESS SURVEY, (1993) *Small Businesses and Their Banks*, Forum of Private Business, Knutsford, Cheshire.

GARNSEY, E. and CANNON-BROOKES, A. (1993) Small high technology firms in an era of rapid change, *Local Economy*, February, pp. 318-33.

MASON, C. and HARRISON, R. (1991) Venture capital, the equity gap and the north-south divide in the UK, in M. Green (ed.) *Venture Capital: International Comparisons*, Routledge, London.

MASON, C. and HARRISON, R. (1992) *The Roles of Investors in Entrepreneurial Companies: A Comparison of Informal Investors and Venture Capitalists*, Venture Finance Research Project Paper No. 5, University of Southampton, Southampton.

MURRAY, G. and LOTT, J. (1992) Have UK venture firms a bias against investment in technology related companies? *Babson Entrepreneurship Conference*, July, INSEAD, Fontainebleau, France.

MURRAY, G. and ROBBIE, K. (1992) Venture capital in the UK, *International Journal of Bank Marketing*, Vol. 10, no. 5, pp. 32-40.

OAKEY R. P. (1984) Finance and innovation in British small independent firms, *OMEGA*, Vol. 12, no. 2, pp. 113-24.

PRATT, G. (1990) Venture capital in the UK, *Bank of England Quarterly Review*, Vol. 30, pp. 78-83.

SAPIENZA, H. J., MANIGART, S. and HERRON, L. (1992) Venture capitalist involvement in portfolio companies: A Study of 221 Portfolio companies in Four Countries, *Babson Entrepreneurship Conference*, July, INSEAD, Fontainebleau, France.

STANWORTH, J. and GRAY, C. (eds.) (1991) *Bolton 20 Years On*, Paul Chapman, London.

STIGLITZ, J. and WEISS, A. (1981) Credit rationing in markets with imperfect information, *American Economic Review*, Vol. 71, pp. 393-410.

STOREY, D. (1993) Should we abandon the support to start up businesses? in F. Chittenden, M. Robertson and D. Watkins *Small Firms: Recession and Recovery*, Paul Chapman, London.

VITTAS, D. (1986) Banks' relations with industry: an international survey, *National Westminster Bank Review*, Feb, pp. 2-14.

VYAKARNAM, S. and JACOBS, R. (1991) How do bank managers construe high technology entrepreneurs? *14th National Small Firms Policy and Research Conference*, Blackpool, November.

CHAPTER 10

The Role of Informal and Formal Sources of Venture Capital in the Financing of Technology-Based SMEs in the United Kingdom

COLIN MASON AND RICHARD HARRISON

Further research is clearly needed on the pattern and causes of initial capitalization of NTBFs founded in...other countries. (*Roberts, 1990, p. 93*)

INTRODUCTION

The financing of technology-based SMEs has attracted a substantial volume of literature (e.g. Roberts, 1990; 1991; Rothwell, 1985; Sweeting, 1991; Freear and Wetzel, 1988; 1990). However, much of this literature relates to the USA and there must be serious concerns about its relevance to the UK, and indeed to Europe as a whole for at least three reasons. First, there are important differences in the structures of the capital markets concerned. The venture capital industry is both much longer established in the USA and, until recently, was much larger relative to GDP than elsewhere. The USA has also had a more fully developed over-the-counter market for companies unwilling or unable to obtain a quotation on the New York or American stock exchanges. This enables fast growth companies to raise further capital to continue growing and also provides an exit route for venture capitalists and other early investors and provides a means whereby entrepreneurs sell a portion of their ownership thereby converting some of their paper wealth into cash. Second, as Rothwell (1989) has pointed out, technology-based industrial development in the USA has been largely in the form of the establishment and growth of new technology-based firms (NTBFs): in Europe, by contrast, such development has largely been through later stage technology development and exploitation within larger, often multinational, corporations. Third, the generalizability of the US literature is further limited by the fact that much of the empirical evidence is drawn from highly specific samples. For example, the influential work of Roberts (1990; 1991) is drawn from companies founded by former employees of MIT laboratories and academic departments in the Greater Boston area and may well be unrepresentative of NTBFs as a whole. As Standeven (1993, p.1) has observed, the 'striking success of a number of US technology companies during the 1980s and their amazing growth have stimulated attempts worldwide...to find ways in which similar stories might be recreated locally'. Venture capital has fuelled most of the high profile US technology success stories; however, the rapid growth of venture capital activity in other developed countries has not been matched by a comparable increase in the supply of capital for early stage ventures and for technology-based firms in particular (Murray and Lott, 1992). In this paper, therefore, we respond to Roberts' (1990) challenge quoted at the outset, by examining the sources of external finance used by technology-based SMEs in the UK. The paper is in five sections, beginning with a review of the conventional model of financing stages in a new, growing venture and highlights differences between the USA and UK in the availability of various sources of venture capital. This review generates a series of propositions concerning the use of venture capital by technology-based SMEs in the UK and the types of finance used at different stages of company development. Details of the survey and data collection are provided in section two of the paper. The third section examines the use and types of outside equity finance used by a sample of UK technology-based firms in order to explore these propositions. The findings highlight a number of ways in which the financing of technology-based firms in the UK contrasts with the situation in the USA. In the fourth section of the paper we seek to explain the reasons for this contrast. The implications of the findings for the development of technology-based SMEs in the UK are assessed in the concluding section of the paper.

FINANCING SOURCES FOR TECHNOLOGY-BASED SMEs: AN OVERVIEW

The technology-based SME evolves through a succession of stages of corporate growth, with each stage having different financial needs in terms of the type and amount of capital required (Bruno and Tyebjee, 1984; Roberts, 1990; 1991). Four stages can be identified through which the growing firm is likely to pass (Roberts, 1990; 1991). The pre-start-up, or R&D, stage involves attempts to determine the commercial applicability of the proposed product or service. At this stage few resources are generally required. The founder or founding team are often still in full-time employment in another organisation and typically undertake the R&D either in their employer's laboratory or in their spare time at home. The start-up stage involves the development of the initial product, demonstration of its commercial viability, initial marketing and securing the first sales. At this stage the firm has significant financial needs, for example, to pay salaries to technical personnel, to purchase equipment and for working capital but has little or no collateral available. At the initial growth stage the company has completed development of the product line, is experiencing growing sales and is operating profitably. However, profits are insufficient to meet the expanding working capital requirements or to finance the purchase of plant and equipment and the recruitment of key staff in various functional areas in order to expand. In addition, at this stage the company is beginning to develop its second and subsequent products. A company which reaches the sustained growth stage will be growing rapidly. It has a variety of customers and a range of products and services. Profits and cash flows are sufficient to meet the majority of the firm's needs but new commercial opportunities are continually being presented. The pursuit of these opportunities will require additional, external finance.

It must, of course, be acknowledged that NTBFs do not constitute a single homogeneous group with comparable needs and prospects. The fact that such firms may have similar initial capital needs, are involved with technology development and would like to raise modest amounts of equity can obscure significant differences in growth prospects and hence in capital and other input requirements. In a background paper for the Six Countries Programme, Standeven (1993) has schematically indicated the development path for three 'typical' NTBFs which illustrate the dangers, from both analytical and public policy points of view, of assuming homogeneity in the sector (see Figure 10.1). Each of these three types is growing rapidly in the early stages, generating approximately similar external financing requirements in the first round, but with significantly

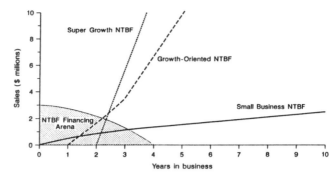

Figure 10.1
The growth of NTBFs: a typology
(Source: Standeven, 1993)

different subsequent financing requirements and growth prospects. Within what Standeven (1993, p. 15) refers to as the 'NTBF Financing Arena' all three companies look very similar in terms of sales revenues and size in terms of employees and total assets. One of the fundamental issues for international and comparative research on NTBF financing, therefore, is an awareness, first, of the existence of heterogeneity in the NTBF sector and, second, of the need for empirical research into variations in the composition of that sector within the framework illustrated in Figure 10.1.

A variety of sources of finance are potentially available to fund the company's capital requirements through the various stages of growth and development (Roberts, 1991) (see Figure 10.2). The majority of firms in the initial stages of development have modest financial requirements which can be met by the personal savings of the entrepreneur or entrepreneurial team, sometimes supplemented by family and friends. Firms will also seek bank overdraft facilities and loans at this stage. However, entrepreneurs in their thirties, the typical 'age launch window', are likely to have limited savings and the amount of personal assets available as collateral will limit access to bank loans. The caution of banks in lending to technology-based ventures, which may be related to evidence that bank managers have problems in distinguishing between good and bad businesses in the high technology sector (Vyakarnam and Jacobs, 1991; Philpott, this volume, Chapter 7), will also limit the access

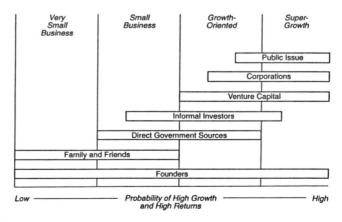

Figure 10.2
Principal equity funding sources by company growth prospects
(Source: Standeven, 1993)

of technology-based businesses to bank loans and overdrafts. Thus, many high tech entre-preneurs will need to turn to external sources of equity finance if the business is to grow.

Private investors, or 'business angels'

Informal investors represent by far the largest source of external equity finance in the USA (Wetzel, 1986; Gaston, 1989). Most have a preference for investing in 'high tech' enterprises (Haar, et al, 1988; Tymes and Krasner, 1983; Wetzel, 1981; 1983). Roberts (1991 p.132) notes that 'the great majority of initial investing in high tech firms by out-side investors has traditionally been undertaken by wealthy individuals.' Informal sources of venture capital also exist in the UK (Harrison and Mason, 1992a; Mason and Harrison, 1994) although it is generally accepted that the size of the informal venture capital pool is significantly smaller than that in the USA (ACOST, 1990; Bannock, 1991). Nevertheless, a significant proportion of investments by business angels in the UK have been in technology-based firms (Mason and Harrison, 1994). Informal investors tend to invest relatively small amounts and their investments are concentrated towards start-ups and early stages. However, US angels are more likely than their UK counterparts to finance start-ups: 56% of informal investments in the US were at the start-up stage compared with just 27% in the UK (Gaston, 1989; Mason and Harrison, 1994). Furthermore, research in Finland suggests that Finnish high technology entre-preneurs are much less likely than those in the UK to have raised finance from informal investors (Lumme et al, 1992; Lumme, Kauranen and Autio, this volume, Chapter 8).

Venture capital companies

Venture capital companies are characterised by careful screening and selectivity of the proposals that they receive. They are looking for companies capable of producing a high rate of return: targets of 50% for start-ups and 30% for established businesses are typi-cal. Companies must have a product which has a clear competitive advantage and have the main elements of a management team in place. As a result of these strict investment criteria venture capital funds invest in only a small proportion of the companies that approach them for finance. Dixon (1989) notes from a survey of 30 London-based funds that just 3.4% of proposals received investment: 75.5% of funding proposals were rejected at the initial screening stage and a further 21% were rejected or withdrawn during the due diligence process. Another UK study suggests that one in 50 or 60 pro-posals receives funding (Sweeting, 1991). In one US study it was reported that on average less than 2% of requests for venture capital financing received a favourable response while nearly half of all funds invested in less than 1% of the proposals received (Maier and Walker, 1987).

Although a few venture capital funds specialise in seed capital funding and so will invest in the early stage of a venture, most prefer later stage investments in established businesses and management/leveraged buyouts (MBOs and LBOs). This is reflected in the size of investments. In the USA in recent years start-ups have comprised only about 10% of the companies which have received financing and just 9% of the total capital invested. By contrast, expansions, LBOs and acquisition financing account for over half of all investments and about two-thirds of the dollars invested (Bygrave and Timmons, 1992). A similar situation prevails in the UK where MBOs have accounted for between half and two-thirds of the finance invested in recent years, whereas investments in start-ups and early stage businesses account for less than 10% of investments by value (BVCA, 1992; 1993a). Indeed, according to Murray (1993), the UK venture capital industry contains only 16 specialist early stage equity providers, and they are of marginal significance in the overall context of the industry (also see Murray and Francis, 1992).

Table 10.1 *Strengths and weaknesses of public sector interventions in venture capital provisions for NTBFs*

SUPPORT TYPE	STRENGTHS	WEAKNESSES
Direct Investment Programmes	• quick to implement and show results • can be tailored to specific company types • programme costs can be controlled • can help train individuals for the venture capital market • can help lever private sector money into deals	• political manipulation for other ends • pressure to invest quickly regardless of opportunity quality • political influence on investment focus • subsidised competition with private sector (displacement effect) • difficult to staff with high quality professionals • ill-equipped to monitor investment progress and performance • exits from investments may be problematic • ability to participate in follow-on financing rounds may be limited • bias to low risk/low growth companies to minimize failure
Indirect Investment Programmes	• improves venture capital infrastructure • can help lever private sector money into market • can be designed to ensure investments are made by professionals • failures not as obvious because government is insulated by a layer of ownership • investment returns higher than direct investment	• can be slow to implement • deal flow/profit may be limited by slow implementation • unwise investments of too much risk underwritten • little opportunity to control investments or otherwise intervene • interest may be low if limited local supply of investors/fund managers • follow-on support may not be available
Cost Subsidies	• helps build venture capital infrastructure • encourages venture capital funds to experiment with early stage investment • low cost relative to direct/indirect schemes • can increase quality of investment decisions	• availability of follow-on finance may be problematic • investment returns for fund may be limited by lack of follow-on participation • additional operating costs from administrative/reporting requirements • investment activity may not increase if investment opportunities are perceived not to exist • low supply of capable/experienced investment managers will reduce returns
Tax-related Measures	• can achieve significant leverage effect • professional fund management can be put in place • the level of informal investment activity can be enhanced • encourages entrepreneurial climate through venture creation	• difficult to estimate programme costs a priori • long elapsed time to build capital pool and make investments • tax-related distortion of risk-return profiles • high marketing and promotion costs • investor protection safeguards may limit fund formation

Table 10.1 *Contd.*

SUPPORT TYPE	STRENGTHS	WEAKNESSES
Tax-related Measures	• awareness/education through large shareholder base • can allow market selection of projects and is less interventionist • reduces legal, administrative, marketing and broker expenses of small programmes	• small pools may become single company investments • direct tax benefits to investors do not lead to fund formation • reporting costs for investors may be high • administrative costs for government may be high • potential for manipulation by tax experts, resulting in unforeseen/undesirable outcomes • investors may decide not to invest in NTBFs

Source: Based on Standeven (1993).

US venture capital funds still show an affinity for 'high tech' sectors, although there has been a shift away from computer hardware technology in favour of computer software, medical/health care and tele/data communications (Bygrave and Timmons, 1992). This is partly a recognition that too much venture funding can result in depressed returns (Sahlman and Stevenson, 1985), with the result that there has been a shift in focus to high growth, but lower capitalisation requirement type opportunities (Standeven, 1993). UK venture capital funds, by contrast, exhibit a reluctance to invest in technology-related companies. Indeed, since the mid-1980s technology investments has become a specialist activity undertaken by a minority of venture capitalists in the UK. The proportion of investments by US venture capital firms in technology-related sectors is three times greater than that of UK funds (even after excluding management buyouts). US venture capital firms also tend to invest at an earlier stage in the development of their investee companies (Murray and Lott, 1992). Murray and Lott (1992) suggest that UK venture capital funds perceive technology investments to be more risky than available later stage alternative proposals. This, in turn, is expressed in more rigorous selection criteria for technology-related projects compared with non-technology projects (e.g. increases in IRRs; demonstration of a supra-national market potential), with a particular reflection in the higher prices imposed for their equity participation, a situation which is also seen in the rest of Europe (Murray and Lott, 1992).

Public sector venture capital funds

These funds have been established by local or state governments using public monies or government pension funds to invest in companies within a particular jurisdiction. Their rationale is to fill regional financing gaps which arise from the concentration of venture capital investments in 'hotbeds' such as California and New England in the USA (Florida and Kenney, 1988a; Florida and Smith, 1990) and South East England (Mason and Harrison, 1991a). The consensus of opinion in the USA is that the impact of public sector venture capital programmes has been modest at best; Thompson and Bayer (1992) conclude that their aggregate activity level and average programme size remain very small compared with the private venture sector, although many funds are targeted at small, innovative ventures that are typically ignored by private venture capital funds. Many of the public sector venture capital funds in the UK are also small, although there are some sizable public sector funds: indeed, funds that are operated by Scottish Enterprise (formerly the Scottish Development Agency), the Welsh Development Agency and by some of the now privatized local authority enterprise boards represent the largest sources of venture capital in their respective regions. However, the investment focus of most of these larger public venture capital funds is with later stage developments and management buyouts (and so their average investment size is towards the upper end of the equity gap) while their appraisal process is no less rigorous than that of private sector funds; indeed, they often review a smaller proportion of the propositions they receive than private sector venture capital firms (Mason and Harrison, 1991b). Overall, public sector interventions in the venture capital market carry more potential weaknesses than strengths (see Table 10.1); as Standeven (1993) has pointed out, public sector intervention in the provision of equity capital to NTBFs may, in the longer run, introduce additional distortions into the market which will increase rather than reduce the ability of NTBFs of all types to meet their external growth capital requirements.

Tax-induced sources

The tax system has been used in a number of countries to encourage private individuals to invest in SMEs either directly or indirectly via pooled funds. In the USA, Small Business Investment Companies (SBICs) were created with tax incentives and low interest leveraged loans. In Canada there is a provincial venture capital company (PVCC) scheme in every province which gives individuals a cash grant or a tax credit for investing, via the PVCC, in SMEs (Moncton Consulting Services, 1991; ACOA, 1992). In the UK the Business Expansion Scheme provided private individuals with tax relief at their top marginal rate for direct and indirect investments (in approved BES funds) in unquoted companies. However, the amount raised through these schemes has been limited. Although important in the 1960s, SBICs have comprised only a very small part of the venture capital pool in recent years and for the most part have not been important in financing cutting edge high technology ventures (Bygrave and Timmons, 1992; Florida and Kenney, 1988b; Roberts, 1991). PVCCs are more significant in Canada, particularly in peripheral regions such as the Atlantic Provinces, but although their investments have been concentrated at seed and start-up, investments in technology-based ventures have been limited (Gadbois, 1986). In the UK investments made under the BES, and in particular by BES funds, have also avoided investments in technology-based sectors, preferring instead property, services and other asset-backed ventures (Mason et al, 1988). On balance, therefore, it appears that tax-based schemes do not have sufficient controls over investment flows to ensure that specific target sectors such as NTBFs benefit (see Table 10.1).

Non-financial corporations

In the USA a number of major 'Fortune 500' companies are willing to provide venture capital to small technology-oriented companies (Winters and Murfin, 1988; Mast, 1991). Their motive is generally to obtain a 'window on new technology': they invest in small entrepreneurial companies as a supplement to their in-house R&D in the hope of gaining access to technology and engineering talent. Their prime investment criteria is therefore the technology. They tend to avoid initial financing, preferring instead later growth financing. They may also provide technological, marketing and manufacturing assistance to companies in which they invest. Many large European companies are also active in corporate venturing. However, 'with a few notable exceptions...UK companies appear to be lagging behind US and even European counterparts in the level of investment in smaller companies, either directly through an in-house venture capital unit or through a professional intermediary' (Pratt, 1990, p. 80). Indeed, ACOST (1990, p. 41) has suggested that 'there is an almost complete absence of corporate venture capital in the UK.' However, one current study suggests that this is an over-pessimistic assessment. Corporate venturing in the UK is not as rare as commonly thought and does have a specific, although not exclusive, orientation to early stage and technology-related investments for financial and strategic reasons (McNally, 1994; 1995).

Going public

Ultimately, a company can turn to the public market. In the USA companies can make an initial public offering (IPO) on the over-the-counter market, the largest of which is NASDAQ, and in other countries they can seek a listing on a junior stock exchange such as the UK's Unlisted Securities Market (USM) and the French second tier market. However, companies must have reached sufficient size and have a trading record in order to meet regulatory requirements. Moreover, because of the significant fixed costs involved in raising finance on the public market, including underwriting fees, legal and accountancy fees and printing costs, it is uneconomic for firms to raise small amounts of finance in this way. In the case of the USM, minimum administrative costs of raising new capital are estimated to be in the order of £100,000, making it costly to raise sums of less than £10m (Hutchinson and McKillop, 1992). Timing is a further factor which may limit access to the public market. The price of the stock will vary over time according to investor sentiment on that industry and market conditions.

The opportunities for going public are greater in the USA than the UK. The preconditions which companies must fulfil are less stringent in the USA, the number of market-makers for each NASDAQ security is greater and the liquidity of NASDAQ is much greater than that of the USM (Bowers, 1992; Buckland and Davies, 1989). The relative underdevelopment of markets on the NASDAQ model represents a constraint in two respects. First, it limits the ability of high growth and high growth potential NTBFs (the 'Super Growth' firms in Figure 10.1) to continue to fund their development, although the ability of non-USA firms to obtain a NASDAQ listing in part overcomes this difficulty. Second, and possibly more significantly, the absence of an effective market limits investor exit possibilities. As most venture capitalists involved in NTBF financings only make a return on their investment when they harvest their position, the absence of a clear exit route will limit willingness to commit to investments at the outset. Accordingly, there may be a consequent reduction in the commitment of otherwise liquid funds to investment opportunities in the absence of clear exit route strategies (Standeven, 1993).

Acquisition

At any stage a technology-based venture may sell out to another, usually larger, company to overcome financial barriers or to enable entrepreneurs and investors to realise their gains. US research suggests that this is not cited by young entrepreneurs as an anticipated future funding source even though many technology-based firms are, in fact, acquired, commonly between their fourth and seventh years (Bruno and Tyebjee, 1984; Bruno et al, 1992). Acquisition of small technology-based companies is thought to be particularly common in the UK (ACOST, 1990). For example, about 50 high tech companies in Cambridge were acquired between 1985 and 1992, in some cases because of resource shortages but in other cases because their technological competences made them attractive to larger companies seeking to enhance their R&D capability (Garnsey and Cannon-Brookes, 1993). While not necessarily undesirable, selling out to a larger company nevertheless carries risks: the new parent company may not understand the nature of the business that it has acquired and faces organisational difficulties in absorbing the acquired company in a way that does not limit its growth or stifle its creativity (ACOST, 1990).

Summary

In summary, the initial capital requirements of most technology-based firms are relatively small and are generally met by the personal savings of the entrepreneur(s), perhaps supplemented by contributions from family and friends in the form of 'love money', plus bank loans. However, with the exception of the 'Small Business NTBF' (see Figure 10.1), the technology-based firm is likely to require significant further finance if it is to grow. Personal and family sources of finance are likely to be quickly exhausted and lack of security or inablity to service debt repayments may limit the scope for further bank borrowing. Thus, the entrepreneur/entrepreneurial team must consider turning to outside suppliers of equity on one or more occasions.

Firms which are successful in raising venture capital are likely to obtain early stage finance from business angels and later stage financing from venture capital funds. Roberts (1990, p. 92) notes that 'angels are far more likely to provide initial funds than are venture capital companies'. Similarly, firms will tend to raise small amounts from angels but larger amounts from venture capital funds. Freear and Wetzel (1988; 1990) report from a study of NTBFs in New England that two-thirds of firms had raised external equity finance, with more firms raising equity capital from private investors than from any other source, including venture capital funds (although the amount raised from venture capital funds was significantly larger). Private individuals were dominant at the seed and start-up financing rounds but their role declined in subsequent stages. Private individuals were also dominant where financing rounds were under $500,000 but their role diminished quite rapidly, relative to venture capitalists, in financing rounds of over $500,000.

However, only a minority of firms will actually successfully raise equity finance from external sources (Roberts, 1991). In some cases the need for finance may not exist. Some firms may not require significant amounts of additional finance because self-generated cash-flow meets their ongoing requirements. Roberts (1991) notes that financing requirements vary by sector, being smallest in consultancy and software and highest in biotechnology. Standeven (1993) has made a similar point in the context of a categorization of the types of NTBFs (see Figure 10.1). In other cases the desire for outside equity may not exist because the entrepreneur or entrepreneurial team wish to retain maximum ownership and control and so will gear their operations to minimize their need for finance, for example by rendering services rather than providing hardware, contracting out production and undertaking custom-oriented development and production for major customers for which they receive stage payments (Roberts, 1991). Other firms will be unsuccessful in their search for external sources, despite the need and desire, and so are forced to use only personal and internally-generated sources. Yet others do not know how to go about seeking external finance and so use their own resources by default. Roberts (1991) suggests that whether firms seek external finance or not, and whether they are successful or not, will be a function of the following factors: size of founding team; personal characteristics (e.g. age, education) and prior work experience of founding team; whether the founding team has specific plans; and the nature of the firm's activities ('software' or 'hardware').

This discussion generates a series of propositions relating to the use of outside sources of equity finance by technology-based firms in the UK which we will explore in the remainder of this paper.

First, given the differences in the size of the informal venture capital market in the USA and UK we anticipate that the majority of technology-based SMEs in the UK will not have raised any external equity finance from either informal or formal sources.

Second, given the differences between the USA and the UK in the investment preferences of both business angels and venture capital funds we also anticipate that investments by both types of investor will be concentrated in the post-start-up stages.

Third, in view of differences in the level of corporate venturing in the USA and UK we anticipate that very few technology-based SMEs in the UK will have raised venture capital from non-financial corporations.

Finally, despite the many differences between the USA and the UK we nevertheless expect the complementarity between informal and formal sources of venture capital in terms of size and stage of investment identified by Freear and Wetzel (1988; 1989; 1990) will also hold in the UK. We therefore anticipate that angels will be more prominent in financing at the early stage of a business venture, and where amounts raised are relatively small, while venture capital funds will be more prominent in later financing rounds and where amounts raised are large.

DATA SOURCES

The data for this study were derived from a postal survey of 'high tech' manufacturing firms and computer software firms. The sampling frame comprised three elements:

● The Northern Ireland Economic Research Centre's (NIERC) establishment database of all high-tech firms in the manufacturing sector, as defined by Butchart (1987), in Northern Ireland, Leicestershire and Hertfordshire (293 firms).
● A listing of high tech firms in South Hampshire extracted from the South Hampshire Databank which lists all manufacturing establishments in the region in 1985 (51 firms).
● Firms listed in various issues of the *Financial Times* Software at Work quarterly survey (80 firms).

This survey achieved 63 usable responses (42 manufacturers and 21 software firms), an overall response rate of 15%. However, it should be noted that the response rate was depressed by our inability to accurately identify and eliminate all companies on these lists that were not independent owner-managed businesses prior to sending out the questionnaires. Thus, some non-usable responses were received from companies that were subsidiaries while it seems reasonable to assume that other non-independent companies would not have responded because the questionnaire was not relevant to them. The response rate will also have been depressed by non-responses from firms that had ceased trading; however, we have no way of estimating this figure (we only received Post Office returns from Northern Ireland and find it difficult to believe that all of the firms in the other regions were still trading).

The ages and sizes of the firms which responded to the survey ranged widely. In terms of age, just under half of the firms were 10 years old or younger (16% were five years old or younger) while at the other end of the age spectrum 24% of firms had been trading for 20 years or more. However, 57 of the 63 firms which responded (90.5%) were still owned by their original founder/founding team. The size distribution was skewed towards the smallest size categories. In terms of employment, 64.5% had less than 25 employees (27.4% less than 10 employees) and only 11.3% had more than 100 employees. In terms of sales, 38.7% had an annual turnover of less than £500,000 while at the other extreme just 14.5% had annual sales of over £5m. The majority of firms had expanded in the 3 years prior to the survey: two-thirds had increased the size of their workforce and 83.3% had increased their turnover.

USE OF VENTURE CAPITAL

Just 10 firms in the sample (15.9%) have raised a total of £6.2m in venture capital. Thus, our first proposition is confirmed: the vast majority of high tech firms have not raised any outside equity finance, supporting findings from other studies (e.g. Monck et al, 1988; Moore et al, 1992; Moore and Sedaghat, 1991) which have also reported the very low use use of venture capital by UK technology-based firms. Furthermore, the proportion of UK high tech firms which have raised external equity finance either at start-up or subsequently is considerably lower than reported by US studies (Freear and Wetzel, 1988; 1990; Roberts, 1991), a contrast which cannot be ascribed simply to differences in sample construction and methodologies. For example, in their study of NTBFs in New England founded between 1975 and 1986, Freear and Wetzel (1988; 1990) found that two-thirds had raised outside equity finance. Similarly, a study of MIT spin-offs by Roberts (1991) found that business angels, venture capital funds, non-financial corporations and public stock issues constituted the primary source of start-up finance for 21% of these firms and were the principal source of post-start-up finance for 56% of firms.

Table 10.2 indicates that of the firms which have not raised any outside equity finance, two-thirds stated that they had no need to do so, in most cases because their financial requirements had been met by other sources, notably retained earnings, bank loans and, less commonly, personal finance. A further 20% of firms specifically chose not to seek external equity finance. The reasons given were varied and included the desire to retain

Table 10.2 *Reasons for not raising equity capital*

	Number of firms	%[1]
THE NEED DID NOT EXIST	35	66.0
• sufficient finance available from other sources (e.g. personal sources, retained profits, bank loan)	27	
• product too specialised: no scope for expansion	1	
• cautious development	1	
• company too small	1	
• no reason given	5	
CHOSE NOT TO SEEK EQUITY FINANCE	11	20.8
• wanted to retain ownership and control	3	
• loan terms were more attractive/less restrictive	1	
• high costs and amount of management time involved	1	
• returns sought by investors are too high	1	
• not large enough to interest investor	1	
• complexity of raising equity finance	1	
• implications of having third party involvement	1	
• other reasons	1	
• no reason given	1	
OTHER REASONS	1	1.9
NO REASON GIVEN	2	3.8
UNSUCCESSFUL IN ATTEMPT TO RAISE EQUITY FINANCE	4	7.5

Note:
1. Expressed as a percentage of firms which have not raised external equity finance (n=53).

ownership and control, the high costs and management time involved and the complexity of the process. Just 4 firms (7.5%) had been unsuccessful in their efforts to raise external equity. Here again there was a wide variety of reasons given: unwilling to release the amount of equity demanded; company profile did not fit the portfolio requirements of the venture capital fund; withdrew because of the delay and amount of incomprehensible paperwork; and advised that venture capital was not the most appropriate method of financing. The majority of firms seem likely to continue with this pattern of self-financing through retained profits supplemented by bank loans and other sources of non-equity finance. Just 6 firms (9.7%), including one firm which had raised venture capital, indicated that they were likely to consider seeking venture capital in the foreseeable future.

One implication of this pattern of responses, within the framework of Figure 10.1 above, is that a high proportion of our UK sample may fall, in terms of business performance and founder/owner attitudes and aspirations, into the 'Small Business NTBF' category. If so, and further systematic research into the performance of NTBFs in the UK is required to test this notion, two implications follow. First, from a public policy perspective, the long-term economic contribution of this type of NTBF, in terms of product development, employment, export sales and tax revenues, may be less pronounced than is normally associated with the – by assumption, high growth – NTBF sector. Second, from an analytic point of view, this sample composition effect may account for the differences between US and UK results in this area: much of the US research (e.g. by Roberts, 1990; 1991 and Freear and Wetzel, 1988; 1990) has been undertaken in the Greater Boston area and has included a high proportion of growth oriented and supergrowth NTBFs. Although initially similar in appearance, as Figure 10.1 makes clear, the development path and financing requirements of a US sample dominated by high growth NTBFs and a UK sample dominated by small business NTBFs will be very different.

The 10 firms in our sample which raised outside equity finance did so in a total of 17 rounds ranging from £10,000 to £1.9m. Four firms raised equity finance on just one occasion, 5 firms raised equity finance on 2 separate occasions and one firm had 3 rounds of external fund-raising. As Table 10.3 shows, there were few cases of firms raising outside finance at seed and start-up stages. Just 3 firms raised a total of 4 rounds of seed or start-up finance from external sources. The majority of outside financing has occurred since start-up (11 out of 17 rounds), supporting our second proposition. Technology-based firms in the USA are also more likely to raise outside equity after start-up: however, the proportion of firms in the USA which have raised seed capital from outside investors is significantly greater than in the UK.

Table 10.3: *Sources of outside equity finance used*

STAGE	SOURCE OF FINANCE					
	VENTURE CAPITAL	INFORMAL INVESTOR	BES FUND/ PROSPECTUS ISSUE	NON-FINANCIAL CORPORATION	NUMBER OF ROUNDS	MEDIAN INVESTMENT SIZE
Seed	1	1	–	–	2	£10,000
Start-up	2	1	1	–	2*	£592,000
Early stage	3	3	–	–	6	£52,500
Later stage	4	–	–	1	5	£600,000
Management buyout/buyin	2	–	1	–	2*	£625,000

Note: Some rounds (indicated by asterisk) involved more than one type of investor hence the number of sources exceed the number of rounds.

Table 10.4: *Sources of outside equity finance by size of financing round*

	SOURCE OF FINANCE				
SIZE OF ROUND	VENTURE CAPITAL	INFORMAL INVESTOR	BES FUND/ PROSPECTUS ISSUE	NON-FINANCIAL CORPORATION	NUMBER OF ROUNDS
Less than £50,000	3	3	0	1	7
£50,000 – £249,000	2	1	0	0	3
£250,000 and over	7	1	2	0	7

Note: Three investments, each involving a total over £250,000, involved more than one source of finance. Two of these investments involved venture capital funds and BED funds and the other involved a venture capital fund and a private investor, investing £650,000 and £10,000 respectively.

Institutional venture capital is the major source of outside equity finance for UK technology-based firms (Tables 10.3 and 10.4). Eight firms raised finance from venture capital funds. Venture capital is also the source of 12 of the 17 outside financing rounds (70.6%), involving a total investment of just under £6m. (This figure includes one round which was syndicated between a BES prospectus issue and a venture capital fund, but the amounts were not separately reported.) In contrast, just 3 firms have raised a total of £140,000 from private investors in a total of 5 financing rounds (in each case the same business angel invested on 2 separate occasions). One of these firms also raised finance from a venture capital fund. This represents a further contrast with the pattern of financing of technology-based firms in the USA where private individuals are the most common providers of outside equity (Freear and Wetzel, 1988; 1990; Roberts, 1991).

Non-financial corporations play a minor role in the financing of technology-based firms in the UK, with just one firm raising finance from this source, supporting our third proposition and confirming the widely held perception in the UK that corporate venturing is extremely limited (ACOST, 1990). In the USA, between 5 and 10% of high tech companies have raised finance from non-financial corporations (Freear and Wetzel, 1988; 1990; Roberts, 1991).

Our final proposition concerns the 'complementarity thesis' which was first highlighted by Freear and Wetzel (1988; 1989; 1990). Their research has indicated that informal investors invest earlier in the life of a firm than venture capital funds and are the primary source of outside equity capital when the total financing per round is small. However, there is little evidence from our survey that informal investors and venture capital funds play complementary roles in the financing of high-tech businesses in the UK. Business angels certainly invest much smaller amounts of finance than venture capital funds. The median amount invested by business angels in the 5 rounds in which they participated was just £15,000 whereas the median investment by venture capital funds was £438,000. However, business angels are a minority source of finance even when the amount involved is less than £50,000 (see Table 10.4). Nor are business angels the most common source of finance at seed and start-up stages. Venture capital funds have been involved at all stages of financing, dominating the later financing rounds and funding or part-funding 3 of the 4 seed and start-up investments whereas private investors were involved in just 2 of these financing rounds (see Table 10.3). This pattern of financing is confirmed in a study of the initial financing of NTBFs in Cambridge which also found that UK firms are more likely to raise start-up finance from venture capital firms (and corporate venturing) than from informal investors (Lumme et al., 1992; Lumme, Kauranen and Autio, this volume, Chapter 8).

ACCOUNTING FOR THE LIMITED ROLE OF INFORMAL VENTURE CAPITAL IN THE FINANCING OF TECHNOLOGY-BASED FIRMS IN THE UK

Our conclusions must inevitably be tentative on account of the limited sample size of the study. But, despite this caveat, it is nevertheless clear that UK technology-based firms are financed differently to their counterparts in the USA, with a much smaller proportion of technology-based firms in the UK raising outside equity finance from both the formal and informal venture capital markets. The much more limited involvement of business angels in the financing of technology-based firms in the UK is particularly marked.

There are a number of possible reasons why business angels appear to play only a minor role in financing technology-based firms in the UK. First, it must be acknowledged that differences in sample characteristics may play a role. Much of the US evidence is for New England which has active informal and formal venture capital markets whereas the evidence presented in this study has been drawn from across the UK. However, the fact that the survey findings are corroborated by the admittedly fragmentary evidence of other UK studies does suggest that the main causes of these UK-USA contrasts in the financing of technology-based firms are more likely to be associated with differences between the two countries in the supply of, and demand for, informal venture capital.

Considering the supply side initially, at least 4 factors may be relevant. First, most business angels are wealthy individuals with an entrepreneurial background. The population of high net worth, self-made individuals is much smaller in the UK than in the USA, thereby limiting the size of the UK's informal venture capital pool. Second, it is likely that the much higher marginal tax rates in the UK compared with the USA will have encouraged tax averse investment behaviour at the expense of investments in unquoted companies. This may well have had a continued psychological effect on investment behaviour even though significant cuts in marginal tax rates occurred during the 1980s in the UK. The capital gains tax regime is also more sympathetic in the USA than the UK.

Third, there is a general lack of familiarity with, and awareness of, the concept of informal venture capital in the UK amongst potential investors, entrepreneurs and professional advisers. As a result, individuals with the appropriate background to become business angels either do not consider this financing option, or reject it on the grounds of their presumed, or actual, lack of expertise. Limited familiarity with the concept of informal venture capital also results in a low awareness of this form of finance amongst entrepreneurs and where consideration is given to the possibility of raising this form of finance there is little understanding of how to find business angels. As a consequence, most firms will rely upon retained earnings or bank finance; those who do seek equity financing will typically confine their search to institutional sources of venture capital, even though they may be unattractive to venture capital funds, for example, on account of their technology, management characteristics or potential growth rate, or else their financial requirements are inappropriate for institutional venture capital.

Fourth, business angels place considerable emphasis in their investment decisions on the need to understand the investee business, and so often make their investments in sectors where they have had experience. For example, a Canadian study of informal venture capital activity found that two-thirds of business angels who were entrepreneurs invested in the same industry as the company that they had founded: however, all of the angels who had founded a technology-based company made investments in technology companies (MacDonald, 1991). Thus, the lack of experienced entrepreneurs in the UK who have built successful technological companies is likely to limit the pool of informal investors who are willing to invest in technology-based enterprises. US business angels express a stronger interest than their UK counterparts in investing in technology-based ventures and make a higher proportion of their investments in high tech businesses (Gaston, 1989; Haar et al, 1988; Mason and Harrison, 1994; Tymes and Krasner, 1983; Wetzel, 1981).

Turning to the demand side, two factors are relevant. Demand for equity finance is concentrated amongst what Timmons (1990) calls high potential firms, those that grow rapidly and are likely to exceed £10m in sales within five years of start-up, and foundation firms which, although growing more slowly, will nevertheless exceed £1m in sales and may grow to £5-£10m over the same period. It is probable that such firms comprise a smaller proportion of the business stock than in the USA. There may also be a greater willingness amongst entrepreneurs in the UK to sacrifice growth if it involves giving up equity, and hence exclusive ownership and control, than in the USA. As we have already suggested above, systematic differences between US and UK NTBFs in terms of growth and performance may be a major feature underlying the results reported in this paper. The use of informal sources of venture capital is also depressed by the existence of market inefficiencies. We have demonstrated elsewhere (Mason and Harrison, 1992; 1994) that most business angels in the UK want to invest more but cannot find sufficient investment opportunities that meet their investment criteria. But at the same time, entrepreneurs seeking sources of equity capital express frustration at their inability to identify business angels. This situation reflects the lack of effective channels for business angels and entrepreneurs to make contact with one another. Because of the considerable time required to search for, and appraise, investment opportunities and the fact that for most investors it is not a full-time occupation, they generally adopt an ad hoc, unscientific and passive approach, placing considerable reliance on friends and business associates for referrals. Thus, serendipity largely determines the number and quality of investment opportunities that come to an investor's attention. Meanwhile, informal investors comprise an unorganised, fragmentated and, because of their desire for anonymity, largely invisible market which renders them very difficult to identify by entrepreneurs seeking private sources of venture capital. Unlike venture capital funds, there are no directories of informal investors that an entrepreneur can consult.

However, the existence of market inefficiencies is not peculiar to the UK informal venture capital market. US studies also report that business angels cannot find enough deals (Gaston, 1989) and are dissatisfied with existing channels of communciation between investors and entrepreneurs seeking finance (Wetzel, 1981; Tymes and Krasner, 1983). But comparison with the USA indicates that the inefficiencies which characterise the informal venture capital market are compounded in the UK as a result of three factors: less effective information networks, leading to lower quality information on investment opportunities and more redundant information; generally less experienced and less sophisticated investors; and the limited involvement of UK business angels in informal investor syndicates (Harrison and Mason, 1992a). These features are reflected in the significantly higher deal flow received by UK informal investors and their lower investment rate compared to their US equivalents, and the higher proportions of UK business angels that are unable to find enough deals and are dissatisfied with existing channels of communication with businesses seeking finance.

POLICY IMPLICATIONS

The central conclusion from this study is that, in contrast to the USA, there is a lack of business angels in the UK to 'seed' NTBFs. As a result, technology-based ventures in the UK are likely to experience greater financial constraints, with implications for their start-up, survival and growth. Using a baseball metaphor, Timmons and Sapienza (1992) refer to business angels as the 'farm system' for the institutional venture capital industry, providing seed and start-up finance and hands-on assistance to enable NTBFs to grow to the stage where they might be of interest to venture capital firms which are increasingly concentrating their activities on later stage investments. Thus, the lack of business angels in the UK also has significant implications for the UK venture capital industry and is likely to be a major reason why venture capitalists in the UK attribute their lack of investments in technology-based ventures to the shortage of convincing investment proposals.

The policy implications which arise from this diagnosis are threefold. First, there is a need to raise awareness amongst wealthy private individuals with a business background, particularly if it is in technology, entrepreneurs and professional advisers (e.g. accountants, solicitors, bankers, consultants) that informal venture capital is a financing option in order to increase both its supply and demand. This can be achieved by means of publicity and promotion of informal venture capital in the specialist financial and professional media and through appropriate business and professional associations. Also appropriate in this context is the need for greater guidance to the entrepreneur on how to find business angels. Two examples illustrate the paucity of information on the informal venture capital market in the UK. First, books aimed at the UK entrepreneur on sources of equity concentrate on the venture capital industry and say little or nothing about informal sources of venture capital (e.g. Sharp, 1992). Second, where informal investors are mentioned the information is often inaccurate and misleading: an extreme example can be found in a recent book on starting a technology business (Allen, 1992) which emphasises the altruistic motivations of business angels, referring to them as 'philanthropists', a view which is contrary to research evidence on their investment motivations (Mason and Harrison, 1994).

Second, there is a need to more effectively mobilize the pool of informal venture capital by establishing mechanisms which overcome the sources of inefficiency in the informal venture capital market, namely the invisibility of informal investors, the fragmented nature of the market, and the high search costs for businesses seeking investors and investors seeking investment opportunities. The most effective means of overcoming these sources of inefficiency is by establishing business introduction services, or 'financial marriage bureaux' which provide an efficient channel of communication between business angels and entrepreneurs. Business introduction services generally operate in one of three ways: publication of an investment opportunities bulletin that is circulated to potential investors; computerised matching which provides investors with details of investment opportunities that meet their investment criteria; and presentations by entrepreneurs to a group of potential investors. As well as enhancing the ability of existing business angels to make investments there is evidence that business introduction services may also lead to an expansion in the size of the informal investor population (Mason and Harrison, 1993). A further way in which business introduction services can stimulate informal investment activity is by educating investors and entreprenurs about various aspects of the informal venture capital market. Indeed, The Venture Capital Network, a long-established and successful business introduction service in New England, runs training workshops in order to raise the competences of investors and entrepreneurs and increase their confidence in their ability to negotiate the price and other terms and conditions of a venture investment (Freear and Wetzel, 1995).

Some business introduction services do exist in the UK (see BVCA, 1993b). Various accountancy firms provide a matching service although at least amongst the bigger firms these tend to concentrate on mergers and acquisition activity. LINC and Venture Capital Report (VCR) are the longest established business introduction services in the UK. VCR operates nationally, publishing a monthly investment bulletin. LINC operates through 9 local enterprise agencies in various parts of the country. Capital Exchange, which was formed in 1992, also publishes a national listing of businesses seeking finance. In 1991 the Department of Employment launched an initiative to provide pump-priming finance to enable five Training and Enterprise Councils in England to establish business introduction services. A number of other TECs and some other not-for-profit organisations are also involved in establishing business introduction services. However, for the most part, business introduction services have had only a very limited impact in stimulating informal venture capital activity in the UK (Mason and Harrison, 1995). Limited budgets have prevented them from undertaking significant marketing activity, hence their awareness amongst investors, entrepreneurs and professional advisors is low and their client base is small. Furthermore, none of the UK business introduction services are specifically aimed at technology-based businesses. This is in contrast to the situation in the USA where Venture Capital Network (VCN), now operated as the Technology Capital Network by the MIT Enterprise Forum, provides a computerised matching service exclusively for high tech firms. The Chalmers Technological University in Gothenburg has recently replicated VCN to serve the needs of high tech university spin-off companies (Landstrom and Olafsson, 1995). Thus, it is important to consider whether 'high tech' businesses and investors interested in investing in technology-based businesses are well served by existing business introduction services which aim to recruit businesses from all sectors and investors with varied investment preferences. Do they require a dedicated business introduction service? Professor William E. Wetzel, founder and President of VCN, has suggested that investors who specialise in investing in technology-based businesses are likely to place less emphasis on location because of the scarcity of investment opportunities in their specialist technology. Thus, it may be inappropriate for a business introduction service specialising in matching technology-based firms with investors to have a geographically-restricted operating area.

Third, and finally, measures to make the tax treatment of equity investment in unquoted companies no less advantageous than other forms of saving are also appropriate as a means of enlarging the pool of informal venture capital in order to encourage private investors to put some of their disposable wealth into smaller companies (ACOST, 1990). However, this should be viewed as a supporting measure rather than a central element in a strategy to promote informal venture capital activity. After all, the major imperfection in the informal venture capital market is the difficulty that investors encounter in identifying businesses seeking finance and vice versa. Offering tax breaks to encourage informal investment activity does not preclude the need for mechanisms to enable investors to identify businesses seeking finance, and vice versa.

The Business Expansion Scheme in the UK did have some success in enabling unquoted companies to raise equity capital from private investors (Harrison and Mason, 1989; Mason et al, 1988), at least until it was extended to include investments in private rented housing. However, as we noted earlier, the BES was unsuccessful in directing significant amounts of finance at start-ups and technology-based businesses. The experience of the BES also indicates that the need for such schemes to have complicated rules in order to prevent abuses limits the role of tax breaks as a means of promoting informal venture capital. First, the complex rules of such a scheme conflict with the desire of most business angels for simplicity. Second, such schemes often attract passive investors seeking a tax shelter whereas genuine informal venture capital investment involves the injection of 'know-how' as well as finance (Harrison and Mason, 1992b). Indeed, in the BES the rules actually prevented investors from being 'closely connected' with their investee companies. Third, although business angels are concerned with capital gains tax they nevertheless treat investments on their merits: a tax break is unlikely to change a poor investment into a good one.

A number of measures were introduced in the two Budgets during 1993 to stimulate informal investment in the UK. The initial measure, in the March Budget, to exempt entrepreneurs from capital gains tax (CGT) on money derived from the sale of shares in their own company which they invest in another company within three years (based on a proposal by the British Venture Capital Association) was extended in the November Budget. To encourage individuals to invest in unquoted companies, liability to CGT arising on the disposal of assets by individuals will be deferred indefinitely when the gains are reinvested in unquoted shares in qualifying companies. This is subject to the provisions that reinvestment takes place within one to three years after the disposal and that a 5% stake in the company is taken. Two other significant initiatives were also announced in the November Budget. First, a new Enterprise Investment Scheme has been introduced to replace the BES, with effect from 1 January 1994. The objective of EIS is to encourage equity investments by individuals in unquoted trading companies. Income tax relief is available at 20% (not at the marginal rate as under BES), there is full income or CGT relief on losses, capital gains are tax free, private rented housing is excluded, investors can become paid directors (unlike under the BES) and companies can raise a maximum of £1m in any 12 month period. Second, Venture Capital Trusts will be set up, probably under legislation in 1995, as a new kind of investment trust to encourage investment in unquoted businesses: dividends will be paid free of income tax and capital gains will not be subject to CGT. None of these initiatives is specifically designed to encourage investment in technology-based companies. It will be of interest, therefore, to observe as these new schemes develop whether they have any greater success than the BES in stimulating equity investment in NTBFs.

However, these policy implications, which focus on the improvement of the mechanisms for the mobilisation of informal venture capital, will require to be accompanied by a more fundamental change in investment culture and attitudes in the UK if they are to be successful in improving the flow of equity finance into technology-based SMEs at start-up and early stages. On the supply side, as we have noted earlier, there is substantial evidence to suggest that the banks, the institutional venture capital industry and informal investors are all averse to considering high tech investments as compared with other investment situations. On the demand side, as the evidence presented in this paper and elsewhere suggests, high tech entrepreneurs in the UK are reluctant to consider taking outside equity partners: it may be that, in the UK at least, the investor/scientist/technologist entrepreneur is more reluctant to relinquish even partial ownership of the business than his counterparts elsewhere. If so, this suggests that there may be a more fundamental issue of the lack of growth orientation among UK high tech entrepreneurs which will significantly affect their ability to fully reap the potential of these enterprises. The attention of future research should therefore turn specifically to an exploration of the wider environmental and systemic constraints on the formation and development of growth-oriented NTBFs in the UK.

ACKNOWLEDGEMENTS

This paper has been prepared under the research project 'Informal Risk Capital in the UK' which formed part of the Economic and Social Research Council's (ESRC) Small Business Research Initiative, and was funded by the ESRC in conjunction with Barclays Bank, the Department of Employment, the Rural Development Commission and DG XXIII of the Commission of the European Communities (Ref W108 25 1017). We are grateful to Dr Mark Hart of the University of Ulster for providing access to his database of high tech manufacturing firms.

REFERENCES

ACOA (1992) *The State of Small Business and Entrepreneurship in Atlantic Canada*, Atlantic Canada Opportunities Agency, Moncton, New Brunswick.

ACOST (Advisory Council on Science and Technology) (1990) *The Enterprise Challenge: Overcoming Barriers to Growth in Small Firms*, HMSO, London.

ALLEN, J. (1992) *Starting a Technology Business*, Pitman, London.

BANNOCK, G and PARTNERS (1991) *Venture Capital and the Equity Gap*, National Westminster Bank plc, London.

BOWERS, D. J. (1992) *Company and Campus Partnership: Supporting Technology Transfer*, Routledge, London.

BVCA (BRITISH VENTURE CAPITAL ASSOCIATION) (1992) *1991 Report on Investment Activity*, BVCA, London.

BVCA (BRITISH VENTURE CAPITAL ASSOCIATION) (1993a) *1992 Report on Investment Activity*, BVCA, London.

BVCA (BRITISH VENTURE CAPITAL ASSOCIATION) (1993b) *A Directory of Business Introduction Services*, BVCA, London.

BRUNO, A. V. and TYEBJEE, T. T. (1984) The entrepreneur's search for capital, in J. A. Hornaday, F. Tarpley, J. A. Timmons and K. H. Vesper (eds.) *Frontiers of Entrepreneurship Research 1984*, Babson College, Wellesley: MA, pp. 18-31.

BRUNO, A. V., MCQUARRIE, E. F. and TORGRIMSON, C. G. (1992) The evolution of new technology ventures over 20 years: patterns of failure, merger and survival, *Journal of Business Venturing*, Vol. 7, pp. 291-302.

BUCKLAND, R. and DAVIES, E. W. (1989) *The Unlisted Securities Market*, Clarendon Press, Oxford.

BUTCHART, R. L. (1987) A new definition of the high technology industries, *Economic Trends*, no. 400, pp. 82-8.

BYGRAVE, W. D. and TIMMONS, J. (1992) *Venture Capital at the Crossroads*, Harvard Business School Press, Boston.

DIXON, R. (1989) Venture capitalists and investment appraisal, *National Westminster Bank Quarterly Review*, November, pp. 2-21.

FLORIDA, R. L. and KENNEY, M. (1988a) Venture capital, high technology and regional development, *Regional Studies*, Vol. 22, pp. 33-48.

FLORIDA, R. L. and KENNEY, M. (1988b) Venture capital and high technology entrepreneurship, *Journal of Business Venturing*, Vol. 3, pp. 301-19.

FLORIDA, R. and SMITH, D. F. (1990) Venture capital, innovation and economic development, *Economic Development Quarterly*, Vol. 4, pp. 345-60.

FREEAR, J. and WETZEL, W. E. (1988) Equity financing for new technology-based firms, in B. A. Kirchhoff, W. A. Long, W. E. McMullen, K. H. Vesper and W. E. Wetzel (eds.) *Frontiers of Entrepreneurship Research 1988*, Babson College, Wellesley: MA, pp. 347-67.

FREEAR, J. and WETZEL, W. E. (1989) Equity capital for entrepreneurs, in R. H. Brockhaus snr, N. C. Churchill, J. A. Katz, B. A. Kirchhoff, K. H. Vesper and W. E. Wetzel jnr (eds.) *Frontiers of Entrepreneurship Research 1989*, Babson College, Wellesley: MA, pp. 230-44.

FREEAR, J. and WETZEL, W. E. (1990) Who bankrolls high-tech entrepreneurs? *Journal of Business Venturing*, Vol. 5, pp. 77-89.

FREEAR, J. and WETZEL, W. E. (1995) Starting a private investor network: reflections on the history of VCN, in R. T. Harrison and C. M. Mason, (eds.) *Informal Venture Capital: Information, Networks and Public Policy*, Woodhead-Faulkner, Hemel Hempstead, forthcoming.

GADBOIS, A. (1986) Provincial venture capital corporations: a comparative analysis, *Journal of Small Business and Entrepreneurship*, Vol. 4, no.2, pp. 14-25.

GARNSEY, E. and CANNON-BROOKES, A. (1993) The 'Cambridge Phenomenon' revisited: aggregate change among Cambridge high-technology companies since 1985, *Entrepreneurship and Regional Development*, Vol. 5, pp. 155-78.

GASTON, R. J. (1989) *Finding Private Venture Capital For Your Firm: A Complete Guide*, Wiley, New York.

HAAR, N. E., STARR, J. and MACMILLAN, I. C. (1988) Informal risk capital investors: investment patterns on the East Coast of the USA, *Journal of Business Venturing*, Vol. 3, pp. 11-29.

HARRISON, R. T. and MASON, C. M. (1989) The role of the Business Expansion Scheme in the UK,

Omega, Vol. 17, pp. 147–57.

HARRISON, R. T. and MASON, C. M. (1992a) International perspectives on the supply of informal venture capital, *Journal of Business Venturing*, Vol. 7 pp. 459–75.

HARRISON, R. T. and MASON, C. M. (1992b) *The roles of investors in entrepreneurial companies: a comparison of informal investors and venture capitalists*, Venture Finance Research Project Working Paper No. 5, University of Southampton/Ulster Business School, Southampton and Belfast.

HUTCHINSON, R. and MCKILLOP, D. (1992) *The Financial Services Industry in Northern Ireland*, Report No. 91, Northern Ireland Economic Council, Belfast.

LANDSTROM, H. and OLAFSSON, C. (1995) Informal risk capital in Sweden, in R. T. Harrison, and C. M. Mason (eds.) *Informal Venture Capital: Information, Networks and Public Policy*, Woodhead-Faulkner, Hemel Hempstead, forthcoming.

LUMME, A., KAURANEN, I., AUTIO, E. and KAILA, M. M. (1992) *New Technology-Based Companies in the United Kingdom and Finland: A Comparative Study*, SITRA, Helsinki.

MACDONALD, M. (1991) *Creating Threshold Technology Companies in Canada: the Role for Venture Capital*, Science Council of Canada, Ottawa.

MCNALLY, K. N. (1994) Sources of finance for UK venture capital funds: the role of corporate investors, *Entrepreneurship and Regional Development*, Vol. 6, forthcoming.

MCNALLY, K. N. (1995) *Corporate Venturing in the United Kingdom*, PhD thesis, University of Southampton, forthcoming.

MAIER, J. B. and WALKER, D. A. (1987) The role of venture capital in financing small businesses, *Journal of Business Venturing*, Vol. 2, pp. 207–14.

MASON, C. M. and HARRISON, R. T. (1991a) Venture capital, the equity gap and the north-south divide in the UK, in M. Green, (ed.) *Venture Capital: International Comparisons*, Routledge, London, pp. 202–47.

MASON, C. M. and HARRISON, R. T. (1991b) The equity gap since Bolton, in J. Stanworth and C. Gray (eds) *Bolton Twenty Years On: the Small Firm in the 1990s*, Paul Chapman, London, pp. 112–50.

MASON, C. M. and HARRISON, R. T. (1992) The supply of equity finance in the UK: a strategy for closing the equity gap, *Entrepreneurship and Regional Development*, Vol. 4, pp. 357–80.

MASON, C. M. and HARRISON, R. T. (1993) Strategies for expanding the informal venture capital market, *International Small Business Journal*, Vol. 11, no. 4, pp. 23–38.

MASON, C. M. and HARRISON, R. T. (1994a) The informal venture capital market in the UK, in A. Hughes and D. J. Storey (eds.) *Financing Small Firms, Routledge*, London, pp. 64–111.

MASON, C. M. and HARRISON, R. T. (1994b) LINC: the Enterprise Agency role in promoting informal venture capital, in R. T. Harrison and C. M. Mason (eds.) *Informal Venture Capital: Information, Networks and Public Policy*, Woodhead-Faulkner, Hemel Hempstead, forthcoming.

MASON, C. M., HARRISON, J. and HARRISON, R. T. (1988) *Closing the Equity Gap? An Assessment of the Business Expansion Scheme*, Small Business Research Trust, London.

MAST, R. (1991) The changing nature of corporate venture capital programs, *European Venture Capital Journal*, March/April, pp. 26–33.

MONCK, C. P. S., PORTER, R. B., QUINTAS, P. R., STOREY, D. J. and WYNARCZYK, P. (1988) *Science Parks and the Growth of High Technology Firms*, Croom Helm, Beckenham, Kent.

MONCTON CONSULTING SERVICES LTD (1991) *Stimulating the Use of Private Sector Venture Capital Financing in Atlantic Canada*, Report to the Atlantic Canada Opportunities Agency, Moncton, New Brunswick.

MOORE, B., MOORE, R. and SEDAGHAT, N. (1992) *Early stage finance for small high-technology companies: a preliminary note*, Paper to an Anglo-German seed capital workshop, Oxford Science Park.

MOORE, B., and SEDAGHAT, N. (1991) *Factors constraining the growth of small high-technology companies: a case study of the Cambridge sub-region*, Paper to the 18th annual conference of the European Association for Research in Industrial Economics, Ferra, Italy.

MURRAY, G. (1993) Third party equity support to new technology-based firms in the UK and Continental Europe, Paper to the Six Countries Programme Conference on Financing the Early Stage Technology Company in the 1990s: An International Perspective, Montreal.

MURRAY, G. and FRANCIS, D. (1992) *The European Seed Capital Fund Scheme: Review of the First Three Years*, Report to the European Community (DG XXIII), Warwick Business School, University of Warwick, Coventry.

MURRAY, G. C. and LOTT, J. (1992) Have UK venture capital firms a bias against investment in high technolgy related companies?, Paper to the Babson Entrepreneurship Research Conference, INSEAD.

PRATT, G. (1990) Venture capital in the United Kingdom, *Bank of England Quarterly Review*, Vol. 30, pp. 78-83.

ROBERTS, E. B. (1990) Initial capital for the new technological enterprise, *IEEE Transactions on Engineering Management*, Vol. 37, pp. 81-94.

ROBERTS, E. B. (1991) *Entrepreneurs in High Technology: Lessons from MIT and Beyond*, Oxford University Press, New York.

ROTHWELL, R. (1985) Venture finance, small firms and public policy in the UK, *Research Policy*, Vol. 14, pp. 253-65.

ROTHWELL, R. (1989) Small firms, innovation and industrial change, *Small Business Economics*, Vol. 1, pp. 51-64.

SAHLMAN, W. A. and STEVENSON, H. H. (1985) Venture capital myopia, in J. A. Hornaday, E. B. Shils, J. A. Timmons and K. H. Vesper (eds.) *Frontiers of Entrepreneurship Research 1985*, Babson College, Wellesley: MA, pp. 80-104.

SHARP, G. (1992) *The Insider's Guide to Raising Venture Capital*, Kogan Page, London.

STANDEVEN, P. (1993) *Financing the Early Stage Technology Firm in the 1990s: An International Perspective*, Discussion paper prepared for the Six Countries Programme Conference on Financing the Early Stage Technology Company in the 1990s: An International Perspective, Montreal.

SWEETING, R. C. (1991) UK venture capital funds and the funding of new technology-based businesses: process and relationships, *Journal of Management Studies*, Vol. 28, pp. 601-22.

THOMPSON, C. and BAYER, K. (1992) *The Geography of 'New Entrepreneurial State' Activity: Public Venture Capital Programs in the United States*, Working Paper No 10, The Robert M. La Follette Institute of Public Affairs, University of Wisconsin-Madison: Madison, Wisconsin.

TIMMONS, J. A. (1990) *Planning and Financing the New Venture*, Brick House Publishing Co, Acton: MA.

TIMMONS, J. A. and SAPIENZA, H. J. (1992) Venture capital: the decade ahead, in D. L. Sexton and J. D. Kasarda (eds.) *Entrepreneurship in the 1990s*, PWS-Kent, Boston: MA, pp. 402-37.

TYMES, E. R. and KRASNER, O. J. (1983) Informal risk capital in California, in J. A. Hornaday, J. A. Timmons and K. H. Vesper (eds.) *Frontiers of Entrepreneurship Research 1983*, Babson College, Wellesley: MA, pp. 347-68.

VYAKARNAM, S. and JACOBS, R. (1991) How do bank managers construe high technology entrepreneurs? *14th National Small Firms Policy and Research Conference*, Blackpool, November.

WETZEL, W. E. (1981) Informal risk capital in New England, in K. H. Vesper (ed.) *Frontiers of Entrepreneurship Research 1981* Babson College, Wellesley: MA, pp. 217-45.

WETZEL, W. E. (1993) Angels and informal risk capital, *Sloan Management Review*, Vol. 24, Summer, pp. 23-34.

WETZEL, W. E. (1986) Informal risk capital: knowns and unknowns, in D. L. Sexton and R. W. Smilor (eds.) *The Art and Science of Entrepreneurship*, Ballinger, Cambridge: MA, pp. 85-108.

WINTERS, T. E. and MURFIN, D. L. (1988) Venture capital investing for corporate development objectives, *Journal of Business Venturing*, Vol. 3, pp. 207-22.

PART IV Intellectual Property

CHAPTER 11

Flexible Specialisation on a Global Basis and the Protection of Intellectual Property: A Problematic Case

ELIZABETH GARNSEY AND MALCOLM WILKINSON

INTRODUCTION

Global alliances are currently hailed as an effective growth strategy in an era of international markets and multinational corporations (Hamel, Doz and Prahalad, 1989). For the small high technology venture, close affiliation with corporate partners as funders, customers and suppliers is often a necessity, and one which is encouraged by government schemes in support of collaboration such as the LINK awards (Moore and Garnsey, 1993). We explore here the experience of a UK semiconductor firm, Anamartic, with a novel integrated wafer scale memory technology which entered into alliances with US, Japanese and German firms as a potential route for growth. The experience of this firm reveals how arduous and problematic such a route can prove, and how the new venture can find itself locked into a trajectory shaped by the needs of powerful corporate partners which reduce its capacity to alter strategy to changing circumstance. The difficulties of building a global business have not been fully recognised by venture capitalists, who not infrequently require international corporate endorsement – and hence a global strategy – as a condition for contributing funding. These difficulties are exemplified by the experience of Anamartic which, despite its much heralded technology and network of corporate backers, proved unable to survive in the 'turbulent waters' of the global computer industry.

Flexible specialisation among a number of supplier and customer firms can provide an alternative to vertical integration within individual firms. Ideally, under this form of production, specialisation in specific activities within a wider value added chain is complemented by flexible technology and responsiveness to changing market conditions (Piore and Sabel, 1984). In the industrial district model (Marshall, 1947, p. 271), conditions of proximity are essential since local demand and supply conditions make it possible for specialisation to be associated with external economies shared among many firms of suppliers and customers. Under current conditions, some of the benefits of specialisation can be achieved without local proximity, for which new technologies of communication and improved transport can substitute. Thus we would distinguish between two forms of flexible specialisation. Those which are based on proximity (the industrial district model) are better known and have been closely studied (Pyke et al. 1990). However, an extended variant of flexible specialisation is also possible, where firms' interactions are not limited by location and industrial networks of specialist suppliers and customers extend across production chains on a national and global scale. The two forms have in common the use of specialist labour, of highly specialised equipment and the close links between customer and supplier/subcontract firms. Local variants of flexible specialisation enjoy many advantages but may fail to access growing international markets, a problem directly addressed by global forms of specialisation. The evidence presented in this paper points to reasons for resorting to global networks and to some of the difficulties of flexible specialisation on a global scale. Though in theory it should be possible for firms to interact as international trading partners with other firms of a similar size, or to retain their autonomy in other ways (e.g. by having a soughtafter product), in practice small firms 'going global' may be pulled into the orbit of larger corporations instead of achieving the balance of market power ideally characterising the interactions of firms in 'industrial districts'. In this case, it proved difficult to capitalise on intellectual property which had been long and arduously built up.

The situation facing Anamartic appeared to be one in which a network of business alliances constituted an effective compromise between hierarchical organisation and narrow market relations (Powell, 1990). However, suitable local suppliers and customers were not available to Anamartic. Instead the company turned to alliances with foreign corporations, in a global variant of flexible specialisation. In the context of the right alliances with successful foreign companies, specialisation appeared to provide a promising growth strategy. However, the case illustrates how a global corporate network can under certain conditions trap an emerging firm and limit its flexibility. The scope for strategic manoeuvres (Evans, 1991) proved minimal as a result of cumulative constraints on the options available to the firm.

STRATEGIC OPTIONS AND CONSTRAINTS

Anamartic was a spin-out from Sinclair Research, incorporated as an independent company in 1986. The expertise of the team assembled by Clive Sinclair by 1984 related to the design, manufacture and application of silicon wafers in the computer industry. The chronology of events at Anamartic is outlined in the Appendix. The location of the company in Cambridge reflected the local expertise in computer science, emanating from the university, which was associated with the emergence of small high technology firms in the area (Garnsey and Cannon-Brookes, 1993). Like all company founders, the members of the new venture had to commit themselves to a strategy in relation to product, market focus and manufacture.

The first decision faced by the founders of Anamartic was how to embody their intellectual property, a technology over 10 years in gestation, in a product. They needed a route whereby their intellectual property could be further extended and used to create value. At the outset the choice appeared to be an easy one, between memory or processor designs on a whole wafer. Memory was chosen firstly because the design was simpler and hence carried lower risk and the promise of a more rapid development cycle, capable of generating revenue faster. Secondly the market was well understood by the Anamartic team and although the wafer technology was new, the product which was selected, solid state disk (SSD), had a significant and growing market. Thirdly, another recent start-up in the USA, Trilogy Corporation, had recently failed in the attempt to make a processor wafer and although the Anamartic engineers believed they could succeed where Trilogy had failed, they expected that financing would be very difficult to obtain for processor design.

Two channels to market were available; firstly, sales could be directly to computer users, facilitated by conforming to certain well defined standards (SCSI or small computers system interface). Secondly, it was believed that a very similar product could also be offered to computer manufacturers to build into their own equipment (the OEM route). It proved difficult to establish consistent priorities here; the product strategy was altered twice during the life of the company, initially because of the financing structure and preferences of one of the major investors. Later there was another change of strategic direction in reaction to the lack of success of the OEM route.

Financing proved to be the initial hurdle to effective take-off, but even after the first round of finance, funding never ceased to be a major source of difficulty. It was clear that close to £3m would be needed for the initial product development. Manufacturing would have to be subcontracted because the capital investment required would have been in excess of £50m which was well beyond the capacity of Anamartic to raise. It was not therefore viable to consider setting up a vertically integrated hierarchical organisation such as another start-up of the same period, NMB Semiconductors, established when it raised over £100m initial financing in Japan and went on to pursue a successful route as manufacturer of memory components. Even with the modest requirement of £3m, Anamartic was not able to raise equity finance from venture capitalists without the endorsement of a major corporate investor. This crucially affected the strategic options available and the route whereby intellectual property could be converted into revenue generating activity. Rather than setting up in production, a means had to be found to generate revenue directly from R&D activity. Although licensing the intellectual property attaching to their designs might have brought in revenue, it was believed that a joint venture with a corporate backer was likely to provide a much better return on the development work carried out since the 1970s and realisation of its future potential.

Thus the perceived need for corporate endorsement set the scene for a growth strategy via strategic alliances. Tandem Computers provided the required support, and a £500,000 grant was obtained from the DTI in 1987 but it was still necessary to raise additional finance through a second phase of equity investment in 1988 to complete development and start to market the product.

These choices effectively constrained the range of options open to Anamartic from this point. The choice of product affected marketing: the UK provides under 10% of the total market for computer memory and it was judged necessary to set up a global operation and to target major potential customers in the USA. Anamartic was driven to use subcontractors for manufacturing. The only US source of supply, Texas Instruments, was moving manufacturing to Japan and in 1988 there were no competitive memory manufacturers in Europe. It appeared necessary to find a Japanese manufacturing partner. Tandem was a favoured customer of Fujitsu's and approached the Japanese company with a view to organising a collaborative undertaking; by February 1988 Fujitsu had agreed to a joint venture activity with Anamartic. Fujitsu were interested in taking an investment stake in the company, and in a wider manufacturing licence, and would perhaps become a user of the technology in their own computer products division. Thus Fujitsu could provide both much needed funding and the promise of major contracts. The Board of Anamartic decided on a step-by-step relationship to motivate the Japanese to collaborate without closing off all other options. In practice, by February 1989, Anamartic was perceived in the industry to have a very strong relationship with Fujitsu, mainly because of the high profile PR which took place and the 'joint' authorship of technical papers at a San Francisco conference in 1989.

The complex strategic alliance thus formed was governed by a joint development agreement with Tandem and a memorandum of understanding with Fujitsu. Tandem paid for the development work and acquired exclusive rights to market the product. Milestones were established setting out what was to be delivered by both parties and a timescale. Tandem was to provide specifications of the product it required and Anamartic was required to effect the detailed design and implementation work. There was cross-licensing of technology whereby Anamartic could use technology developed in the course of the project as long as it was not in the same area of application as Tandem's products. In the case of Fujitsu, the memorandum of understanding covered the development and manufacturing phases of the wafer memory development work. Fujitsu required to be sole supplier and in return agreed to supply all Anamartic's needs at competitive prices.

The relationship with Fujitsu had positive and negative aspects. Fujitsu was viewed as a very high quality supplier to the computer industry and this provided credibility to Anamartic with customers. However, Fujitsu's sole sourcing rights effectively locked out any other supplier. This arrangement made it very difficult for Anamartic to apply pressure on Fujitsu to provide genuinely competitive prices for the memory components even at times when there was a glut on the world market of 1 Megabyte chips. There was another factor which could have either positive or negative implications. In taking on the manufacturing capability for wafer scale integration, Fujitsu would also acquire the technological competence required to convert Anamartic's intellectual property into revenue generating activity. This was a positive development for the new venture only so long as Anamartic benefited from the transfer to and development of these competencies in another company.

The relationship with Tandem was also proving to have a down side. The endorsement of the technology by Tandem had triggered the initial financing, but Tandem had also offered its own candidate as chief executive. In the event this nominee proved unable to cope with the intense pressures that members of the young company were experiencing. His inexperience also led to the setting of unrealistic goals and a breakdown in self confidence and motivation of the team.

In terms of product specification, Tandem had decided to use the technology in its own computer products, but instead of taking the SCSI standard product which Anamartic had proposed, had requested its own proprietary interface which could not be sold by Anamartic to other computer manufacturers or users. Anamartic engineers focused on the delivery of the product for Tandem and as a result the standard SCSI product was almost a year late in reaching the market, and suffered from an inferior mechanical and performance specification in relation to what had originally been envisaged. The application of Anamartic's intellectual property to the development of a proprietary product for another company represented an unanticipated diversion from the planned route whereby intellectual property would be used to develop a generic product of wide application.

On the marketing side, Anamartic found itself tightly constrained as a result of its strategic partnerships. The Anamartic SSD product had a wealth of features but was expensive to manufacture and highly priced, because no competitive pressure could be exerted on Fujitsu. Thus Anamartic had to focus on the high value added end of the market where the volumes were low and as a result the production volumes never reached a level attractive for a second source, even had one been available. The use of a non-standard interface meant that Anamartic could not address the rapidly growing market for SCSI solid state disk products and other manufacturers, including NEC, were able to enter the market before Anamartic. The main marketing efforts up to 1989 were spent on pursuing OEM customers – trying to find another 'Tandem' – but with little success.

It was only with the advent of a new CEO, Peter Cavill, in 1990 that the earlier strategic decisions were reviewed and reversed. Major efforts were made during 1990 to find a second source and to focus sales of the SCSI product through resellers and system integrators to end users of computer equipment. Both these efforts were success-

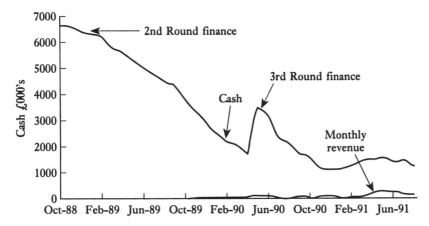

Figure 11.1
Anamartic: revenue and cash 1988–91

ful. Siemens and Anamartic began a joint development to replace the now ageing Fujitsu design and in the meantime Anamartic's marketing efforts in Europe were bearing fruit, with British Telecom becoming a major customer.

However, this success came too late for Anamartic (see Figure 11.1). The cash flow from product sales was insufficient to support the large development team and with the failure to raise further equity finance from the City of London in 1991, the company had to wind down its operations early in 1992.

THE INDUSTRIAL ENVIRONMENT

In the 20 years it took to bring the technology from the laboratory into the market place, the global computer industry itself travelled from infancy to maturity, undergoing change which affected the prospects for radically new computer technologies. The pioneering British computer industry failed to take off, unsupported by the British electronics industry which had focused on military and aerospace markets. The consumer electronics industry in Britain did not provide a significant market for semiconductor products. These changes in the wider industrial environment impinged on Anamartic's prospects, making delays highly costly. The fluidity of the industry diminished and in some respects it became increasingly difficult to launch a radically new semiconductor technology as the influence of proprietary and standardised production processes and products took hold (Hobday, 1990). Yet the computer industry was in other respects very open to change and remained subject to waves of innovation through the continual introduction of changes in technology which offered cost and functionality advantages. A feature of this continual instability in the computer industry was a resurgence of small specialised semiconductor firms in Silicon Valley from the mid-1980s. This occurred at the same time as the established semiconductor firms in the region were suffering from over capacity and declining profits.

> More than 85 new semiconductor firms were started in Silicon Valley during the 1980s. This new wave of chipmakers represents the state-of-the-art in semiconductor design and product innovation and has generated some 25,000 jobs and more than $2 billion in annual sales.
>
> (Saxenian, 1990)

The supporters of Anamartic's technology believed that the venture stood a good chance of success of the kind enjoyed in the 1980s by new specialised semiconductor start-ups in Silicon Valley.

FLEXIBLE OR RIGID SPECIALISATION?

Small high technology firms have been extolled for their flexibility and capacity to adapt rapidly to technological developments and market opportunities (Gilder, 1989). Through specialisation in activities they are best suited to carry out, they are said to overcome the rigidities of larger, vertically integrated companies. Yet under the conditions in which it was forced to operate, Anamartic's specialist role gave rise to a certain immobility rather than flexibility. The decision to avoid vertical integration in the form of a specialised fabrication unit in the locality was forced on the company by funding shortages. The decision to use a Japanese manufacturer followed from this resource deficit and from the difficulties in finding European or US manufacturers capable of providing a competitive memory technology. But once tied in to a manufacturing venture with Fujitsu, which had an equity stake in Anamartic, the new venture had no leverage over costs and limited influence on Fujitsu's adherence to their specifications. We have seen that since they could not turn to another supplier, Anamartic was to a certain extent immobilised by the partnership with Fujitsu.

Ultimately it appears that Fujitsu will obtain control over the venture's intellectual property. Negotiations are underway to find a way to pay for unsold work-in-progress for Anamartic at Fujitsu by providing Fujitsu with the licence to Anamartic's intellectual property. Fujitsu had already developed the competence in the technology through the technology transfer aspects of undertaking the manufacturing process. This was achieved through intensive 'coaching' of Fujitsu personnel by Anamartic's development engineers, as was necessary if the manufacture of the wafer scale product was to be carried out to a high standard. In this respect, the case may appear to support the argument of Florida and Kenney who hold that excessive specialisation in R&D by Western firms which lack local manufacturing support has the effect of channelling innovative products into the Japanese corporations which undertake manufacture through subcontracting arrangements or alliances. The manufacturing capabilities of the Japanese corporations enable them to reap the major revenue gains of innovations through volume output (Florida and Kenney, 1990).

However, in this instance it is not clear that Fujitsu intended to put the technology to use. The investment was a costly experiment for the Japanese firm and it is not certain whether it will bear fruit. The quality and the cost of existing technologies had improved with massive Japanese investment in raising chip yields, so reducing the short-term competitive edge of Anamartic's designs. However, the scanning of new technological developments and conversion of emerging intellectual property into revenue generating potential (whether or not immediately realised) is part of the innovation strategy of Japanese corporations. The joint alliances with new ventures which ensue (witness the many Japanese corporate alliances with Silicon Valley firms) can have relatively long-term objectives because Japanese firms are not under pressure to show immediate profit from capital expenditure. This is in direct contrast to the situation in Britain where short-term pressures contribute to the cautious approach evidenced by British electronics and computer companies in relation to new technologies developed outside their own R&D facilities.

As to Anamartic's relationship with the major customer, there was at first enthusiasm at having obtained the support and the endorsement of their technology from an innovative company with Tandem's reputation. However, two major difficulties ensued. In the first place, Tandem proposed a CEO who had development but no general management experience. One of his assets was experience in working with Japanese manufacturers which was held to compensate for his lack of management experience given the objective of finding Japanese funding and production facilities. In the event, the new CEO proved unable to retain the confidence of staff at Anamartic at a time when effective leadership was crucial to the company's success. Moreover, Anamartic was forced to customize to Tandem's specifications. Since reaching these specifications was a highly demanding target, it was beyond the capacity of a small specialist firm to support the parallel development of a major generic product.

DYNAMIC OR STATIC NETWORKS?

Flexible specialisation refers not only to the characteristics of the firm itself, but also to its interactions with other firms. Specialised firms benefit from productive relationships with other specialised companies through a 'dynamic network' in the ideal model of innovation which has been used to characterise Silicon Valley (Saxenian, 1990). Anamartic formed part of a global network, of which the most significant circuits centred on Tandem in California and Fujitsu in Japan, but the network included also SGS Thomson and Siemens. The practical difficulties of running the company on a global scale should not be underestimated. Both the technical director and Peter Cavill, the CEO appointed in 1990, felt in retrospect that their energies had been dispersed by networking activities which reduced to a minimum the time they had available to deal with internal problems of running the new venture. Managing teams of development engineers in the USA and Britain while teaching Japanese engineers the WSI technology was highly taxing for the development staff. These tasks rendered more difficult the job of creating a sense of common purpose among the development team and between development and sales staff in Cambridge.

The dynamism of the global network consisted above all in continual change of circumstance, as when Tandem encountered problems of recession in the computer industry and reduced its orders just as Anamartic's product delivery process had been established. In other respects there were static elements to the global network, in that Anamartic was not free to reconfigure or enter new networking relationships.

The global network of which Anamartic formed part was in strong contrast to the relative isolation of the firm locally. The company did not form part of a dynamic regional network of firms. The location of the company in Cambridge reflected local expertise. Cambridge University had pioneered computer development, the Atlas computer had been one of the two most powerful in the country and its Computer Science Department had been engaged in novel and important work for over 20 years. Sinclair Research was able to draw on local talent and to provide industrial opportunities for computer scientists. There were other small Cambridge computer companies, notably Acorn Computers, now part of Olivetti, whose staff knew each other. Nevertheless, staff at Anamartic were working largely in isolation. No one else in Cambridge or indeed in Britain was working on the commercial application of wafer scale integration and there was a minimum of interaction with other British companies. Local contacts had been necessary for recruitment and for attracting finance. But once the company was set up and running, global networking took precedence over local links, which were only with a few suppliers. These circumstances made Anamartic's network very different from flexible specialisation on the industrial district model, characterised by close knit linkages between firms in a regional economy. Cultivating global partnerships could in principle open up international markets closed to firms caught within the economy of the local district, but in this case there was no open sesame. It proved very difficult for Anamartic to compensate for limitations of national supply and demand conditions.

This was desirable because of developments in the domestic economy. By 1990 there was no major British computer manufacturer left and memory chips for foreign-owned computer companies were being supplied predominantly from Japan and Korea. Sinclair's interest in Anamartic had stemmed from his vision of a parallel supercomputer, which was not shared elsewhere in Britain at that time. A small British semiconductor company planning to raise more revenue than could be achieved by licensing its designs had no real choice but to look to global markets and to choose between joint venture with foreign firms or being acquired, given the difficulty of raising finance for advanced technology ventures on British capital markets. Under conditions of the kind Anamartic experienced, the licensing of the venture's designs and software, despite its limited revenue generating potential, is a less risky route than subcontract manufacture.

CONCLUSIONS

Anamartic's story is a cautionary tale from many angles. The promise which the company held out led many talented engineers and some well-informed financiers to invest much time, energy and over £20m in promoting this technology. The strategy, though pragmatic, was carefully thought out, with an awareness of new developments in the industry.

The joint alliances undertaken by the new venture were designed to position the company in a production chain which would substitute for vertical integration. The product made in Japan to their design would be delivered to customers in California, via the capabilities of their corporate allies. The network was set up with a view to introducing checks and balances into the power relationships of such alliances. Small ventures are often acquired by their distributors and the aim was to retain the new company's independence. There were advantages therefore in an alliance with a supplier which had joint equity in the new company to reduce dependence on the customer. The original plan was to have other corporate customers to balance the power of Tandem, but in the event the product range required for such a strategy proved beyond the resources of the new venture, which could not satisfy SGS Thomson and Siemens at the same time as meeting Tandem's requirements. The need to collaborate in complex global joint ventures cornered the company into exclusive relationships with manufacturing and customer firms which created dependencies limiting the flexibility of the venture. Specialisation under these conditions reduced Anamartic's ability to exact its price for the exploitation by its partners of its own intellectual property.

When conditions are propitious, flexible specialisation can prove a viable and productive mode of operation. Propitious conditions include capital markets well attuned to the needs and prospects of high technology ventures and a local dynamic network which can be used to recruit experienced managers to run a start-up company. But under less favourable circumstances, such as Anamartic encountered, the pursuit of a new technology through specialisation within a global network can give rise to rigidities and diseconomies of scope which can vitiate the prospects for a new technology.

Michael Porter has cautioned those contemplating strategic alliance:

> Alliances with foreign companies have become another managerial fad and cure-all...In reality, however, while alliances can achieve selective benefits, they always exact significant costs; they involve co-ordinating (at least) two separate operations, reconciling goals...creating a competitor and giving up profits. (Porter, 1990)

It can be added to these points that where the intellectual property of an innovative

R&D company is made available to a corporation through a manufacturing alliance, there is also the danger that the R&D venture fails to develop crucial technological competencies required to realise the value of their intellectual property through production. Ultimately there is a danger of loss of control over intellectual property. The dangers of uncoupling R&D from production has recently been signalled in the USA (Ferguson, 1990; Florida and Kenney, 1990). In the enthusiasm for specialist high technology activity in R&D it was assumed in the 1980s that for high technology ventures, manufacturing was an activity which could be readily subcontracted because the real value inhered in the intellectual property developed during the research and design phases. Critics of the uncoupling of R&D from production argue that intellectual property in design is highly imitable in the absence of an effective manufacturing facility, and the latter is required to realise adequately the value of intellectual property embodied in R&D work. The manufacturing facility may be achieved through the close monitoring of the production of subcontract and supplier firms, but success requires direct involvement in the manufacturing activities of this network of firms, a role which cannot be safely delegated.

Larger corporations can choose whether to enter into alliances. Emerging ventures have fewer degrees of freedom. Anamartic's alliances gave rise to precisely the costs identified by Porter, which stemmed in turn from the company's inability to fund its own development route. The case does not imply that global alliance and flexible specialisation are strategies to be avoided by emerging firms. Such an argument could not in any case be based on the experience of one firm, presented here not as a typical case but to demonstrate difficulties which can in principle arise in global ventures. On a broader basis, it is difficult to evaluate the success of joint ventures, since the criteria by which partners judge the alliance may differ. In one of the most extensive studies available, it was found that the success of the ventures was contested by at least one of the partners in over half of the cases (55% of a sample of 895 joint ventures) (Harrigan, 1986). The small partner is more likely to express dissatisfaction according to the evidence of certain studies (Dodgson, 1993). Problems are experienced not only by smaller companies, however; larger Japanese corporations also have difficulties in undertaking joint ventures and it has been argued that successes are few (Imai, 1990; cited in Dodgson, 1993). Counter cases of successful global alliances could no doubt be cited. Experienced entrepreneurs are increasingly embarking on strategic start-ups which involve professionally organised alliances in a network of partnerships between international corporations and venture capitalists, who take balanced equity in the new venture, with control of the new venture vested in the hands of its management. Substantial funding is thereby raised to avoid the resource shortages which plagued Anamartic's managers. Mutual interest in the successful outcome of the venture is built into the arrangement. General Magic in California and Electronic Office in Cambridge, England, could be cited as examples of strategic ventures of this kind, which call for further study.

The experience of Anamartic shows that the potential consequences of various scenarios need to be traced out fully. These strategies must be pursued under appropriate conditions if flexibility is to be retained. Though they may be successful under specific conditions, global alliances provide no panacea for dealing with the growth problems of emerging high technology firms.

NOTE

A version of this paper is to appear in *Long Range Planning*, December 1994, as 'Global alliances in high technology: a trap for the unwary'.

ACKNOWLEDGEMENTS

Thanks to all members of Anamartic who gave generously of their time, and especially to Ian MacGregor for his help with the chronology. Thanks to Sir Clive Sinclair, David Hall and Matthew Bullock of Barclays Bank for their help with the case study.

APPENDIX:
Brief summary of developments at Anamartic

1973 Ivor Catt patented idea for a fault tolerant wafer scale chip technology.

1974 Catt enlists support of Middlesex Polytechnic staff.

1975 Catt's project taken up and then dropped at Plessey. Catt enlists Wilkinson (also at Middlesex Polytechnic) in support of WSI technology.

1977 Wilkinson moves to Burroughs and enlists McGregor's support for a wafer scale integration (WSI) project. As technical director and general manager at Burroughs Cumbernauld, McGregor is able to make £60,000 available for WSI project in 1981. WSI project moved to new Burroughs research centre at San Diego and runs into technical difficulties; then dropped.

1983 Catt convinces Sinclair of the viability and importance of WSI. Work on WSI continues at Sinclair Research. Wilkinson and two others who had been at Burroughs are recruited to work at SR on WSI.

1984 Sinclair Research runs into serious problems in computer market shake out. In an attempt to salvage WSI from Sinclair Research difficulties, the idea of an autonomous company concerned with WSI is launched. Rob Wilmot ex-CEO from ICL, helps to draw up business plan.

1986 Anamartic is incorporated after complex deal to restructure Sinclair Research is negotiated with Barclays and venture capitalists. Thirteen people move from SR to start this company. Attempts to enlist support of large British companies and MOD fail. SGS Thomson Italy prepared to support another development, a bipolar device project. This has to compete with resources for WSI development at Anamartic.

1987 Support of Tandem, James Treybig's innovative Californian company, is obtained. First round financing including Barclays and Tandem. Bipolar and WSI programmes financed. CEO from Tandem joins Anamartic in Cambridge.

1988 Fujitsu agree to WSI joint development programme. Second round financing: $10m and Fujitsu has 10% of equity. Strains emerge in staff-CEO relations. Explosive meeting with Tandem over difficulties in meeting specifications and dates. December: CEO resigns.

1989 Ex-CEO required to quit interim post and leaves Cambridge. D. Hall joins company as temporary CEO. Bipolar programme reprieved and new objectives set. Finance Director appointed. First wafer product delivered to Tandem in March. Bipolar programme cancelled by Board. Lack of support from SGS Thomson. Prototype samples to Tandem in October. P. Cavill joins company as CEO in November. New funding requirements identified and process of refinancing begins.

1990 Major recruitment for Engineering division. Abortive financing attempt (£13m sought). Barclays, Tandem and Fujitsu put together interim finance package until money is raised. Tandem insist on a lower cash requirement by building a licensing strategy for the technology into projections. Fujitsu agree unwillingly. 4Mbit programme started with Siemens. No new finance forthcoming. Decision in May to close US engineering operation and transfer SCSI development to Cambridge. Tandem product launch problems in August. Finance continuing on month by month basis. Problems with SCSI product and wafers from Fujitsu.

1991 65 employees in engineering. Poor revenue stream. No confidence in financing. 42 redundancies including 25 in engineering. Siemens 4MBit and JESSI programmes cancelled. 16MBit with Fujitsu cancelled. Further redundancies.

1992 Final reduction of workforce. Company continues to trade. Negotiations with Fujitsu over intellectual property rights.

1993 Closure

REFERENCES

DODGSON, M. (1993) *Technological Collaboration in Industry: Strategy Policy and Internationalisation in Innovation*, Routledge, London

EVANS, J. (1991 Strategic flexibility for high technology manoeuvres: a conceptual framework, *Journal of Management Studies*, Vol. 28, no. 1 January, pp. 69-89.

FERGUSON, C. (1990) Computers and the coming of the US Keiretsu, *Harvard Business Review*, July-August, pp. 55-70.

FLORIDA, R and KENNEY, M. (1990) *The Breakthrough Illusion; Corporate America's Failure to Move from Innovation to Mass Production*, Basic Books, USA.

GARNSEY, E. and CANNON-BROOKES, A. (1993) The Cambridge phenomenon revisited: aggregate change among Cambridge high technology companies since 1985, *Entrepreneurship and Regional Development*, Vol. 5, no 1, pp. 179-207.

GILDER, G. (1989) *Microcosm*, Simon and Schuster, New York.

HAMEL, G., DOZ, Y. and PRAHALAD, C. (1989) Collaborate with your competitors and win, *Harvard Business Revue*, January-February.

HARRIGAN, K. (1986) *Managing for Joint Venture Success*, Lexington Books, Lexington Mass.

HOBDAY, M. (1990) Semiconductors: creative destruction or US industrial decline? *Futures*, July-August, pp. 571-85.

IMAI, K-I. (1990) Japanese business groups and the structural impediments initiative, in K. Yamamura (ed.) *Japanese Economic Structure: Should it Change?*, Society for Japanese Studies, Washington DC, University of Washington, cited in Dodgson, 1993.

MARSHALL, A. (1947) *Principles of Economics*, Macmillan, London.

MOORE, I. and GARNSEY, E. (1993) Funding for innovation in small firms: the role of government, *Research Policy*, Vol. 22, pp. 507-19, forthcoming.

PIORE, M. and SABEL, C. (1984) *The Second Industrial Divide: Possibilities for Prosperity*, Basic Books, N.Y.

PORTER, M. (1990) The competitive advantage of nations, *Harvard Business Review*, March-April.

POWELL, M. (1990) Neither market nor hierarchy: network forms of organisation, *Research in Organisational Behaviour*, Vol. 12, pp. 295-336.

PYKE F., BECATTINE, F. and SENGENBERGER, W. (eds.) (1990) *Industrial Districts and Inter-Firm Cooperation in Italy*, International Institute for Labour Studies, Geneva.

SAXENIAN, A. (1990) Regional networks and the resurgence of Silicon Valley, *California Management Review*, Fall, pp. 89-112.

CHAPTER 12

The Impact of Institutional Intellectual Property Policy on the Propensity of Individual UK Universities to Incubate NTBFs

KERRON A. HARVEY

INTRODUCTION

If we may judge by the 'Route 128 phenomenon', the 'Cambridge phenomenon' and similar phenomena, major research universities in the UK should in theory be such fruitful incubators of NTBFs as to create a critical mass in their immediate vicinity. In practice, despite the fact that Segal, Quince and Wicksteed's (1986) work on Cambridge University seems to be the only comprehensive study of NTBFs incubated directly and indirectly by an individual university, it is commonly claimed that relatively few enterprises have spun off from UK universities, that there is no critical mass in the vicinity of other UK universities. In short, the 'Cambridge phenomenon' is widely regarded as atypical in the UK context.

The results of parallel studies of other UK universities would be interesting – perhaps even surprising. We may hazard a guess that such studies have not been undertaken due to inherent methodological difficulties. Any attempt to establish the incidence and identity of NTBFs via a survey which focuses on the university itself is liable to be distorted by the 'iceberg effect' which Roberts (1972) encountered in the USA. An alternative, company-centred approach would almost certainly be required. Even if it could somehow be demonstrated that there was no 'iceberg effect', establishing that university x had incubated y NTBFs over z years – compared to only p NTBFs at university q – would have limited value. We would want to know how to account for the discrepancy. Our curiosity would also extend to discrepancies between the incubation record of major research universities in different countries, if such discrepancies were demonstrated.

The supposed discrepancy between the extent to which UK and US research universities incubate NTBFs seems to be attributed most frequently – not only by UK politicians and the media, but also by UK academics (see, for instance, Sharp, 1985) – to the non-entrepreneurial nature of UK academics as a 'breed'. This very one-dimensional 'explanation' seems to be rooted in the entrepreneur-centred work of pioneering entrepreneurship researchers in the USA; early empirical studies often focused almost exclusively on differences in the innate and socialisation-derived characteristics of academic and non-academic entrepreneurs.

Subsequently, however, the focus shifted from the characteristics exhibited by entrepreneurs to the context in which they became entrepreneurs. Context might be macro (e.g. the extent to which the nation as a whole was deemed to have an 'entrepreneurial culture') or micro (e.g. the organisation in which the entrepreneur was previously employed). At the micro level, efforts were made to compare the 'spin-off rates' of large corporations, government research laboratories, and universities; this resulted in US universities being characterised as more effective incubators of NTBFs than large corporations or government research laboratories. Explanations were sought for variations in the 'spin-off rates' of organisations of the same type – variations both within and across countries. It was proposed that US research universities were more effective incubators of NTBFs than their European counterparts because features of the US university system were facilitative, whereas features of European university systems were inhibitive. Facilitative features of the US university system which were highlighted ranged from the difficulty of obtaining tenure, widespread use of 9-month contracts of employment and strong competition for research funding to the freedom to undertake consultancy. Inhibitive features of the UK university system, in particular, were said to range from job security and the continuing pursuit of academic goals in academics' 40s and 50s, to constraints (both attitudinal and time and/or earnings-related) on consultancy activities etc.

THE IMPACT OF INSTITUTIONAL IP POLICY ON NTBF FORMATION

One contextual feature which has received little attention in the literature is the potential impact of institutional intellectual property (IP) policy on the propensity of universities to incubate NTBFs. If a university does not routinely assert ownership of intellectual property rights (IPR) – that is to say, where ownership is not predetermined, as it is in Europe, for example, by EC funding programmes and as it has been in the UK by certain SERC collaborative programmes – then it has no control over the manner in which that IPR is exploited. Thus, neither the university itself nor its academic staff will be in a position to found NTBFs to exploit IPR generated within the university, unless a licence can be 'wrested' from the owner of the IPR. Similarly, if a university asserts ownership but then routinely transfers technology by assigning it or by granting an exclusive licence to an existing company, members of the academic staff are denied the opportunity to found NTBFs to exploit their IPR.

This is an interesting research area because it readily permits comparisons between individual universities within one country and comparisons between the university systems of different countries. Comparison between the UK and the USA would be particularly interesting because, where the exploitation of IPR arising from publicly-funded research is concerned, the university systems in the two countries are ostensibly operating under very similar conditions.

In 1980 the US federal government passed the Uniform Federal Patent Policy Act (also known as the Bayh-Dole Act), which gave US universities the right to retain ownership of IPR arising from publicly-funded research, to determine how that IPR was exploited, and to exploit it themselves, or via their academic staff, if they wished. This Act, together with the Small Business Innovation Development Act 1982, was described in a joint ACARD/ABRC report (ACARD/ABRC, 1983) as 'the two main steps of interest' for the UK government when it came to considering how to improve the outward technology transfer process from UK universities. This report influenced the government's 1983 decision to remove the British Technology Group's (BTG's) long-standing 'right of first refusal' with regard to the exploitation of IP generated in the course of Research Council-funded projects.

When the government finally removed the BTG's so-called 'monopoly' in May 1985, rights and responsibilities which it previously enjoyed were formally offered to UK universities. The Department of Education & Science (DES) document[1] accompanying the offer letter from Sir John Kingman, then Chairman of the SERC, indicated that universities should accept this offer only if they were prepared to give academic researchers 'the fullest opportunity and scope' to assume responsibility for the exploitation of the IP which they generated. It was made clear that academics should be permitted – indeed, 'encouraged' – to found NTBFs to exploit their IP, if they wished, and that their university should give them 'guidance and help'. If individual academics did not wish to assume this kind of responsibility, the university itself should feel free to exploit the IP via NTBFs, where appropriate. This document acknowledged that on occasion academics' attempts at exploitation might be 'less than optimal' but explicitly stated that it was 'right to incur this risk to secure the gains that will come from giving researchers...more responsibility and more incentive'. Thus, in order to be authorised to assume the rights and responsibilities previously enjoyed by the BTG, universities were expected to have formulated IPR policies which permitted – indeed, facilitated – NTBF formation.

A COMPARATIVE ANALYSIS OF POLICY AND PRACTICE IN NINE UK UNIVERSITIES

This paper reports the findings of a study which sought, among other things, to ascertain whether UK universities did, in fact, act upon the commitment they made in this respect. The significance of this commitment should have been underlined by the fact that the Exploitation Scrutiny Group (ESG)[2] – that is to say, the group which scrutinised universities' responses to the Kingman letter before deciding whether or not to authorise universities to assume the rights and responsibilities previously enjoyed by the BTG – was prepared to (and did) enter into correspondence with universities with a view to clarifying the potential role of the academic researcher in the exploitation process.

The investigation adopted a research design based exclusively on case studies. Nine cases were selected including the Universities of Bristol, Durham, Glasgow, Hull, Kent, Liverpool, Strathclyde and York, and the City University. The investigation adopted a grounded rather than a logico-deductive approach to data collection and theory development. The fieldwork took place in the academic session 1989/90. Data were elicited principally through face-to-face tape-recorded interviews with informants nominated by the universities themselves as the most appropriate sources of information on IPR policy and practice. Initial interviews were both lengthy (2-4 hours) and highly structured (informed by a lengthy literature review). Follow-up interviews became increasingly less structured, however, and additional informants were interviewed, where appropriate. Data from histories, documents and records were also elicited, where possible.

OPERATIONALISING THE RESEARCH OBJECTIVE

The relatively vague phraseology of the document accompanying Sir John Kingman's offer letter presented a problem when it came to trying to establish objectively whether the 9 universities did, in fact, give members of their academic staff opportunity and scope to assume responsibility for exploiting their own findings and ideas – and if so, whether what they offered amounted to the fullest opportunity and scope or whether it fell short in some way. It was therefore necessary to define – for the purposes of the study, at least – what constituted 'fullest opportunity and scope', and what was meant by 'assume responsibility for exploiting' and 'findings and ideas'.[3,4]

The phrase 'fullest opportunity and scope' was the hardest to define. It was decided to attempt a definition in terms of criteria which would need to be fulfilled in order for researchers to have the fullest opportunity and scope to assume the kind of responsibility for exploiting tangible forms of IP (i.e. excluding expertise). Under the provisions of the 1977 Act, employers may assert ownership of inventions made by employees in the course of their duties. However, this same Act makes provision for employees to acquire sole right to IP generated in the course of their duties. Patent law overrides most other types of law, excepting the law of equity, which deals with trade secrets and confidential information. Contract law cannot override the rights of employees as specified by the Patent Act 1977. However, employers can choose to yield their rights under the 1977 Act. Thus, because Cambridge University has no wish to own IP generated by members of its academic staff, as a matter of policy it uses these provisions to immediately assign to inventors any rights which might be conferred on it by the 1977 Act by virtue of being their employer. The provisions of the Copyright, Designs and Patent Act 1988 – and, indeed, earlier Copyright Acts – also allow employers to yield to employees first ownership rights to copyright material and designs created by those employees in the course of their work; again, as a matter of policy, Cambridge University uses these provisions to immediately assign rights in designs and copyright material to their creators. If Cambridge chose to, of course, it could avoid the need for separate documentation in respect of every piece of IP to be assigned; it could simply waive its rights on a global basis. In the light of this, it was felt that the simplest, most unequivocal criterion of 'the fullest opportunity and scope' was a positive, unqualified answer to the following question:

> Do researchers, as a matter of policy, immediately acquire sole ownership of the IP they generate in the course of their duties?[5]

It was felt that the DES document offered support for this approach: it appeared to suggest that universities should, as a matter of policy, conditionally assign all their rights to researchers who wish to assume responsibility for exploiting their 'findings and ideas'.

If this criterion was fulfilled in the 9 participating universities, these researchers would, like their colleagues in parts of Europe, have the exclusive right to exploit their IP in whatever manner they see fit. If this criterion was not fulfilled, fulfilment of a second criterion could still give researchers considerable power to determine how their IP is exploited, though it falls short of 'the fullest opportunity and scope' to assume responsibility for exploiting their inventions which sole ownership confers. The provisions of the Patent Act 1977 and the Copyright, Designs and Patent Act 1988 allow employers to partially yield to employees their rights in inventions, copyright material and designs, as an alternative to wholly yielding those rights. Universities could use those provisions to give their employees joint ownership of IP they generate; this would confer on employees the same rights as employers enjoy when it comes to determining how their IP should be exploited. This falls short of 'the fullest opportunity and scope' to assume responsibility for exploiting their inventions which sole ownership confers, because joint ownership means that both parties must agree on the manner in which that IP is exploited. Academics who are joint owners could be prevented by their university from exploiting their IP in the manner they saw fit. On the other hand, they could equally prevent their university from exploiting their IP in a manner which did not meet with their approval. The value of joint ownership from the perspective of the academic is that it confers the legal right to have an equal say in how their IP is exploited.

This second criterion would be fulfilled if the following question received a positive, unqualified answer:

Do researchers, as a matter of policy, immediately acquire joint ownership of the IP they generate in the course of their duties?

If this second criterion was not fulfilled either, the situation becomes more complex. A series of alternative criteria need to be taken into account. A university may elect to assert ownership of the various types of IP generated by members of the academic staff; however, it may subsequently elect to assign those rights to a third party, rather than retain ownership. If the academic is not party to this decision, he could find himself unable to exploit the IP intellectually, let alone exploit it commercially.

There is considerable evidence to suggest that in many fields a discovery is more likely to be commercially exploited – and successfully exploited – if it is 'protected' in some manner, rather than put into the public domain. A university may elect to retain ownership of a discovery; however, unless the academic has the right to try and ensure that the IP in question is 'protected' in an appropriate way, he may be denied the fullest opportunity and scope to assume responsibility for exploiting it.

It may also be important for the academic to determine the way in which the IP is 'protected'. With some types of tangible IP, there is a choice between 'protecting' it overtly or covertly (patent versus secret know-how), formally or informally (registered design versus design right); in some industry sectors the choice may be critical. Finally, unless an academic has the right to decide who is allowed to commercially exploit that IP, his options are limited. He could opt to start a company to exploit his discovery, only to find that the university insists on licensing to existing companies, rather than to his proposed NTBF.

This complex situation can be expressed in terms of the following criteria. In order to have 'the fullest opportunity and scope' to exploit IP they have generated, where academics routinely acquire neither sole nor joint ownership of their IP, they need as a matter of policy to be able to determine:

- the subsequent ownership of IP they generate;
- how that IP is protected;
- who is granted use of the IP.

We may consider all the above criteria to be absolutely fulfilled if question (a) below gets a positive, unqualified answer. We may consider them to be only conditionally fulfilled if question (b) gets a positive, unqualified answer. Whether they acquire joint ownership or no ownership, we may, however, consider these criteria to be absolutely fulfilled if each of questions (c)–(e) gets a positive, unqualified answer:

(a) Do academics, as a matter of policy, immediately acquire sole ownership of the IP they generate in the course of their duties?
(b) Do academics, as a matter of policy, immediately acquire joint ownership of the IP they generate in the course of their duties?

If not, do academics, as a matter of policy, have the right to:

(c) determine the subsequent ownership (if any) of IP they generate?
(d) determine how that IP is protected?
(e) determine who is allowed to commercially exploit the IP they generated?

Finally, of course, irrespective of whether they have sole, joint or no ownership, in order to be able to entrepreneurially exploit IP they have generated rather than be obliged to license/assign it to a third party, do academics have:

(f) the freedom to found/co-found a business to exploit their IP while retaining their academic status?

If question (f), question (a) or any of questions (c)-(e) received a negative or a qualified answer in the 9 universities, and if question (b) received a positive answer, it was likely to indicate that academics in the university concerned did not have the fullest opportunity and scope to assume responsibility for exploiting the IP they generated. It was recognised as essential to establish whether negative (or positive) answers to these questions were a matter of policy or policy-implementation. It was felt that the number – or, perhaps, the nature – of the criteria which were not fulfilled should give some objective measure of the extent to which academics in any given university were denied such opportunity and scope. Establishing whether positive or negative answers were a matter of policy or policy-implementation should also give an idea of the underlying processes.

FINDINGS

The answers to all of these questions revealed a situation which was far more complex than had been anticipated. Analysis of the data suggested that this complexity stemmed from a range of factors which interacted in varying permutations in each university.

Ownership of intellectual property

The possibility that these universities might adopt a different approach to ownership of IP generated by academics had been forseen. What had not been forseen was the fragmented approach which some of them adopted to the different types of IP.

As Figure 12.1[6] shows, whereas Bristol, Durham, Glasgow, Strathclyde and York all asserted sole ownership of inventions, software, designs and other types of tangible IP, City had opted for joint ownership of inventions, software and other types of tangible IP, but waived even joint rights to designs unless they were connected to a patent. Hull and Liverpool had opted for joint ownership of inventions but asserted sole ownership of software, designs and other types of tangible IP. Kent asserted sole ownership of inventions, but had reached no decision in respect of software, designs and other types of tangible IP; effectively this meant that academics were free to assert sole ownership of these types of IP, if they were so minded.

In all four cases there appeared at first to be an association between this fragmentation and the date when these universities had formulated their original IP policy. Thus, Hull and Liverpool had acquired their original IP policy in the wake of the Patent Act 1977 by virtue of adopting wholesale recommendations in a document circulated by the Committee of Vice-Chancellors and Principals (CVCP, 1978). The policy of Kent and City were also formulated in the wake of the 1977 Act.

On the other hand, Strathclyde's original IP policy dated from the 1970s, while Bristol's and Glasgow's dated from the early 1980s; Bristol's, Glasgow's and Strathclyde's policies did not exhibit this kind of fragmentation, while City's sole deviation from a consistent approach to all forms of IP derived from a conscious decision that it had no interest in IP covered by design right. The fragmentation exhibited by 3 of the 9 universities is, in fact, symptomatic of a failure to conduct an in-depth and informed review of institutional IP policy – either on receipt of Sir John Kingman's offer letter or in the wake of the 1988 Act. By 1990 Kent had done nothing in respect of either. Liverpool's administrator had simply misread the terms of the university's (by now 11-year-old) patent policy (concluding that it indicated sole, rather than joint ownership) and extended this misreading to the 1988 Act. Hull went so far as to have a working party examine and extend its IP policy; unfortunately, the working party does not seem to have been as well informed as it might have been, also mistaking its earlier policy of joint ownership as indicating sole ownership.

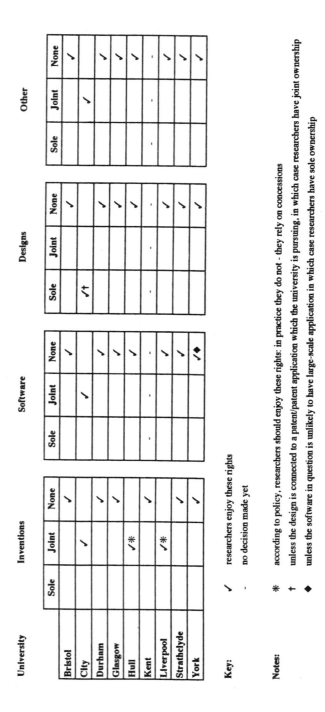

Figure 12.1
Summary of the IP rights of researchers in the nine participating universities (1989/90)

Retaining ownership or assigning it: who decides?

As a result, deploying the rights conferred by sole ownership, policy-implementers in every university except City could determine, if they chose to, whether ownership of an academic's IP was retained or assigned to a third party.

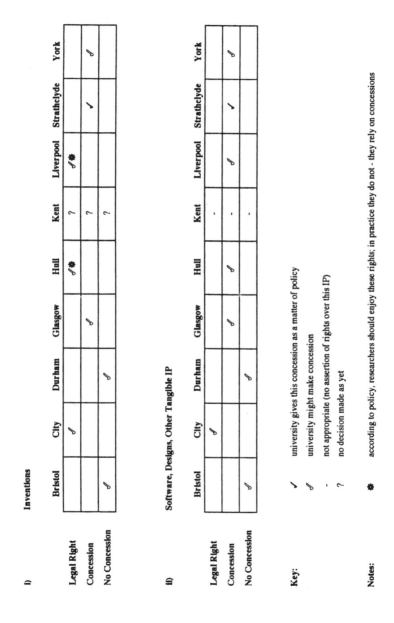

Figure 12.2
Researchers' ability to determine whether ownership of their IP is retained (1989/90)

As Figure 12.2 shows, most of the universities investigated indicated that they would probably, on a purely concessionary basis, take account of an academic's views in this respect. Only Strathclyde had made this a matter of policy, however. Ironically, despite City's policy of vesting ownership jointly in the university and the academic(s) concerned, City's policy-implementer seemed to regard it as a concession on his part rather than acceptance of an academic's legal rights if he took account of academics' views as to whether ownership should be retained or assigned. In a joint ownership situation, of course, both sides may have to compromise in order to reach agreement on how to proceed.

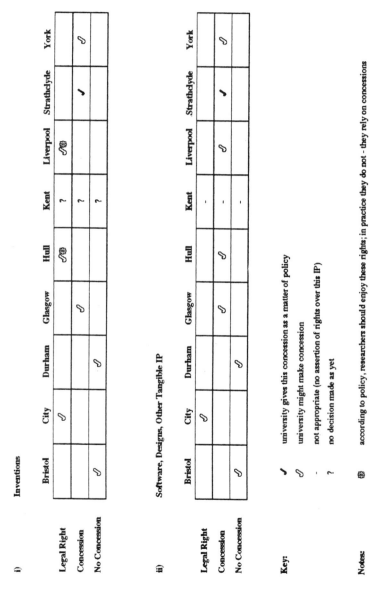

Figure 12.3
Researchers' ability to determine how their IP is protected (1989/90)

Protecting intellectual property: who decides whether and how?

In theory, deploying the rights conferred by sole ownership, policy-implementers could also determine whether and how academics' IP was protected. Figure 12.3 shows the extent to which academic inventors in the nine universities investigated might have been able to influence these decisions.

Policy statements/guidelines to policy-implementers regarding exploitation mechanisms

Only 5 of the 9 universities (City, Glasgow, Hull, Liverpool and York) had formal, written IP policy statements. With regard to NTBF formation, at least 2 were couched in terms likely to deter academics from coming forward with a view to exploiting their IP within some entrepreneurial framework, while none explicitly indicated that this was a possible, let alone an acceptable option. Only City and Strathclyde had used other means (e.g. the university newsletter) to convey to the academic community that NTBF formation was, in principle, an option.

Very few of the 9 universities had drafted guidelines specifically for their policy-implementer, and even when they had, the guidelines tended not to cover the issues raised in questions (c)-(e) above. In 6 of the 9 universities there was no standing policy-maker or group of policy-makers who could guide and monitor the activities of the policy-implementer, either. In some cases, this had profound consequences in relation to questions (c)-(f). For instance, in contravention of their written policy, policy-implementers at both Hull and Liverpool vested patents in the university alone, rather than jointly – and no-one noticed.

Choosing licensees: who decides?

This widespread absence of policy statement or detailed guidelines meant that policy-implementers tended to exercise the rights conferred by sole ownership to determine what kind of organisation might be granted a licence, and whether licensees are granted an exclusive or non-exclusive licence. In practice, this often seemed to boil down to personal preferences.

Figure 12.4 reveals the diversity of policy-implementers' preferences in respect of the kinds of organisations which might be granted a licence. Thus, even though academics in all 9 universities were free to found/co-found a business provided they sought permission, Durham's policy-implementer regarded any type of NTBF spun out of the university as an unacceptable licensee; in Durham it was the policy-implementer's practice to grant licences to large, existing companies rather than existing SMEs or start-ups – a practice noticeably at odds with Durham University Business School's entrepreneurial aims and objectives for the North East. Although no other policy-implementer operated so inflexibly, several others regarded certain types of NTBF (e.g. joint ventures as opposed to independent academic spin-off companies) as more acceptable than other types. As Figure 12.4 shows, however, this was motivated more by a wish to ensure that the NTBF succeeded by bringing in other shareholders, and, hopefully, their expertise (as well as the expertise of a professional manager with a track record) than by an inherent mistrust of NTBFs as a vehicle for exploiting IPR generated in the university.

There were only 2 universities where the policy-implementer was not entirely free to deploy the rights conferred by sole ownership in a dictatorial way. In Strathclyde it was policy to let the academic(s) concerned carry out every procedure and make every decision entailed in the exploitation process except the terms of the licence which was granted to their (joint venture) NTBF; these were negotiated. The only limitation

	Bristol	City	Durham	Glasgow	Hull	Kent	Liverpool	Strathclyde	York
BTG									
Uni. Institute	∂	✓	∂	?	∂	✓	✓	∂	∂
Existing Co. - small	✓	✗	✗	✗	✗	✗	✗	?	✓
- large	✓	✓	∂	✓	✓	∂	✓	✓	✓
Campus Co. - dedicated	✓	∂	✓	∂	✓	?	∂	✗	✓
- umbrella	✗	✗	×	✗	✗	?	✗	✗	×
Jnt. Venture - academic manager	✓	✓	×	✗	✓	∂	∂	✗	✓
- professional manager	∂	∂	×	✓	∂	∂	✓	∂	∂
Indep. Ac. Co. - academic manager	✓	∂	×	✗	✓	✓	∂	✗	✓
- professional manager	∂	∂	✗	✗	∂	∂	∂	✓	∂

Key:

✓   university prefers to license to this type of organisation

∂   university might license to this type, depending on circumstances

✗   university would prefer not to license to this type

×   university would not usually license to this type

?   no decision taken

Note: where professional managers in joint ventures or independent academic spin-off companies are concerned a may be taken to imply that the university would allow it, but does not have the skills/contacts/time to locate and vet such a manager itself and has not sufficient interest to locate other agencies to do this for it

✓

Figure 12.4
Types of organisations which could be granted use of IP – universities' preferences (1989/90)

related to NTBFs wishing to exploit 'hard' IP; these had to be joint ventures rather than independent academic spin-off companies or wholly-owned university companies. In City, joint ownership ensured that the academics concerned had equal rights to the policy-implementer; academics could therefore prevent the university from licensing to a third party, but could obtain a licence for an NTBF in which they played an entrepreneurial role only if they were sufficiently persuasive.

To summarise, then, in 8 of the 9 universities, policy-implementers were minded to accommodate academics' wishes with regard to the exploitation of their IP, as far as university policy or their personal philosophy allowed them to. However, in 6 of the 8, academics were effectively dependent on concessions which were not formally articulated anywhere. When policy-implementers moved on – as they seemed to with surprising frequency – their replacements could (and often did) adopt a less concessionary approach.

CONCLUSIONS

Two of the 9 universities (Liverpool, Hull) were (mis-)implementing an IPR policy dating from the 1970s which took no account of their commitment to facilitate NTBF formation. Another (Durham) had finalised its policy after receiving Sir John Kingman's offer letter – yet that policy consciously militated against NTBF formation. Two universities with a policy which was intended to facilitate NTBF formation (i.e. Bristol and Kent) either failed to communicate that support to their policy-implementer or failed to monitor his activities in this respect, with the result that academics could be denied the opportunity to form NTBFs to exploit their IP. Only one of the 9 (Strathclyde) actively promoted and facilitated NTBF formation; it also had IP policy and practice to match. IP policy and practice in the remaining 3 (City, Glasgow, York) neither inhibited nor facilitated NTBF formation – yet noticeably all 3 universities had incubated a number of highly successful NTBFs. It would appear, then, that institutional IP policy – and practice – can have a facilitative or an inhibitive but apparently not a neutral impact on the propensity of individual UK universities to incubate NTBFs.

ACKNOWLEDGEMENT

The study described in this paper was funded by the SERC. Thanks are also due to the City University and the Universities of Bristol, Durham, Glasgow, Hull, Kent, Liverpool, Strathclyde and York, which bravely agreed to be subjected to scrutiny and to be named in the analysis which followed.

NOTES

1. 'The Exploitation of Research Council Funded Inventions', effectively a written answer given by Sir Keith Joseph, Secretary of State for Education and Science, in the House of Commons on 14 May 1985, recorded in the House of Commons Official Report: Parliamentary Debates (Hansard), Vol. 79, no. 116, cols. 97-100.
2. The Exploitation Scrutiny Group was established by the Science & Engineering Research Council in mid-1985, with representation from the other four Research Councils, the University Grants Committee (subsequently the University Funding Council), the Department of Education & Science, the Department for Trade & Industry, the Treasury and the Committee of Vice-Chancellors and Principals. Subsequently, the Cabinet Office, the Polytechnic & College Funding Council and the Committee of Directors of Polytechnics were represented on the ESG, too.

3. It was unclear whether 'assume responsibility for exploiting' was intended to be interpreted in a narrow sense, meaning that academics themselves should exploit IP which they generate, by means of spin-off companies, university companies, commercial arms of their Department or some other entrepreneurial means. It could also be interpreted in a wide sense, meaning that academics could exploit their IP themselves and/or arrange to have it exploited by one or more third parties. In the latter case, assuming responsibility for exploiting would entail identifying, contacting and negotiating with appropriate companies. It was felt that this second, wider definition provided an absolute against which participating universities could be measured. This, in turn, raised an additional problem, however: it was unclear whether assuming responsibility in this way should be construed as the academic taking the necessary steps under his university's direction or taking the necessary steps on his own initiative – or some kind of intermediate position. Once again, it was felt that the academic taking the necessary steps on his own initiative provided an absolute against which participating universities could be measured.

4. 'Findings and ideas' was just one of a number of equally woolly phrases employed by the DES. For the purposes of this study, it was necessary to define this far more rigorously. Information provided by the BTG suggested that the term 'inventions', when used in connection with the BTG's so-called monopoly, was not interpreted in the exclusive manner defined by the 1977 Patent Act, for its own purposes. 'Inventions' was a far more encompassing concept than this, though there were clearly limits to the BTG's rights which can best be described in the following way. IP comes in a number of forms, as evidenced by the variety of ways in which it can be protected. It can be divided into two broad groups – tangible and intangible. Tangible IP includes patentable inventions; computer software, books, musical compositions and so on, which are copyrightable; registered designs, unregistered design rights, etc. It also includes what – for the purposes of this study – we shall call 'know-how', that is to say, tangible IP which cannot be protected in any of these ways, or which the owner of the IP chooses not to protect in any of these ways. The term 'know-how' is sometimes used to denote intangible IP; in order that there should be no confusion, for the purposes of this study such intangible IP was deemed to be expertise, that is to say, the kind of background knowledge which any academic might be expected to have in order to be appointed in that discipline, or in a specific area of that discipline. These two broad groups of IP have been referred to in the course of this study as 'hard' and 'soft' IP respectively. For the purposes of this study, therefore, 'findings and ideas' was defined as 'hard' or tangible IP. Where appropriate, the analysis further distinguished between inventions, computer software and other forms of 'hard' IP.

5. 'Immediately' in this context means without having to wait several weeks/months while the university makes up its mind.

6. Figures 12.1–12.4 are taken from K. Harvey (1993) Managing the exploitation of intellectual property: an analysis of policy and practice in nine UK universities, PhD thesis, University of Stirling, and are reproduced with the author's permission.

REFERENCES

ACARD/ABRC (1983) *Improving Research Links Between Higher Education and Industry*, HMSO, London.

CVCP (1978) *Report of a Working Party on Patents and the Commercial Exploitation of Research Result*, Committee of Vice-Chancellors and Principals, London.

ROBERTS, E. (1972) Influences upon new technical entrepreneurs, in A. Cooper and J. Komives (eds.) *Technical Entrepreneurship: A Symposium*, The Centre for Venture Management, Milwaukee, Wisconsin.

SEGAL, QUINCE and WICKSTEED (1986) *The Cambridge Phenomenon: The Growth of High Technology Industry in a University Town*, Segal, Quince and Wicksteed, Cambridge, England.

SHARP, M. (1985) The new biotechnology: European governments in search of a strategy, *Sussex European Papers 15*, Science Policy Research Unit, University of Sussex.

CHAPTER 13

Technology and Intellectual Property Strategies of Taiwan's Semiconductor Firms: Implications for International Product Life Cycle Models

JONG–TSONG CHIANG

INTERNATIONAL PRODUCT LIFE CYCLES IN FOLLOWER COUNTRIES

A simplified model

As a basis for later specific examples, a classical model of the international product life cycle[1] is described as an introduction to this paper. First, all countries are categorized into three aggregated groups: the innovator country, other (moderately) industrialized countries, and developing countries. Second, suppose that a globally important innovative new product (i.e. a product and the associated system producing it) or a new product class appears in an innovator country. With respect to world trade flows and industrial transplantation, the following sequential stages of exploitation will probably happen:

STAGE 1: The original innovator is the only producer. Most of the output of the newly innovated product is directed at the domestic market, with only a small proportion of total output exported to other industrialized countries displaying similar levels of sophistication and consumption.

STAGE 2: The export from the original innovator to other industrialized countries expands greatly, while exports to the developing countries also begin to increase significantly.

STAGE 3: Manufacturers in other industrialized countries begin to produce the original product, either by importing the necessary technology as part of an agreement (i.e. licences), (sometimes accompanied by the innovator's capital), or by imitating or developing the technology themselves. These follower firms in industrialized countries also begin to compete with the original innovator for markets in developing countries.

STAGE 4: Firms in other industrialized countries increase their market share in developing countries and start to export the products back to the country of the original innovator. Meanwhile, the developing countries also begin to implement an import substitution and indigenization strategy by importing or imitating foreign technology. Thus, the original innovator gradually moves its production sites to these developing countries, with a view to lowering production costs and keeping or acquiring local and international markets. Other industrialized countries also follow this track but often fall a little behind the original innovator.

STAGE 5: The developing countries begin to pursue an export expansion strategy, partly for the sake of foreign exchange, and export their products to the original innovator nation and other industrialized countries. Their products have usually been standardized, and might be of lower quality than those of the innovator nation or other industrialized countries, but much of the time these products are better than those previously exported by the innovator.

Challenges to follower countries

If the product life cycle is long enough, then most countries will sooner or later benefit economically from any given innovation. And if the followers can take advantage of the relatively low uncertainty at the later development stages of a product's life cycle and concentrate their limited resources on some appropriate strategic fields, their lag behind the forerunners might be effectively reduced over time.

However, if product life cycles in a given sector are somewhat shortened, then it is likely that before the international trading of an initial product evolves from an industrialized country to stage 4 or 5, another new product class will appear and replace the old one. In this case, followers will be in an unfavourable situation, either because of their inability to exploit the non-existent later stages of a product life cycle, or, more seriously, because the production is never directly transplanted to them by the original innovator. Some countries below a certain development level will thus be excluded from potential economic prosperity brought about by more frequent innovations. Conversely, the innovators or pioneers, if equipped with strong production capability – including production cost reducing process innovations – will retain most benefit. In fact, the recent incorporation of modern information technology (IT) into product and process design and the automation of production in many advanced countries has already exerted the far-reaching impact mentioned above. This new trend not only shortens the time needed to complete R&D and introduction of new products and processes, but it can also reduce the comparative advantage of low labour cost in many developing countries.

Another crucial factor in the international transfer of technology lies in the emergence of more comprehensive global strategies and networks developed between multinational corporations. These strategies include global deployment of the elements of 'value chain' across national boundaries from the very beginning, or at early stages in a product's life cycle, therefore making the traditional sequential strategy described above no longer relevant. For example, the prevalent 'triad alliances' among world class corporations in the United States, Western Europe and Japan[2] are just well-known examples of such collaboration. Although their sustainability remains to be seen, due to the inherent instability rooted in many possibilities for strategic divergence between firms due to the difficulty of blending competition and cooperation, global collaborations of this kind will no doubt deprive many developing countries of many opportunities.

FORERUNNERS AND FOLLOWERS IN THE SEMICONDUCTOR INDUSTRY

Technological progress and competitive patterns

The semiconductor industry is a particularly appropriate example of the difficulties faced by follower countries for several reasons. First, this sector allows considerable scope for follower countries to enter the market. Second, the technological dynamics of production continues at a strong pace, especially in terms of the drive to minimize feature size, for memory ICs. Third, the capital investment necessary for producing new generations of products has increased very rapidly. These combined effects are exemplified by the minimum investment required for a wafer fabrication plant in different years: $0.5m for 16-bit RAM ICs in the mid-1960s; $1m for 256-bit ICs in 1970; $2m for 1K-bit ICs in 1974; $5m for 4K-bit ICs in 1978; $10m for 16K-bit ICs in 1980; $50m for 256K-bit ICs in 1984; $100m for 1M-bit ICs in 1986; $200m for 4M-bit ICs in 1987. In 1990, SEMATECH in the USA estimated that $750m would be required for a typical, state-of-the-art semiconductor facility.[3] In fact, the skyrocketing trend of capital reinvestment required in this field is a very big challenge for any network or potential player (notice that the above figures relate only to the fabrication plant). A brief review of the actors in this industry can explain the situation.

Most of the radical or revolutionary semiconductor innovations took place in the USA. This was in part because of the overall economic and technological superiority of US firms in the early postwar era, and in part because of the mission oriented programmes of the Defense Department and NASA that emphasised performance and quality and, therefore, encouraged many US firms, some small and medium-sized, to develop systems and products that embody radically novel or cutting edge technologies. However, the competitive environment following these initial breakthroughs changed for later entrants. The organisational characteristics of later followers in Japan and Western Europe partly explain this changed competitive regime.

In Japan, Hitachi, Fujitsu, NEC, Toshiba, Mitsubishi and Matsushita – 6 of the world's 10 largest semiconductor companies in the late 1980s – are all highly vertically and horizontally integrated firms. They can draw resources from other divisions for huge reinvestments. In the USA, only AT&T and IBM are similar to these Japanese firms. Most other merchant semiconductor producers could not keep pace with Japanese investments. As a result, on the average, the Japanese firms have consistently been able to invest a greater percentage of their sales in manufacturing equipment and R&D than their US counterparts.[4] In Europe, virtually only Philips and Siemens, similarly integrated firms, can participate in this industry without substantial government support. In France, the government has never discontinued its heavy subsidies since the mid-1970s to Sescosem, which was later merged with Italy's SGS-Altes into Thomson-SGS in the mid-1980s. In the UK, Inmos – created by the government in 1978 to produce standard ICs – suffered heavy losses and was finally abandoned by the Conservative government in the early 1980s.

The above mentioned development of the semiconductor industry roughly fits a general model concerning the locus of interactive product innovation and process innovation.[5] In the first phase, product designs are fluid; manufacturing processes are loosely and adaptively organized; generalized capital is used; competition is mainly amongst markedly different product designs; and so product innovation emphasizing functional performance prevails. In the next phase, one product design or a narrow class of designs emerges as promising 'dominant' technology; competition shifts from a specification to price basis and away from product design; scale and process innovation becomes more important, leading to large investment in specialized capital equipment; accordingly, process innovation aimed at efficiency and cost competition is crucial. Finally, both the product and processes become rather mature; hence innovation at this stage is typified by incremental improvement.

For developing countries, the above conceptual model suggests that their firms should enter the market at the incremental improvements and higher efficiency stage. However, the entry barriers for them to the semiconductor industry must have seemed insurmountable, because, even in the industrialized world, only a small number of very large firms with vast resources (and, preferably, large captive markets) could survive at this mature stage due to the severe selection process rooted in very rapid technological progress and the huge static and dynamic economies of scale.

The environment and practices concerning intellectual property rights

Needless to say, developing countries are at a disadvantageous position in terms of intellectual property right (IPR). Indeed, the recent development of the US IPR judicial institution has put developing countries in a more difficult situation than ever before. In the USA, the effectiveness of patents as a tool for competitive advantage has undergone a major change in the past decade. This new era began with the 1982 formation of the Court of Appeals for the Federal Circuit (CAFC). Since then, appeals of District Court patent case decisions are heard only by CAFC. Therefore, CAFC's decisions become powerful precedents in the field of patent law. CAFC has created a new environment for corporate IPR strategy for the following reasons:

CAFC has upheld lower court decisions on patent validity over 80% of the time, as opposed to 27% in the prior system.

CAFC has upheld both preliminary and permanent injunctions. A preliminary injunction can be granted by a Federal District Court when it is convinced that there is a high probability that a patent will be judged to be infringed. The hearings on a request for preliminary injunction can become almost a mini-trial. An injunction will require cessation of commercial activities by a patent infringer.

The magnitude of monetary awards against infringers has grown; if infringement is deemed deliberate, there could be a trebling of damages.

Thus, it is no surprise that patent owners have become more offensive in their IPR strategy and patent litigation and enforcement activities are on the increase. In the meantime, preliminary injunctions are often quickly followed by out-of-court settlements of the dispute rather than full trials on the merits of the case, because even if the enjoined party wins the subsequent full trial, the disruption to manufacturing, marketing and other production functions due to the injunction may be hard to overcome.[6]

For follower countries, this new trend in the USA represents a very serious threat for several reasons. First, semiconductor patents are very widespread within the sector, and consequently very difficult to avoid. Second, US firms own most of the semiconductor patents. Third, the gross margin of a follower firm may not be high enough to support legal licensing of necessary technologies for production from the many patent owners.

Moreover, rapid technological progress produces a confused intellectual property environment which, although often creating a good opportunity to make inventions and improvements, may lead well established large firms to infringe existing patents. However, the process of negotiation for compensation or for licensing is not easy since the agreement or contract is costly to each and even incomplete, and an incomplete contract tends to induce opportunistic behaviour. In other words, the transaction cost for settling patent disputes is very high. To solve this problem, many firms have negotiated for the cross-licensing of one another's patents in some fields to reduce transaction cost.[7] However, normally only leading firms with roughly equal strengths in similar technological fields will pool their patents in this way. Therefore, followers are excluded. This further aggravates the competitive position of followers because leading firms' 'offensive' IPR strategy can concentrate more on 'non-club members'.

Taiwan as an exceptional follower

For reasons explained previously, few countries outside the industrialized world have shown considerable capability in the semiconductor industry. South Korea and Taiwan may be regarded as two exceptions. However, firms in these two countries are very different in many respects. In Korea, players are all very large integrated companies, such as Samsung, Hyundai and Goldstar, mainly producing standard memory ICs. In Taiwan, nearly all players are fairly small in size relative to their counterparts in the

USA, Japan, Western Europe and Korea. The assets of the three largest firms in 1991 were as follows: United Microelectronics Co. (UMC), $400m; Taiwan Semiconductor Manufacturing Co. (TSMC), $360m; and Winbond, $300m.[8] In the semiconductor industry, Korea's main strategy of large firm size is rather comprehensible if based on the success of Japan, where firm size is also large.[9] However, if large size is essential it would be of strategic value to enquire how Taiwan's relatively small firms can survive the severe competition of such large enterprises.

As regards IPR strategy, the firms in Korea and Taiwan also show different styles. Korean firms primarily license necessary technologies from foreign firms and pay about 7-9% of their revenue for royalties. Taiwan's firms, despite their much less revenue and thus much smaller bargaining power, pay about 5% of their revenue for royalties to foreign firms and adopt a variety of strategies to cope with IPR challenges from abroad.[10] While Korea's main strategy, which is to avoid the patents of others or to license them, seems reasonable, Taiwan's alternative strategic approach deserves further investigation.

TAIWAN'S STRATEGIES

The role of the government R&D Institute

In Taiwan, the Electronics Research and Service Organisation (ERSO) has played a central role in cultivating the domestic semiconductor industry. ERSO was established by the government under the institutional framework of the Industrial Technology Research Institute (ITRI) in 1974. ERSO's most important mission at the time of formation was to develop semiconductor technology. In this regard, it had first to select a specific technology within the broad semiconductor industry.

Although in the early 1970s CMOS's (complementary metal-oxide-semiconductor) market share was smaller than PMOS's (P-channel metal-oxide-semiconductor) and bipolar's, and its computing power was lower than NMOS's (N-channel metal-oxide-semiconductor) and bipolar's, ERSO's selection of CMOS technology in 1974 proved to be a correct decision. One reason is that CMOS technology then was not yet mature, so ERSO had the opportunity to catch up by virtue of this early entry and learning. Another reason for success was that CMOS's price was lower and suitable for many downstream products, such as electronic watches, calculators and personal computers, that later became Taiwan's internationally competitive IT products.

After the evaluation of several US companies' proposals and the negotiation with some of these companies, ERSO chose RCA as the technology licensor of the chosen technology. In terms of technology transfer, RCA had effective and comprehensive programmes that subsequently helped ERSO. In terms of IPR, RCA, along with IBM and AT&T, was among the pioneers in CMOS process and device technology, so its IPR 'umbrella' largely protected ERSO and few foreign firms challenged ERSO in CMOS technology. Although RCA requested $6m plus 7.5% of total revenue for 10 years (the highest technology transfer fees among those proposed to ERSO), the cost was not, in fact, as high as it initially appeared. First, ERSO basically was established to perform for R&D and consequently its revenue from CMOS products was small relative to what it would have been from commercial production. Second, RCA later withdrew from the semiconductor industry and, after an agreed period, did not ask ERSO for further technology royalties, thus leaving ERSO to freely build and improve on RCA's CMOS technology. ERSO's alliance with RCA also more or less alleviated the IPR difficulties of some domestic firms when they used CMOS technology transferred from ERSO. In fact, in the 1970s RCA's main business with Taiwan was TV and CRT, so it did not pay much attention to the business with ERSO in semiconductor technology.

In fact, ERSO's R&D was not solely confined to CMOS technology, although it has hardly ever been charged with IPR infringement associated with their non-CMOS work. This is not because ERSO has not infringed upon others' patents, but mainly because ERSO's moderate revenue was not sufficient to attract foreign firms into taking action for IPR infringement. Moreover foreign firms were less likely to challenge ERSO in its role as a national laboratory sponsored by the government. The former motivation is based on an economic consideration; the latter, on a political consideration.

Another crucial decision made by ERSO was to establish a demonstration plant soon after its establishment to produce 3-inch wafers at the scale of 4,000 pieces per week instead of the originally planned 500 pieces per week. The main reason for this strategy was the achievement of the minimum economic scale in order for ERSO's products to really compete in the commercial markets. It transpired that ERSO's production actually performed very well. The production yield rates reached the objectives set by RCA within half a year. Besides, ERSO sold its IC products successfully and profitably (with electronic watches as main carriers) in the competitive markets. After this first stage, ERSO supported the establishment of several commercial firms, in particular UMC, TSMC and Winbond, in the 1980s by transferring technology and human resources to them.

UMC, established in 1980, received roughly 40% of ERSO's total capabilities, including ERSO's deputy director (becoming UMC's president), 3 department managers of testing, marketing and quality assurance, and 2 division heads of the fabrication department. In 1986 TSMC commenced and received about 50% of ERSO's then capabilities; in the meantime, TSMC's chairman was also ITRI's president. In 1988 Winbond was started and led by ITRI's planning chief, a former ERSO deputy director. On this occasion Winbond absorbed most of ERSO's capabilities related to commercial operations.[11] In terms of number of professionals, UMC, TSMC and Winbond obtained 180, 150 and 100 people from ERSO respectively.

Though approximate, and perhaps rather subjective, the above evidence nevertheless generally illustrates that UMC, TSMC and Winbond (three leading semiconductor firms in Taiwan) benefited greatly from ERSO's provision of the manufacturing learning experience, and business management expertise for the semiconductor industry. It should also be noted that these three firms are currently all led by former ERSO or ITRI top managers. This arrangement may, to a considerable degree, explain the success of ERSO's support of these firms.

Another 'extra' benefit these firms may have received from ERSO was the transfer of technologies that were patent protected but were difficult to detect or not immediately obvious when they were in use.

Economies of scale and production efficiency

In addition to the national strategy executed and promoted by ERSO mentioned above, Taiwan's corporate strategies also merit discussion.

To survive, a firm's gross margin times sales volume must be large enough to cover overheads and support further investments. In Taiwan's semiconductor firms, the cost side is mainly determined by the efficiency of the foundry for wafer fabrication. Take the present production of the 6-inch wafers as an example. To be efficient, a single plant must produce about 20,000 wafers per month at the average unit cost of US$400–450 (with half of this scale at US$550–600). This calls for an investment of nearly US$500m in fixed assets.[12] In Taiwan, only the recent new plants of TSMC and UMC could meet this requirement. However, despite the scale disadvantage, many other firms perform excellently in production. Although they rely on imported sophisticated equipment, they are able to finely tune the equipment, such as lithographic machines, even better than the suppliers, like Philips. Therefore, Taiwan's firms, generally speaking, have high yield rates to partly compensate for their disadvantage in scale economies. Some experiences in Acer and TSMC exemplify this competitive advantage.

Around 1990, Acer cooperated with Texas Instruments in establishing a 4 M-bit DRAM (dynamic random access memory) plant. Although the plant could produce only 10,000 wafers per month, its recent yield rate was 84%, the highest in the world. As to TSMC, its production performance was so good that Philips, a shareholder in TSMC, found it unattractive to continue the cooperation with Siemens and Thomson-SGS in the JESSI programme for semiconductor production technology and thus withdrew from that programme.

Another strategy adopted by Taiwan's firms is to increase the sales price through the production of more sophisticated products. Therefore, few firms produce standard memory ICs. Instead, application-specific ICs (ASICs) of various kinds are the main products of Taiwan's semiconductor industry. Because short delivery time is usually a requirement of ASICs, the geographical proximity of the ASIC producers to local designers and buyers offers a locational advantage over more distant competitors.

Intellectual property strategies

In the 1980s, the infringement of foreign firms' IPR emerged as a crucial strategy in Taiwan. In the early years when Taiwan was considered to be poor, IPR infringements seldom brought about international lawsuits because local firms had little to lose in financial terms. Ironically, the recognition of Taiwan's capability to infringe patents helped attract orders from advanced countries, and make Taiwan an important manufacturing base. In the past decade, however, Taiwan has been regarded as financially rich, as indicated by its huge foreign exchange reserves. Local industry, and in particular the semiconductor IT industries, were thus under serious IPR threat from foreign firms.

Basically, Taiwan's semiconductor firms adopt several strategies to withstand this threat, different firms having different combinations. The first strategy is to simply license the technology. This is a common practice and easy to understand. A second strategy is to establish an alliance with world leaders (that cross-license with other major world players) and allow them an equity holding of 20%. By this arrangement, Taiwan's firms only have to pay royalties to the allied partners. Thus, TSMC is allied with Philips, and Acer with Texas Instruments.

A third strategy is only to manufacture and market products in places where the patents of foreign firms have not been filed, because patents offer protection only in the countries where they have been registered. Indeed, patent application is an economic decision. Usually the value of patents becomes clearer with time, but the costs covering patent registration (in foreign countries), prosecution, filing and maintenance are obvious and perhaps high enough to deter patent application in a number of countries. Moreover, after public disclosure (definition of which varies between countries) for a certain period of time, some governments may refuse to grant patents to some inventions or improvements that have already received patents elsewhere. Following this strategy, some semiconductor firms in Taiwan target only markets in Southeast Asia and Mainland China. To avoid being charged with patent infringement, these firms usually do not set up subsidiaries in the USA. In this strategic category, UMC is a typical case.

A fourth strategy is to use new suppliers' products provided at lower prices, and leave any patent disputes to the new suppliers and the patent owner.

Finally, because IPR enforcement is costly in many cases, IPR infringement may exist in some fields of technology at the margin. This most traditional behaviour may also be deemed a fifth IPR strategy.

Although it remains to be seen whether, and for how long, the above IPR strategies will continue to work, Taiwan's semiconductor firms have been largely successful in their attempts to cope with the IPR threats presented by foreign firms.

CONCLUDING REMARKS

Generally speaking, to compete with forerunners, followers need to establish strong complementary assets – including manufacturing, distribution, maintenance and service capabilities, as well as close relations with key customers. In the semiconductor industry, this principle is particularly applicable. However, the new international IPR environment adds further strategic dimension deserving keen attention. Taiwan's experiences suggest that both national and corporate strategies are essential to ensure the survival of domestic semiconductor firms.

NOTES

1. A representative scholar in this field is Raymond Vernon. See, for example, Vernon (1979).
2. Ohmae (1984) was among the first thoroughly explaining this phenomenon.
3. These estimates are from Arnold and Guy (1986), pp. 26-7; Sharp and Shearman (1987), p. 105; SEMATECH, Operating Plan 1991, p. 5.
4. Many articles discuss this. See, for example, Bar et al. (1989), pp. 25-6.
5. For a simplified model, see Abernathy and Utterback (1978).
6. For the development of IPR environment in the USA, see Berkowitz (1993).
7. This is a typical issue of market vs. hierarchy, and the decision is to reduce transaction cost. For this transaction cost approach, see Williamson (1981).
8. According to China Credit Investigation Co., Top 500 Corporations 1989-1992 (in Chinese).
9. See Amsden (1989) for Korea's general industrial strategy emphasizing large firm size.
10. The estimates about Korean and Taiwanese firms in paying royalties were made by the author according to the interviews with the chairman of MXIC Co. and an employee of Goldstar Semiconductor Co. No published data are available to the author.
11. These estimates were made by ERSO's founding director, who led ERSO until the mid-1980s and then became ITRI's vice-president. Around 1990 he became chairman of MXIC Co.
12. These estimates were given by the chairman of MXIC Co.

REFERENCES

AMSDEN, A. H. (1989), *Asia's Next Giant*, Oxford University Press, New York.

ARNOLD, E. and GUY, K. (1986) *Parallel Convergence: National Strategies in Information Technology*, Frances Pinter, London.

BAR, F., BORRUS, M., COHEN, S. and ZYSMAN, J. (1989) The evolution and growth potential of electronics-based technologies, *STI Review*, April, pp. 7-56.

BERKOWITZ, L. (1993) Getting the most from your patents, *Research-Technology Management*, March-April, pp. 26-31.

OHMAE, K. (1984) *Triad Power*, The Free Press, New York.

SHARP, M. and SHEARMAN, C. (1987) *European Technological Collaboration*, Routledge and Kegan Paul, London.

VERNON, R. (1979) The product life cycle hypothesis in a new international environment, *Oxford Bulletin of Economics and Statistics*, Vol. 41, no. 4, pp. 255-67.

WILLIAMSON, O. E. (1981), The economics of organization: The transaction cost approach, *American Journal of Sociology*, Vol. 87, no. 3, pp. 548-77.

PART V Policy

CHAPTER 14

Technology Policies and Small Firms: An Evolutionary Perspective

J. S. METCALFE

My purpose in this paper is to draw together two lines of current thinking in relation to evolutionary economic change and the innovation process in small firms: the central purpose being to provide a framework for technology policy in which the support of smaller firms has an explicit rationale. It has long been recognised that smaller firms are a natural locus of entrepreneurial business experimentation, that they are important elements in the competitive process and that they are important vehicles for technological change (Acs and Audretsch, 1990). To understand their significance a framework for dynamic analysis is required, one which is automatically at home with the idea of innovation driven competition. Such a framework is provided by an evolutionary perspective (Nelson and Winter, 1982) and provides us with a convincing set of ideas with which to better comprehend technology policy and the smaller firm.

ARGUMENTS FOR TECHNOLOGY POLICY

It is convenient to begin with an outline of some of the traditional arguments used to rationalise policy interventions. Much of the economic theory of technology policy is concerned with the so-called 'market failures' which prevent the attainment of Pareto equilibria by violating one or other of the conditions for perfect competition (Hall, 1986; Stoneman, 1987; Wolf, 1987). The most important of these violations are related to missing or distorted markets. Put briefly, future markets for contingent claims in an uncertain world do not exist in any sense sufficiently for individuals to make inter-temporal decisions and to trade risks in an optimal fashion and establish prices which support the appropriate marginal conditions. Because the appropriate price structure is missing, distortions abound and the policy problem is to identify and correct those distortions. Missing markets imply constrained efficiency and constrained effects of policy intervention. Moreover, missing markets imply the need for agents to form expectations on the likely private values of innovating activities, expectations which policy can certainly influence. In such cases the question naturally arises of whether non-market processes – direct bargaining or political activity, for example, – should be promoted to improve resource allocation (Newberry, 1990). Since the development of technology is uncertain and future orientated it is certainly susceptible to these missing market distortions. The innovation process both generates and is influenced by uncertainty and this aspect of market failure is particularly damaging to the possibility of a Pareto efficient allocation of resources to invention and innovation. It is not uncertainty about future states of nature which matters here, whether tomorrow will produce rain or an earthquake, but rather the uncertainty which comes from the anticipation that individuals and organisations will behave in a way which cannot be fully or even partially anticipated. The difficulty is deeply embedded in the nature of technical knowledge, the creation of which depends upon the establishment of information asymmetries (Dosi, 1988). In a quite fundamental sense, innovations and information asymmetries are one and the same phenomena. Indeed such asymmetries can scarcely be termed market imperfections when they are necessary conditions for any technical change to occur in a market economy. As Stiglitz (1991) makes clear, the resulting unequal distribution of knowledge creates multiple problems of adverse selection and moral hazard which in turn deny the possibility of Pareto optimal market processes. Notice that this involves much more than a trade-off between dynamic and static efficiency. Rather it is saying that innovation and information asymmetries are inseparable and thus innovation and Pareto optimality are fundamentally incompatible.

While problems of asymmetric information are at the heart of technology policy, other aspects of market failure are also relevant. Appropriation externalities have always been recognized as a major constraint on the incentives to innovate, as reflected in the fact that the patent system is one of the longest established instruments of technology policy. Patents are the institutional device by which market economies seek to cope with the peculiarities of knowledge production: limiting appropriability at the cost of creating temporary monopoly rights in exploitation. Similarly, the public good attributes of scientific and technological knowledge imply that market solutions to the allocation of resources to innovation will not be efficient. Finally, the indivisibilities inherent in the innovation process imply that there are increasing returns to the exploitation of technology and that it will be necessary for firms to retain some market power if they are to recover the costs of innovation. At best, an innovating industry can be monopolistically competitive. Hence, and from a different angle, Pareto efficiency and innovation are seen to be incompatible (Dixit, 1988; Dasgupta and Stiglitz, 1980).

While the case for technology policy as a corrective to market failure is well established, one needs to recognize also that government interventions can fail as well (Krueger, 1991). For a variety of reasons, imperfect information, the separation between those who benefit and those who pay, bureaucratic capture, pressure group activity, and political myopia, governments may undertake mistaken interventions (Eads and Nelson, 1971; Henderson, 1971; Wolf, 1987). It does not automatically follow that government policy will be welfare improving. This is particularly so with respect to innovative activities, the formulation of which entails access to detailed microeconomic and social information. Indeed it has long been recognized that the strength of a market economy vis-à-vis a centrally planned economy is precisely the efficiency of and flexibility of the former in terms of the decentralized and distributed gathering, storing and communicating of detailed information (Nelson, 1987; Nelson and Winter, 1982).

THE EVOLUTIONARY PERSPECTIVE

At this point we turn to the evolutionary approach to technical change and the implications for policy. Firmly rooted in the behavioural theory of the firm its focus is upon learning capabilities and adaptive behaviour and the interactions between these behaviours and various economic selection mechanisms. The central policy issue that it prompts is the contrast between efficiency and the innovative creativity of firms.

Creativity is intimately connected to uncertainty and the discovery processes by which firms find and exploit their own choice sets, that is, innovation possibility frontiers. Whether it is because of organization, the individuals involved or historical happenstance, no two firms are expected to innovate in an identical fashion and it is this emphasis on the decentralized emergence of technological diversity which is a defining characteristic of the evolutionary approach. If a firm is not sufficiently creative it is unlikely to survive in the long term. If it is not appropriately efficient it will not survive in the short-term. Somewhere a balance has to be struck and the striking of this balance is complicated greatly by the fact that forms of organisation and business conduct which promote efficiency are not necessarily those which promote creativity. Indeed, any organisation which devotes all its attention to the maximisation of efficiency will not, by definition, have the resources to devote to creativity. It is one of the oldest puzzles in evolutionary thinking that evolutionary change is contingent upon elements of redundancy, waste and inefficiency. By themselves, creativity and efficiency are not sufficient to explain economic evolution, a third element is needed, expressed in terms of the growth of firms. Superior economic practices can only have their desired economic impact if they are diffused into the economy and this requires that the associated firms grow faster than inferior rivals. The smaller firm must grow if its quality is to be reflected in national welfare.

While there are a number of evolutionary approaches (Hodgson, 1993; Witt, 1991), they have in common a fundamental concern with processes of economic change. In assessing the contribution which they can make to technology policy, it is vital to understand the ways in which they jointly represent a change in perspective from the equilibrium viewpoint. For present purposes, evolutionary economics can be reduced to two central concerns, namely the processes which determine the range of available innovations, and the processes which alter the relative contributions which different innovations make to economic welfare. The fundamental issues are dynamic and intimately connected to a quite different view of competition from that deployed in equilibrium theory. Moreover, this is not to be interpreted as change in response to exogenous changes in data but rather change which occurs endogenously without reference to adjustment to some equilibrium state. This entails a shift from perceiving competition in terms of price alone to viewing competition in terms of those decisive cost and quality advantages which arise from innovative behaviour. It entails a shift from perceiving competition in terms of states of equilibrium characterized by different market structures, to competition as a process of change premised on the existence of the differential behaviour of firms and other economic agents (Downie, 1958; Nelson & Winter, 1982; Metcalfe & Gibbons, 1989). It is only with this process perspective that the role of entrepreneurial behaviour becomes intelligible, since an equilibrium theory cannot, as a matter of logic, determine the rewards to entrepreneurship which are necessarily transitional. It is only in the process perspective that many competitive behaviours of firms are explicable, behaviours which from an equilibrium perspective are typically interpreted as anti-competitive market imperfections. Indeed as we have already suggested it is central to the evolutionary perspective that economic progress is only possible in what, from an equilibrium viewpoint, is an inefficient world. It is not in the least surprising therefore that scholars with a concern to understand historical patterns of technical change have begun to develop evolutionary theory. Equally, it is not surprising that together with concepts of individual equilibrium they have abandoned optimization as the route to explaining individual behaviour and replaced it by adaptive learning and the creation of novelty. It is by this change in approach that attention is switched to the strategic, cognitive and organizational aspects of firms which explain why they behave differently. In this context a central purpose of policy becomes that of stimulating the technological and innovative capabilities of the economic system;

enhancing the learning processes in firms and other institutions to generate variety in behaviour. The focus of attention ceases to be market failure per se and instead becomes the enhancement of competitive performance and the promotion of structural change (Mowery and Rosenberg, 1989). Evolutionary policy is fundamentally tied up with the creativity of firms and supporting institutions, and, arguably, there is no more powerful source of differential behaviour than that provided by technological innovation. This granted the problem in understanding reduces to the economic significance of diverse behaviour and here the distinctive feature of evolutionary theory is its intrinsic capacity to make sense of variety. Once this step is taken, one can immediately recognize that evolutionary economic processes are essentially open ended and unpredictable. As Austrian and other subjectivist economists are fond of emphasizing, there is an irreducible element of discovery in the working of the market process (Hayek, 1948; Buchanan and Vanberg, 1991). Nonetheless, although the emergence of novelty is unpredictable, the processes which translate novelty into coherent patterns of change are not, and it is on this distinction that the role of technology policy hinges. There is nothing unscientific about this, science is much more than prediction, at least it is for a historical science such as the economics of technological change (Gould, 1990).

For present purposes, evolution means two things: the gradual unfolding of phenomena in a cumulative and thus path dependent way; and, quite separately, a dynamics of system behaviour which creates change and emerging structure out of the presence of variety. From the technology policy viewpoint, change is to be interpreted in three different and interdependent ways: the emergence of genuine novelties in the form of new product and process design configurations; the internal development of existing design configurations through sequences of innovations; and the comparative diffusion of competing alternatives in a market environment. It follows that two questions traditionally have defined the scope of evolutionary analysis: the origin of variety and the nature of selection. In biology the answer to the first question is found in the concept of blind variation, that is variation which is independent of selective advantage (Campbell, 1987). In economics, this obviously is not the whole story: while no treatment of innovation can ignore a stochastic element, it is also true that innovation represents guided and intentional variation (Hodgson, 1991) purposely undertaken in the pursuit of competitive advantage. Economic agents learn from experience and anticipate future states of the selective environment in a way quite unknown in biological or ecological selection. Naturally, this greatly enriches the scope of the theory. Indeed, as Nelson has repeatedly stressed (1980, 1990) it is this guided element in innovation which explains the rapid and sustained rates of progress in capitalist market economies. The concept of a selective environment also requires careful handling. In the simplest cases, it can be equated to a market mechanism within which users and suppliers interact in traditional fashion. However, this represents only one level and mode of selection. Any framework in which agents interact in order to choose between competing patterns of behaviour has selective properties. In particular, any organization creates its own internal selection environment to choose between competing alternative futures and their associated patterns of behaviour. As the discussion below of innovation systems indicates, the degree of matching between choices made at different levels of technological selection exerts a strong influence on patterns of technological change. Beyond the traditional two questions, a third must also be raised, that of the outcomes of selection processes feeding back into the subsequent generation of variety. All selection processes consume the available variety, and if evolutionary change is to continue, variety must be continually recreated by some other mechanism. Two issues are important here: first, the role of inertia and institutional limits in setting bounds to the generation of variety; and second, positive feedback mechanisms which link the generation of variety to the exploitation of increasing returns and endogenous innovation, that link it back to the selection process. That one can have a theory of variety generation is too far fetched, it is not possible to treat novelty as if it were an analytical concept (Witt, 1992), and it is certainly not possible to anticipate the emergence of novelty. However, one can make considerable progress in identifying important feedbacks which keep a balance between variety generation and competitive selection. The significance of this balance lies in the elementary fact that evolutionary processes destroy the variety on which they depend so that some regeneration mechanism is required if evolution is not to grind to a halt. At this point we sense a clear framework for policy analysis is already emerging which distinguishes policies which influence variety generation from policies which influence various selection processes. Not surprisingly, the small firm sector has a particularly important role in variety generation. As far as variety generation is concerned one of the major contributions of the evolutionary school has been its insistence that the pattern of technological innovation depends on much more than the behaviour of individual firms. This leads us directly to the idea of technology systems and national systems of innovation. Similarly, the treatment of selection processes leads us to the treatment of technological competition and the diffusion of innovations. From this general background we can move more specifically to the role of small firms in the generation of economic variety and the competitive process.

SMALL FIRMS: FORMATION AND GROWTH

It is hardly a surprise to find that the small business unit plays an important role in this evolutionary perspective on economic policy. Small firms are an essential source of the mutations in technology, organisation and markets which continually redefine the longer term pattern of economic activity and generate the growth of economic wealth (ACOST, 1990). On this the historical record is clear but it is also essential to delve deeper into the mechanisms involved. Here we distinguish between the mechanisms which lead to the formation, birth, of new business units, whether founded independently or as a branch of a larger, umbrella organisation, and the mechanisms which result in the growth of 'superior' experiments at the expense of 'inferior' rivals. Growth involves absolute expansion but this is not enough. What matters is that the superior businesses increase in relative importance, that is, they they are selected to account for a greater share of the creation of wealth in a particular market. Economic weight is the important issue at stake because the economic impacts of a particular business firm increase in proportion to the share of economic activity which that firm accounts for.

Of course, it is the role of the competitive process to ensure the increasing relative importance of superior business practice whatever its origin. The converse to growth is decline and eventual elimination from the market and this is just as important an element in the evolutionary picture. Translated into the language of policy this implies two concerns: policy with respect to the formulation of new business units; and policy with respect to market selection and growth. Essential to our understanding at this point is the idea that not all business experiments can succeed. Evolution requires a necessary level of redundancy and waste, failures provide useful lessons about mutations which are to be avoided.

I shall devote most of my comments now to the problems of small firm growth. Here the distinction between absolute and relative growth is important. The idea that as firms grow absolutely they pass through distinct stages with identifiable transition points captures one aspect of evolution – the unfolding patterns of development in individual firms (Tiler et al, 1993). The idea that the relative growth of firms is a function of economic selection captures the second dimension of evolution. For the second mechanism

to operate competing firms must have distinctive differences with respect to their efficiency and ability to grow. Profitability is here a key issue: the firm with better
products and lower unit costs has superior profit margins and the basis for a faster rate
of growth. Whether this is achieved or not depends on the willingness to grow, which
cannot be presumed, and upon the ability to manage growth. The oft used observation
that the entrepreneur who founds a firm is not always the appropriate individual to
manage its subsequent growth is relevant here. At this point a summary of the barriers
to growth of firms is worth listing. These are:

- The growth of its market, dependent on the growth of the overall market and the
  firm's competitive advantages relative to rivals;
- The resources available to fund and manage growth, not least of which are external
  capital and managerial talent;
- Technological capability sufficient to keep the firm up with the leaders in the
  market;
- A managerial and organisation structure appropriate to each stage in the firm's
  growth.

It is obvious that many other factors besides technology constrain the formation and
growth of small firms. The role of the capital market and formal and informal sources
of venture capital provides one example among many (Mason and Harrison, 1993).
Nonetheless the technological dimension is important and it is a central concern of
policy makers in many industrialised nations.

NATIONAL SYSTEMS OF INNOVATION

At this point the question arises of how one might categorize technology policy for
smaller firms in the light of the above observations. A useful place to begin is with Justmann and Teubal (1986) who have advocated a distinction between policies directed
(strategically) at the infrastructure of elements in the economy which facilitate innovation, and those which are directed (tactically) at the development of specific
technologies. More recently the infrastructure aspects have been brought together with
the concept of a national system of innovation (Freeman, 1987; Lundvall, 1988, 1992;
McElvey, 1991). A national system of innovation is that set of distinct institutions
which jointly and individually contribute to the development and diffusion of new technologies and which provide the framework within which governments form and
implement policies to influence the innovation process. As such it is a system of inter-
connected institutions to create, store and transfer the knowledge, skills and artefacts
which define new technologies. The element of nationality follows not only from the
domain of technology policy but from elements of shared language and culture which
bind the system together, and from the national focus of other policies, laws and regulations which condition the innovative environment. In the operation of national systems,
governments play an important part in their support of science and technology generally
and in their procurement of specific technologies to meet the needs of the executive. To
define such a system empirically one must locate the boundaries, its component institutions and the ways in which they are linked together (OECD, 1992). Many institutions
are involved: private firms working individually or in collaboration; universities and
other educational bodies; professional societies and government laboratories; private consultancies and industrial research associations. Each national system reflects a strong
division of labour, and due to the economic peculiarities of information, a predominance
of co-ordination by non-market means. When organized appropriately national systems
can be a powerful engine of progress (Nelson, 1992a). Poorly organized and connected
they may seriously inhibit the process of innovation (Freeman, 1987).

Among modern industrial societies, private firms with an explicitly defined R&D function are key elements in any national system of innovation. Their motivation is to improve profitability through product and process innovation, by creating technology of an essentially proprietary nature. They are the primary institutions for designing and developing new technological artefacts and for applying them in the search for competitive advantage. In the process they also have a major impact on the skill and knowledge dimensions of technology particularly the development of tacit knowledge (Pavitt, 1990). Some large firms also make considerable efforts in many applied and engineering sciences. The research budgets and facilities of some of these firms would be the envy of many a well-founded university department. By contrast, universities and other educational establishments are only minimally concerned with the development of artefacts, and make their major contributions in terms of knowledge and skills. Universities are composed of highly specialized groups of individuals, advancing knowledge and training students in the basic methods, findings and operating procedures of distinct disciplines. Unlike firms, universities and the science and engineering departments they contain are essentially open institutions committed to widespread dissemination of knowledge (Nelson, 1987). Some of the research is fundamental in nature but substantial proportions of university research effort are devoted to the applied or so-called transfer sciences (OECD, 1992), which act as a bridge between fundamental science and technology. Computer science, civil engineering, pharmacology, plant breeding science, medical science are typical transfer sciences, each one tied to identifiable technological activities while drawing on insights from a range of fundamental disciplines. Universities not only create new knowledge, but also act as repositories of the stock of established knowledge which may have important generic implications for a whole range of technologies including traditional ones. Indeed the closeness of different industries to the science base varies considerably, and within industries it can change markedly over time. Public research laboratories often play important roles either in transfer sciences or in underpinning the infratechnology of standards and metrology which is vital to the innovation system (Tassey, 1991). Private consultancies, professional societies and industrial research associations also play significant roles as bridging institutions between the worlds of industry and academic research.

While it is sensible to identify differences between science policy and technology policy there remains from the national innovation system perspective a crucial interface around which policy must be integrated. This interface is concerned with more effectively drawing scientific and engineering knowledge into the design and development activities of firms. Management of this interface creates a number of difficult problems. Since science and technology compete for many of the same skills, how should policy influence the distribution of creative talent between the two worlds? What should be the appropriate balance between research and skill formation in higher education institutions? If science is to be directed more to supporting innovation a number of questions need to be addressed. Is there to be more emphasis on the transfer sciences, or a greater use of extrinsic, non-scientific criteria in the allocation of scientific funds (Wienberg, 1967)? Would closer links with technology together with research sponsorship from industry undermine the openness of science and thus its capacity to verify results and stimulate competitive development (Gibbons, 1987)? Is it best to design a policy to foster 'exploitable areas of science' through existing university institutions or through new bridging research institutions closely linked with industry? While these questions do not at all exhaust the domain of science policy proper they cover a highly significant proportion of the policy issues on which national innovation systems must depend.

To summarise, national innovation systems are to various degrees pluralistic in nature. Strongly based on the division of labour their component institutions make complementary contributions to the innovation process but they differ significantly with respect to motivation and with respect to a commitment to dissemination of the knowledge they generate. Science is not fully open, nor is technology fully closed, rather they lie towards different ends of the spectrum. They also differ in size and in the mechanisms by which they accumulate knowledge. These differences are of considerable significance in understanding how well the various components of a national system interconnect.

In practice, connectivity is achieved via a variety of mechanisms. Mobility of scientists and technologists in the labour market and collaboration agreements to develop technology are important formal mechanisms linking firms. Links between firms and universities are often instituted through grants and contracts for research, especially in the transfer sciences. In recent years increased emphasis has been devoted to the various informal networks which provide the connections within national systems. In this regard, Lundvall (1988) and Anderson (1992) have emphasized links between user firms and their suppliers, while von Hippel (1988) and Schrader (1991) have drawn attention to the significance of informal but 'balanced' 'trading' of knowledge which takes place between engineers in different firms in the same industry. Such informal networks are important routes for technology transfer and for the transfer of more tacit knowledge. They reflect the important fact that scientists and technologists are members of common communities of practitioners with a common background in the methods of approach to problem solving: to use de Solla Price's phrase, they share common 'instrumentalities' (1984). De Bresson and Amesse (1991) have made the useful suggestion that we see networks as economic clubs acting to internalize the problems of effective knowledge transmission. To this degree, networks are a substitute both for formal markets and for organizational integration. They fall within the perimeter of non-market devices by which firms seek to co-ordinate their activities with other firms and with other knowledge-generating institutions (Richardson, 1972; Langlois, 1992). However, much remains to be discovered about the operation of different kinds of networks, scientific, technological and industrial, and in particular the ways in which different networks may interact. The costs of and time taken to establish networks are also little understood at present as are the role of networks in limiting the decision horizons of firms, locking them into conventional technological attitudes which become self-reinforcing (Torre, 1992). Moreover, as McDonald (1992) has emphasized, formal collaboration and informal network mechanisms may be in conflict as innovative support mechanisms.

Although much remains to be clarified in this area, the concept of innovation systems is of crucial importance to the policy debate even though they vary considerably across countries (Nelson, 1992b). They encourage policy makers to think in terms of institutions and their connectivity and thus to address the mechanisms by which policy is translated into shifts in the innovation possibility frontiers of firms. National boundaries clearly define the domain for policy making in the first instance, although increasingly policy making can be interpreted in a multi-country context as with the European Framework programme (Eilon, 1992). The issue for policy making is to be aware of how different technologies are promoted by different accumulation systems, and the extent to which these systems are connected internationally.

TECHNOLOGY POLICY AND SMALL FIRMS

We can now link the general aspects of innovation systems to the more specific question of innovation in small firms. More attention has been devoted in recent years to the distinctive innovation processes in smaller firms (ACOST, 1990; Acs and Audretsch, 1990), and this has been reflected in the way technology policies have developed. In general terms we can think of technology policies in terms of their impact on the opportunities, incentives, resources and capabilities of smaller firms to develop and apply new technology. Enhancing opportunities is very much a question of the operation of the national innovation system and the way in which it connects smaller firms with science and technology generating institutions. The development of science parks in higher education institutions and the creation of regional technology centres are illustrative of connection policies for smaller firms. Much of the debate about these issues falls under the general heading of technology transfer. On incentives, one issue is the protection of intellectual property in smaller firms, not so much in terms of the mechanisms and cost of patenting but more in terms of the legal costs of protecting patents which have been challenged or ignored. More important is the effect of risk in limiting incentives to innovate, since developing a technology can often mean betting the future of the company. This is a greatly under-researched issue in relation to smaller firms.

Resources to innovate has traditionally been recognised as the major constraint on the ability of smaller firms to develop new technology, particularly when step changes in its knowledge base are required. This is a matter which is clearly linked to the supply of equity capital to smaller firms (Mason and Harrison, 1991), and also relates to the operation of the tax system, the treatment of capital gains and the incentives to develop venture capital funds. Finally, in relation to the capability to innovate we have one of the advantages of smaller firms, their inherent creativity. Informal organisation and entrepreneurial management have long been recognised as essential characteristics of smaller firms which make them effective experimental institutions and the most likely source of radically new technologies.

From the evolutionary perspective the requirement is to ensure that capabilities are backed up by resources, opportunities and incentive structures. In this regard the UK has seen major shifts in policy since 1980. The standard instrument of UK technology policy until then was the innovation grant, tied to a particular project or firm. The general rationale for this approach was the failure of the capital market to support adequately investment in innovation. It is generally agreed that the system of support which provided monetary resources was dominated by large R&D-intensive firms. After 1984, this policy was abandoned under the general principle of not supporting near-to-market technology development. Policy shifted towards the development of more generic knowledge and skills, pre-competitive research, often in the context of collaborative work between firms and other research institutions. The Alvey programme in advanced information technology was the flagship of this approach (Georghiou, 1989) but equally significant was the LINK programme with its explicit emphasis on collaboration between firms and higher education institutions. This general thrust of policy, of course, was reinforced by the parallel development of European Community technology policy on pre-competitive lines. These shifts in policy have been problematic for smaller firms. Their short-term planning horizons and inevitable new market emphasis to innovative activities are not matched to the idea of longer-term pre-competition research: it is a luxury that few can afford. Secondly, collaboration with larger firms creates formidable difficulties in relation to the protection of intellectual property and the managerial overheads of collaboration programmes which fall with disproportionate emphasis on the smaller firm. Because of this 'incompatibility' between a pre-competitive R&D policy and the needs of smaller firms, two aspects of UK policy, the SMART and SPUR programmes, require particular mention (Moore, 1993; Garnsey and Moore, 1993). Both schemes provide innovation grants, SPUR for companies with less than 500 employees in the manner familiar before 1980. SMART differs in that it applies to firms with less than 50 employees and is delivered by means of regional competitions. Moreover, the grants are awarded in two stages, to develop initial feasibility and subsequently to develop the technology to a prototype stage.

In the last two years there have been further developments in UK policy which reflect the national systems perspective discussed above. Policy is now more concerned to develop explicitly the innovation infrastructure, encouraging the formation of innovation networks and stimulating technology transfer and innovation awareness. Combined with the SMART and SPUR schemes these recent changes constitute a significant technology policy shift in favour of smaller firms. More significantly it reflects a more evolutionary perspective on the nature of the links between innovation and wealth creation. Since one cannot predict in advance which firms will develop new technology it is pointless to give general stimulation in the form of R&D tax incentives – the deadweight loss of the policy is too great. A mechanism is required for firms to identify their innovation intentions as a prerequisite for targeted support, and this is where the innovation infrastructure is important. By encouraging innovation awareness and the formation of technology networks it helps firms identify opportunities to innovate and to come forward with claims on schemes such as SMART and SPUR. Clearly, in stimulating a greater demand for innovation support in smaller firms, it will be essential to provide an adequate supply of innovation grants if the policy is to have the required effect. Taken together these policy changes have considerable potential to develop new technology business experiments along the lines implicit in the evolutionary approach. Variety generation is a necessary prerequisite of a competitive process of wealth creation. It is not sufficient because much depends on the ability of firms to grow and diffuse new technology into the economy. But then technology policy conducted in isolation from policies for business growth and the maintenance of open competition has never been a realistic way of proceeding in a market economy.

CONCLUSION

Downie (1956) has neatly summarized the conditions for a progressive evolutionary process as follows: efficient firms must be able to grow relative to less efficient rivals; firms must have sufficient resources to experiment with new technologies; and they must have sufficient incentives, that is a sufficient degree of appropriability of innovation, to justify the risks of investment. From this perspective small firms clearly play a major role as loci of new innovation experiments, a limited number of which we expect to grow into major economic activities. From the evolutionary perspective two major policy questions follow. Is the national innovation system an adequate experimental system in that it generates an appropriate pattern of technological change consistent with policy objectives? If so, it is likely to be a pluralist system supporting many different sources of innovation with an emphasis on the diversity of micro level activity rather than a centrally driven conception of the innovation process. In such a context the coupling together of institutions in the national system is of prominent importance. Enhancing the operation of the national system is the major route to increasing the creativity of firms. The second major issue is the openness of the competitive process; that every established market position can be challenged by some other innovating firm. Barriers to innovative entry and the efficiency of market selection processes are major concerns of the policy maker here, and it is clear that they are inseparable from aspects of competitive policy more generally. In conclusion one of the major contributions of the evolutionary school has been its insistence that the pattern of technological innovation depends on much more than the behaviour of individual firms. It is this that has lead us directly to the idea of technology systems and a national system of innovation, and it is around the operation of these systems that policy towards small firms should be formed.

REFERENCES

ACOST, (1990) *The Enterprise Challenge: Barriers to Growth in Small Firms*, HMSO, London.

ACS, Z. J. and AUDRETSCH, D. B. (1990) *Innovation and Small Firms*, MIT, Boston.

ANDERSON, E. S. (1992) Approaching national systems of innovation from the production and linkage structure, in B. Lundvall (ed.) *Towards a New Approach to National Systems of Innovation*, Frances Pinter, London.

DE BRESSON, C. and AMESSE, F. (1991) Networks of innovators: a review and introduction to the issue, *Research Policy*, Vol. 20, pp. 363-79.

BUCHANAN, J. and VANBERG, V. (1991) The market as a creative process, *Economics and Philosophy*, Vol. 7, pp. 167-86.

CAMPBELL, D. (1987) Blind variation and selective retention, in creative thought as in other knowledge processes, in G. Radnitzky and W. Bartley (eds.) *Evolutionary Epistemology, Theory of Rationality and Sociology of Knowledge*, Open Court, New York.

DASGUPTA, P. and STIGLITZ, J. (1980) Industrial structure and the nature of innovative activity, *Economic Journal*, Vol. 90, pp. 266-93.

DIXIT, A. K. (1988) A general model of R and D competition and policy, *Rand Journal of Economics*, Vol. 19, pp. 317-26.

DOSI, G. (1988) Sources, procedures and microeconomic effects of innovation, *Journal of Economic Literature*, Vol. 36, pp. 1126-71.

DOWNIE, J. (1956) The control of Monopoly II, *Economic Journal*, Vol. 56, pp. 573-7.

DOWNIE, J. (1958) *The Competitive Process*, Duckworth, London.

EADS, G. and NELSON, R. (1971) Government support of advanced creative technology, *Public Policy*, Vol. 19, pp. 405-29.

EILON, S. (1992) R&D policy in the European Community, *International Journal of Technology Management*, Vol. 17, pp. 113-28.

FREEMAN, C. (1987) *Technology Policy and Economic Performance*, Frances Pinter, London.

GARNSEY, E. and MOORE, I. (1993) Pre-competitive and near-market research and development: problems for innovation policy, in M. Dodgson and R. Rothwell (eds.) *Small Firms and Innovation: The External Influences*, a special publication of the *Journal of Technology Management*, pp. 69-83.

GEORGHIOU, L. (1989) Overview of assessment and evaluation practice, in L. Georghiou and E. Davis (eds.) *Evaluation of R&D: A Policy Maker's Perspective*, HMSO, London.

Gibbons, M. (1987) Contemporary transformation of science, in M. Gibbons and B. Wittrock (eds.) *Science as a Commodity*, Longman, London.

GOULD, S. (1990) *Wonderful Life*, Hutchinson, London.

HALL, P. (ed.) (1986) *Technology, Innovation and Public Policy*, P Allen, Oxford.

HAYEK, F. (1948) The meaning of competition, in ibid, *Individualism and Economic Order*, Chicago University Press.

HENDERSON, D. (1971) Two British errors and their probable consequences, *Oxford Economic Papers*, Vol. 35, pp. 159-205.

HODGSON, G. (1991) Evolution and intention in economic theory, in P. Saviotti and S. Metcalfe (eds.) *Evolutionary Theories of Economic and Technological Change*, Harwood, London.

HODGSON, G. (1993) *Economics and Evolution*, Polity Press, London.

JUSTMANN, M. and TEUBAL, M. (1986) Innovation policy in an open economy: A normative framework for strategic and tactical issues, *Research Policy*, Vol. 15, pp. 121-38.

KRUEGER, A. O. (1991) Economists' changing perceptions of government, *Weltwertschaftliches Archiv*, Vol. 63, pp. 417-31.

LANGLOIS, R. N. (1992) Transactions cost economics in real time, *Industrial and Corporate Change*, Vol. 1, pp. 99-127.

LUNDVALL, B. (1988) Innovation as an interactive process: from user-producer interaction to the national system of innovation, in G. Dosi et al. (eds.) *Technical Change and Economic Theory*, Frances Pinter, London.

MCDONALD, S. (1992) Formal collaboration and informal information flow, *International Journal of Technology Management*, Vol. 7, pp. 49-60.

MCELVEY, M. (1991) How do national systems of innovation differ, in G. Hodgson and E. Screpanti (eds.) *Rethinking Economics: Markets, Technology and Economic Evolution*, Edward Elgar, Aldershot.

MASON, C. and HARRISON, R. (1993) Strategies for expanding the informal venture capital market, *International Small Business Journal*, Vol. 2, no. 4.

MASON, C. and HARRISON, R. (1991) The small firm equity gap since Bolton, in J. Stanworth, and C. Gray (eds.) *Bolton 20 Years On: The Small Firm in the 1990s*, Paul Chapman, London.

METCALFE, J. S. and GIBBONS, M. (1989) Technology, variety and organisation: a systematic perspective on the competitive process, *Research in Technological Innovation, Management and Policy*, Vol. 4, pp. 153-93.

MOORE, I. (1993) Government finance for innovation in small firms: the impact of SMART in M. Dodgson and R. Rothwell (eds.) *Small Firms and Innovation: The External Influences*, a special publication of the *Journal of Technology Management*, pp. 104-18.

MOWERY, D. and ROSENBERG, N. (1989) New developments in US technology policy: implications for competitiveness and international trade policy, *California Management Review*, Vol. 32, pp. 107-24.

NELSON, R. (1980) Assessing private enterprise: An exegesis of tangled doctrine, *Bell Journal of Economics*, Vol. 97, pp. 93-111.

NELSON, R. R. (1982) The role of knowledge in R&D efficiency, *Quarterly Journal of Economics*, Vol. 97, pp. 453-70.

NELSON, R. (1987) *Understanding Technical Change as an Evolutionary Process*, North Holland.

NELSON, R. (1990) Capitalism as an engine of progress, *Research Policy*, Vol. 19, pp. 193-214.

NELSON, R. R. (1992a) National innovation systems: a retrospective on a study, *Industrial and Corporate Change*, Vol. 1, no 2, pp. 347-74.

NELSON, R. R. (1992b) The role of firms in technical advance: a perspective from evolutionary theory, in G. Dosi, R. Gannetti and P. Toninelti (eds.) *Technology and Enterprise in a Historical Perspective*, Oxford.

NELSON, R. and WINTER, S. (1982) *An Evolutionary Theory of Economic Change*, Holland Press.

NEWBERRY, D. M. (1990) Missing markets: consequences and remedies, in F. Hahn (ed.) *The Economics of Missing Markets, Information and Games*, Oxford.

OECD (1992) *Technology and the Economy: The Key Relationships*, OECD.

PAVITT, K. (1990) What do we know about the strategic management of technology? *Californian Management Review*, Vol. 32, pp. 17-26.

RICHARDSON, G. B. (1972) The organization of industry, *Economic Journal*, Vol. 82, pp. 883-98.

SCHRADER, S. (1991) Informal transfer between firms: cooperation through information trading, *Research Policy*, Vol. 20, pp. 153-70.

DE SOLLA PRICE, D. (1984) The science/technology relationship, the craft of experimental science and policy for the improvement of high technology innovation, *Research Policy*, Vol. 13, pp. 3-20.

STIGLITZ, J. E. (1991) The invisible hand and modern welfare economics, in D. Vines and A. Stevenson (eds.) *Information, Strategy and Public Policy*, Blackwell.

STONEMAN, P. (1987) *The Economic Analysis of Technology Policy*, Oxford.

TASSEY, G. (1991) The functions of technology infrastructure in a competitive economy, *Research Policy*, Vol. 20, pp. 345-61.

TILER, C., METCALFE, S. and CONNELL, D. (1993) Business expansion through entrepreneurship: the influence of internal and external barriers to growth, in M. Dodgson and R. Rothwell (eds.) *Small Firms and Innovation: The External Influences*, a special publication of the *Journal of Technology Management*, pp. 119-32.

TORRE, A. (1992) Untraded and technological interdependencies: some new developments and conclusions, Communication to the Conference of the International Joseph A Schumpeter Society, Kyoto, August.

VON HIPPEL, E. (1988) *The Sources of Innovation*, Oxford University Press.

WEINBERG, A. M. (1967) *Reflections on Big Science*, Pergamon, London.

WITT, U. (1991) Reflections on the present state of evolutionary economic theory, in G Hodgson and E. Screpanti (eds.) *Rethinking Economics: Markets, Technology and Economic Evolution*, Edward Elgar, Aldershot.

WITT, U. (1992) Evolutionary concepts in economics, *Eastern Economic Journal*, Vol. 18, pp. 405-19.

WOLF, C. (1987) Market and non-market failures: comparison and assessment, *Journal of Public Policy*, Vol. 7, pp. 407-25.

CHAPTER 15

How NTBFs Acquire, Accumulate and Transfer Technology: Implications for Catching-Up Policies of Less Developed Countries such as Portugal[1]

MANUEL LARANJA

INTRODUCTION

It is believed that new technology-based firms (NTBFs) have an inherent innovation potential, which allows for the industrial structural change of backward and mature regions (Rothwell, 1989). Some writers (Freeman, 1989; Perez, 1990; Soete, 1985) claim that there are 'windows of opportunity', for less developed regions to 'catch-up', based upon the emergence and spread of a new 'cluster of technological innovations' related to Information and Communication Technologies (Freeman, 1987). However, the con-

Table 15.1: *Business innovation centres in Portugal, location, founding and supporting organizations*

BIC	LOCATION	STARTED	FOUNDING AND SUPPORTING ORGANISATIONS
AITEC	Lisbon	1986	INESC, IPE
CEISET	Lisbon South	1987	Almada city council, various banks, EBN New University of Lisbon FLAD
NET	Oporto	1987	Oporto city council, EBN INESC, INETI FLAD
CPIN	Lisbon	1991	ITEC, Higher Technical Institute of Lisbon, EBN
NIDE	Oporto	1991	Youth Foundation from the State Secretariat of Youth ANJE-Young Entrepreneurs Association

Source: interviews
Notes:
INESC – Institute of Engineering and Computer Systems, university based research institute
ITEC – Institute for the European Community, is a university liasion and administrative office
INETI – National Institute of Engineering and Industrial Technology
FLAD – Portuguese-American Foundation
EBN – European Business Network supported by DGXVI

tention that new technology-based firms could drive regional 'catch-up' has been challenged by studies claiming that, in depressed areas, the jobs generated by new firms are, to a large extent, dependent on the previous mature industrial structure and that, in any case, NTBFs have relatively low employment potential (Storey, 1982).

In Portugal, the NTBF phenomena is relatively recent. It appears to be related to the relatively low entry barriers associated with 'knowledge intensive' businesses, the Portuguese economic climate of the late 1980s that has favoured investment and demand for technology intensive products and services, and the emergence of Business Innovation Centres (BICs) during this decade. Obviously, the pre-existence of a 'pool' of technical engineering also played an important role in enabling higher levels of local technical entrepreneurship.

As in other European countries (Audretsch, 1991; Conti et al, 1991; Sternberg, 1989), Portuguese BICs are becoming important mechanisms for the stimulation of technical entrepreneurship. While in 1986 there was only one BIC in Lisbon, in 1992 5 BICs were fully operational (see Table 15.1). BICs such as AITEC and CPIN are strongly related to the engineering activities of the Higher Technical Institute of Lisbon and its associated Institutes of Research (INESC and ITEC), while other BICs (NET, CEISET and NIDE) are promoted by various other organisations such as city councils, banks, Portugese-American Foundation etc.

The research presented in this paper is based on a survey of 62 NTBFs, 49 of which were based at 5 Business Innovation Centres located in several parts of the country. A selection of a sub-sample of firms from the main sample allowed further analysis on their origins, their product-market strategies, and their funding difficulties. BIC and off-BIC firms, ranging from 6 months to 10 years old, are very small and fragile, and only a small minority will become, in the long-term, important local employers. Nevertheless, despite their small size and their overall low employment potential (in total the 62 firms currently employ 830 people), the evidence gathered from this survey and case studies suggests that NTBFs are 'Shumpeterian vehicles' for high risk technological ventures that effectively bring new technologies into local markets. The common mode of product-market entry, for surveyed NTBFs (see Figure 15.1), is achieved through launching new products in 'existing markets', although from the entrepreneur's viewpoint these 'existing markets', are often perceived as new market niches.

UPSTREAM LINKAGES: TECHNOLOGY INPUTS

Of the total 62 firms in the sample, 28 (45%) have already established, while 18 (29%) have actively sought to create and maintain strong R&D formal (contract R&D and joint R&D projects) linkages with local public and private research organisations. Formal R&D interactions with universities and their associated private non-profit institutes of research (i.e. the Higher Technical Institute of Lisbon and INESC - Institute of Engi-

N=62   Product/service

		Existent	New
Market	Existent	14	39
	New		9

Figure 15.1
NTBFs innovation potential

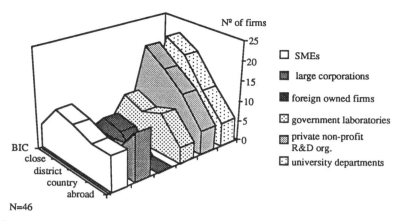

Figure 15.2
R&D formal linkages

neering and Computer Systems) were relatively more common (see Figure 15.2), although other small firms and government R&D laboratories were also important secondary sources of technological inputs. As Figure 15.2 shows, there is some evidence to support the contention that formal R&D interactions depend upon physical proximity, while physical proximity was even more relevant to 'informal' R&D linkages.

Although differences in the number of linkages between firms of different BICs were not statistically significant, due to the small size of this sub-sample, the research found that firms associated with university-based BICs (AITEC and CPIN) and off-BIC firms located in Lisbon and Oporto close to the main engineering universities were relatively more active in creating and maintaining R&D links. 'University spin-off' firms (15 out of the total 62 firms), founded by former researchers, were also relatively more active in fostering formal R&D collaboration.

Reasons underlying R&D formal collaborations with local universities and other R&D organisations were essentially related to the technical and product development activities of firms concerned. However, given their difficulties in recruiting highly qualified personnel, formal R&D collaborations with local universities (and institutes of research) are

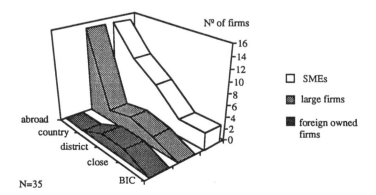

Figure 15.3
Agencing-in contacts

often used as channels of access to additional local skilled R&D labour markets.

Another important mechanism used by Portuguese NTBFs as a technological input appears to be 'product agencing-in' from other firms abroad in which foreign manufactured products were sold by survey firms (see Figure 15.3). Although the firms in the sample are quite recent start-ups, 21 (34%) firms already have agencing-in agreements, 14 (23%) were seeking to have such an agreement, while the remaining (43%) do not intend to act as sales agents for other companies.

Searching for companies abroad from whom to source new products was acknowledged by 35 firms in the sample (56%). Such firms were not biased in favour of a location based at a BIC or strongly associated with a university. However, the reasons underlying agencing-in vary. NTBFs that rely on their own internal R&D, complemented with local external R&D interactions as the basis for product or service innovations, explained agencing-in as an activity that enabled them to enlarge and complement their own product range. To a substantial number of other NTBFs, however, product-agencing, complemented by value added servicing to local clients (so called VARs – Value Added Reselling services), was their main business activity.

The patterns of R&D and product-agencing upstream linkages suggest that NTBFs located in less developed countries, such as Portugal, are extensively linked with two sources of technological know-how comprising local universities and small firms abroad. However, the ability of NTBFs to adapt and further extend their technical knowledge base, acquired from those sources, depends on the firms' ability to develop strong linkages with local clients. In the next section we turn to this subject of customer linkages.

DOWNSTREAM LINKAGES: THE DIFFUSION OF TECHNOLOGY

NTBFs within the survey were strongly tied to local clients, which essentially comprised other small firms in industrial or services sectors. The research found no geographical clustering of clients in the districts where NTBFs are located, and no particular bias in favour of either industrial or services sector clients, although NTBFs promoting their own products within industrial sectors find relatively less demand since

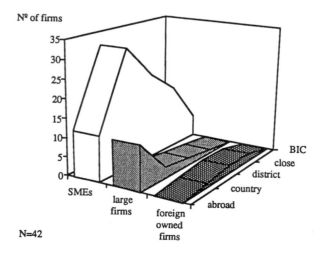

N=42

Figure 15.4
Agencing-out contacts

there are fewer clients that might value their expertise. Rothwell and Dodgson (1992, p. 5) support this argument by pointing out that:

> As NTBFs in less endowed regions develop their unique technological competencies, they often faced problems when attempting to market highly innovative products through being located in an area lacking in innovation demand.

An agencing-out agreement for the firm's own products is an alternative that some NTBFs are choosing as a response to lack of innovative demand, in order to rapidly penetrate and expand beyond their local markets. From the total 62 firms in the sample, 18 firms (29%) already used sales agents, 24 (39%) were seeking to find agents, while the remaining 20 (32%) did not intend to establish agencing-out agreements.

Firms that have (or seek to have) agents, look at the whole country as their potential agencing area and not just to their local district. Therefore, there are no significant regional effects in agencing-out (see Figure 15.4).

The firms that do not intend to use agents (32%) prefer direct contact with their customers. In many cases direct contact with the client is a vehicle for the firm's value added servicing activities. While most companies would prefer direct contact with the customer, their motivation to use sales agents is essentially related to geographical distribution and reduction of distribution costs.

In the next section, fast growing NTBFs providing highly specialised products and services, through direct contact with the customer, are analysed. It is argued that local large users may provide 'innovative' demand, contributing to the development of such firms and to their cumulative processes of learning.

LESSONS FROM FAST GROWING NTBFS

Selected case studies of fast growing NTBFs discussed below show that a key to their success lies in the management of upstream and downstream external linkages and in the synergies that 'in-house' technical and managerial skills derive from such external interactions.

An IT provider

This firm has developed and commercialised Electronic Office Systems software and equipment, based on a differentiation strategy to meet local user requirements such as: Portuguese language, user support facilities, and software portability to different mini-computer systems marketed by the large computer manufacturers who are preferred by large local clients, such as Public Administration. By fostering software portability, and establishing marketing agreements with local sales-subsidiaries of large computer manufacturers, the company has achieved a significant share of the Office Automation segment of the public sector procurement market. By specialising in this segment of large public procurement accounts, the firm was forced to develop a package of complementary services in the areas of user training, office and bureau organisation, and system configuration. Such 'product localization' and servicing complementary skills are essential for the firm's differential advantage over local subsidiaries of large multinationals and other competitors.

Electronics alarms manufacturer

Another case study, concerning a firm specialising in 'electronic alarm systems', revealed a similar pattern of activity. The company had relatively modest sales turnover until it found a large local customer. In this case the customer required the design and development of an 'SOS motorway emergency system'. The local NTBF was able to outperform foreign competitors by fostering strong interactions with INESC and the university, on the one hand, and strong user-producer relations related to 'prototype' testing, on the other hand (Lundvall, 1988).

This research also found two cases of fast growing NTBFs that resulted from the decision of large users to become 'suppliers' by backwards integration through starting their own NTBF subsidiaries. This provides further evidence to support the importance of the relationship between large user and small technology supplier firms. Examples of such firms, included in the survey, are: a software company founded by the airports systems maintenance and construction (large public sector company), and an information technology management company founded by the national electricity producer and distributor. Obviously, in these cases, the symbiotic user-producer relationship is reinforced by capital ownership linkages and 'interlocks' (Håkanson, 1987).

Moreover, such cases suggest that large user sectors, such as electricity production and distribution, the local telecommunications operators, or foreign owned assembly operations, could stimulate local technology-based markets through their 'local' technology procurement. This would favour the formation of large-user small-producer industrial clusters, that are of fundamental importance for the development and accumulation of technical skills. The importance of large users to NTBFs can be summarised in the following manner:

> Large users, may provide NTBFs with a steady demand over a considerable period of time. This demand often starts as a niche opportunity, but niches may grow, or they may disappear. When they grow they attract competition from other (larger) firms. As niches grow the supplier NTBF confronts itself with the learning associated with competition and with satisfying large orders to sophisticated customers (von Hippel 1986). This situation is highly conducive to accumulation of the marketing and managerial skills that are often lacking in young technically oriented firms.

Large users may also be willing to try local products instead of foreign imported technology, and provide 'early-users' trading expertise and 'test-sites' for the small technology-based suppliers. This situation also facilitates learning that leads to improved products and services that are of sufficient quality to meet competition from abroad.

For the small supplier, large users provide the 'bread and butter' product-market that enables sustainable accumulation of endogenous technological and managerial skills (Perez, 1990). In many ways this is a situation similar to that of the small high technology companies in the USA that depended upon defence procurement (Markusen, 1990). However, in the Portuguese case, new technology-based firms are not necessarily high technology firms, and public procurement does not come from defence but rather from public administration and public enterprises. Following the same analogy, in the USA, this strong relationship between large users in the public sector and small NTBFs spills over to the rest of the productive sphere in the long term. The same process could happen in Portugal, where such spill-overs from public sector patronage could also contribute to the technological catching-up of traditional industrial sectors.

On the other hand, fast growing NTBFs in this sample were found to be those that developed an explicit 'technology strategy' based upon collaborative R&D activity with university-based research facilities. The importance of these relationships can be summarised in the following manner:

> Local universities (and university-based research institutes) may provide NTBFs with access to state-of-the-art technologies. Such institutions often provide valuable technical information, and in some cases 'prototypes' are transferred to new firms that bear the risks of creating and developing local markets for new technological intensive products and services.

Local universities are also fundamental sources of qualified human resources that NTBFs need to support their development.

It is from their remarkable customer-orientation, based upon strong user-producer interactions (Lundvall, 1988), that fast growing NTBFs derive their differentiated market advantages (Doyle et al., 1986). Such firms effectively work as local agents of technology diffusion. On the other hand, it is because of their explicit and informal strong interactions with universities that NTBFs are effectively 'university-industry' technology transfer agents.

FINANCE BARRIERS

An important barrier to the development of NTBFs is their access to sources of finance (Baber et al., 1989). Oakey (1984) in his study of regional innovation resources in Scotland, South East England and San Francisco Bay area of California, found that small firms' personal savings and an incremental approach based on retained profits reduces the risks to the venture team, when compared with faster loan-based financing schemes.

To a large extent, Portuguese NTBFs have obtained their initial and subsequent increases of capital from the entrepreneurs' own savings or from retained profits (see Table 15.2). While agreeing that loan reimbursement commitments could originate serious cash-flow imbalances that are sometimes fatal, many Portuguese entrepreneurs were not against the idea of having venture capitalists as share owning partners.

In Portugal, venture capital operations are relatively recent and they appear to be a consequence of the growth and diversification of financial services, industrial conglomerates and public sector venture capital. The large majority of Portuguese venture capital operations reflect the business interests of their sponsors. While the proportion of Portuguese venture capital investment in start-ups is considerably higher than the rest of Europe, none of these start-ups is in the technology intensive areas of, for example, computers, software or biotechnology. Portuguese venture capitalists are investing primarily in the technological upgrading of traditional and mature sectors. Little effort has been made by venture capitalists to contact BICs, technical universities or individual

Table 15.2: *Number of firms that used the listed sources of start-up capital, in a given proportion of total capital needs*

SOURCES OF START-UP CAPITAL	0-24%	25-49%	50-74%	75-100%
Self finance (entrepreneurs)	1	4	4	44
Business innovation centre	1	3		
Public sector				
Banks			1	
PEDIP			1	
Private sector				
Large corporations	1		2	2
Individual investors				
Banks	1			
Small firms		4	1	1
Private non-profit origanis	1			
Special funds				
Awards (IAPMEI-CGD)			1	

Notes: N = 59, 3 non-respondents
Source: interviews

Table 15.3: *Percentage of firms in each row that considered the listed services as important*

	BUSINESS PLAN ASSISTANCE	ADMIN ACCOUNTING LEGAL RECRUITMENT	COMMON SERVICES (FAX PHOTOC)	USE OF BIC'S IMAGE FOR ADVERTISING	REDUCTION COST OF SPACE	SHORT OR LONG TERM FINANCING	FINDING TECHNICAL AND MARKET INFORMATION
CPIN N = 5	40%	40%	80%	100%	60%	15%	37%
CEISET N = 12	75%	57%	83%	58%	58%	31%	57%
AITEC N = 17	47%	35%	53%	59%	47%	47%	40%
NET N = 8	25%	27%	88%	63%	88%	9%	46%
NIDE N = 7	14%	29%	100%	57%	86%	7%	21%

Source: interviews

technical entrepreneurs. Government sponsored venture capital, however, is starting to collaborate with Business Innovation Centres, although up to now there are only a few cases where public sector venture capital funds have actually flowed into new technology-based ventures.

BICS' INFLUENCE IN STIMULATING LINKAGES

It is likely that differences in an ability to accumulate technological and marketing know-how can be explained by variations in access to the 'rich' technology and business opportunities environment, in which BICs are embedded. BIC-firms, however, replied that 'common services' (use of fax, photocopier, switchboard, etc) are the most important type of support provided (see Table 15.3), which suggests that BICs may have little influence in the creation of technical linkages with university-based research or with public research establishments.

Despite the apparent poor contribution of BICs for the formation of technical linkages, NTBFs appear to be able to create strong technical informal flows of information with external sources. Such is the case of AITEC firms, who appear to benefit from facilitated access to INESC (university-based research institute) and INESC's associated organisations – such as the telecommunication operators, technical universities, FUN-DETEC (the Fund for the Development of Vocational Training in areas of Information and Electronic Technologies), TECNINESC (equity investor) etc. It appears that INESC and AITEC-firms are embedded in an 'informal transactions network' or 'innovative millieu' (Aydalot and Keeble, 1988) that effectively conveys informal technical information, reduces uncertainty for the firms and stimulates technical entrepreneurship.

CONCLUSIONS: THE ROLE OF NTBFS AND POLICIES OF SUPPORT

The role of NTBFs

The characteristics of the NTBFs surveyed in this study are of some consequence to the process of technological catching-up in less developed European countries, such as Portugal, and the development of appropriate policies of support to such a process. The most important characteristics of the firms are:

- Their upstream linkages suggesting that, to some firms, local technical universities appear to be an essential source of technological inputs. Similar small firms abroad are also an important source of technological inputs through product-agencing. Most firms did not appear to have had any constraints in accessing sources of technology, that is, in creating and maintaining upstream linkages.

- Their downstream linkages suggest that, while the large majority of companies are tied with small local clients, a few have established strong links to local large customers.
- Their internal technological and managerial skills complement and determine the creation, effectiveness and evolution of upstream and downstream linkages.

Therefore, NTBFs perform an important role as local technology agents from abroad, introducing new products in local markets, and supporting the risk associated with new product-market development. A few firms are strongly tied to local technical universities and are effectively contributing to the technological upgrading of large public sector companies or public administrations and, in the long term, they may generate technological skills spill-overs to other sectors. It is in their 'bridging' function between local or international sources of technological know-how and their local clients (small or large) that NTBFs in less developed countries find their role as elements capable of acquiring, accumulating and diffusing technologies. Given their important contribution to the process of technological modernisation, NTBFs should be the target of a specific policy of support.

The role of government in the support of NTBFs

Recognising the important role of NTBFs, governments in Europe have increased their range of mechanisms to support these firms (Rothwell and Dodgson, 1989, 1992),

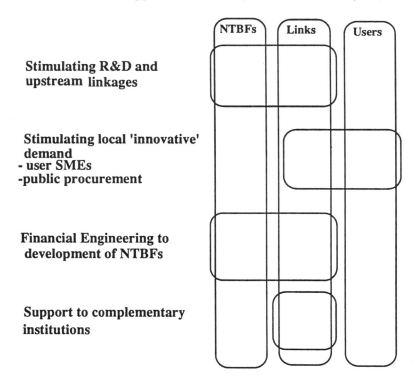

Figure 15.5
Impact of Policies of Support to NTBFs in lagging regions on the firms, their linkages and their clients

including instruments such as BICs and special financing schemes. However, such schemes are often based upon non-integrated demand and supply side instruments, making poor use of 'interface arrangements' such as a central agency that could help in the creation of 'intangible relational assets' by NTBFs (de Bresson, 1990; Rothwell, 1990) associated with their upstream and downstream linkage interactions.

Figure 15.5 summarises the recommended policy guidelines for implementing policies of support to NTBFs in the context of lagging regions. Those guidelines derive from the characteristic upstream and downstream interactions of these firms, and point to the need to improve interfaces at the inputs and outputs of NTBFs' business activities.

Given the extensive upstream linkages of NTBFs in terms of R&D, and their efforts towards continuous technological innovation, support consisting of a subsidy for research and technological development should be available to NTBF applicants to stimulate the formation of linkages to local technical universities, joint projects or contract research between NTBFs and universities (and/or associated institutes of research). Assistance to NTBFs in retraining, and post-graduate education, through subsidies that, for example, pay students' fees, would also be an important aspect of improving upstream linkages and internal levels of technological skills.

Stimulating local 'innovative' demand

The downstream linkages of NTBFs suggest that stimulation of demand should be based upon two different sets of policies: procurement policies in public sector administration and enterprises, and policies directed at industrial SMEs.

While in the context of more advanced regions, government has provided opportunities for technology intensive firms in the areas of defence, chemical and oil industries (Rothwell, 1992), in the context of less developed regions, central and local government may create opportunities for technology intensive firms through promoting technological modernisation of their own administrative structures and public companies. This, however, does not mean that the public sector should favour local technology suppliers instead of foreign suppliers. 'Infant industry' protection arguments appear not to be relevant (Bell et al., 1982) as Portuguese NTBFs should be capable of competing and establishing cumulative level technological competitiveness, provided they create and maintain upstream linkages and close 'user-producer' interactions with their clients. Local public procurement markets should promote rivalry between local technology intensive firms, and equivalent products/services provided by sales-subsidiaries of foreign firms. As a substantial part of client-downstream linkages of NTBFs, however, are directed to industrial SMEs, policies to support SMEs in their efforts to adopt and use new technologies would significantly impact on the expansion of local markets for NTBFs. Support to user SMEs should include 'fast' access to small subsidies for an initial 'needs analysis' survey followed by larger subsidies to fund an agreed project of technology adoption.

Financial engineering to development of NTBFs

The financial difficulties that NTBFs face as they develop suggest that access to funds and the promotion of stronger technological and business interactions should be the role of a central agency of support to NTBFs. The 'Fund' could have a mixture of financial instruments based upon subsidies, loans and venture capital, including, amongst other facilities:

- Seed capital
- Expansion capital

- Joint venture capital support
- Loans at lower than market rate
- Conditional loans (repayable if successful)
- Loan guarantees

Support to complementary institutions

However, policies to reinforce and further develop upstream and downstream linkages are not sufficient in the context of less developed regions, where not only 'innovative demand' is lacking, but also infrastructures that directly or indirectly provide and promote conditions for NTBFs to evolve are scarce. Therefore, it is important to provide support to organisations such as:

- Business Innovation Centres that effectively provide 'tangible' support in the form of financial capital, and indirect support to development in the form of access to a network of business, technical information and training services.
- Technological infrastructures such as technical universities, research institutes, technology centres, etc., that provide technical support to NTBFs.

Another extremely important area for effective support of NTBFs is technical education. One of the major constraints of Portuguese NTBFs is their difficulty in finding technically skilled personnel. Therefore, government may play an important role by providing funds for the creation of new technical training courses, and the expansion of the existing ones. Finally, local venture capitalists should also be stimulated to invest in technology intensive start-ups. Public sector sponsored venture capital also could play a major role in two ways: by providing 'seed' capital directly to 'would be' entrepreneurs or by implementing 'matching' and 'syndicate' schemes with other financial organisations.

NOTES

1. The author acknowledges his gratitude to JNICT-CIENCIA and the British Council Lisbon, for the support given to his research work.

REFERENCES

AYDALOT, P. and KEEBLE, D. (eds) (1988) *Technology Industry and Innovative Environments: The European Experience*, GREMI (Groupe de Research Europeen sur les Millieus Innovateurs) Routledge, London.

AUDRETSCH, D. B. (1991) The transfer of technology from the university to small and medium-sized firms, OECD Case Studies on Germany, Paper presented at OECD expert meeting on *Technological resources and competitiveness strategies of Small and Medium-sized Enterprises (SMEs) and the access of SMEs to the research system*, Paris, 21 May.

BABER, J., METCALFE, S., and PORTEOUS, M. (eds.) (1989) *Barriers to Growth in Small Firms*, Routledge, London and New York.

BELL M., SCOTT-KEMMIS, D. and SATYARAKWITZ, W. (1982) Limited learning in infant industry: a case study, in Frances Stewart and Jeffrey James (eds.) *The Economics of New Technology in Developing Countries*, Frances Pinter, London, pp. 138-56.

CONTI, ARNOLDI, BIONDIDINO, ENRIETTI, SEGRE (1991) Universités et transfert de l'information technologique aux PME: la geographie complexe Italienne, OECD étude des cas sur l'Italie, Paper presented at the OECD expert meeting on *Technological resources and competitiveness strategies of Small and Medium-sized Enterprises (SMEs) and the access of SMEs to the research system*, Paris, 21 May.

DE BRESSON C. (1990) Networks of innovators: introduction and highlights of issues, Paper presented as the introduction to the conference *Network of Innovators Workshop*, Montreal. Canada, 1-3 May.

DOYLE, P., SAUNDERS, J. and WONG, V. (1986) Japanese marketing strategies in the UK: a comparative study, *Journal of International Business Studies*, Vol. 17, no. 1.

FREEMAN, C. (1987), The challenge of new technologies, Prepared for the Symposium marking the 25th aniversary of the OECD, *Interdependence and Co-operation in tomorrow's world*.

FREEMAN, C. (1989) New technology and catching up, in Charles Cooper and Raphael Kaplinski (eds.) *Technology and Development in the Third Industrial Revolution*, pp. 85-99, Frank Cass, London.

HÅKANSON, H. (eds) (1987) *Industrial Technological Development: A Network Approach*, Croom Helm, London.

LUNDVALL B. (1988) Innovation as an interactive process: from user-producer interactions to the national system of innovation, in G. Dosi, C. Freeman, R. Nelson, G. Silverberg and L. Soete (eds.) *Technical Change and Economic Theory*, Frances Pinter, London, pp. 349-69.

MARKUSEN, A. (1990) The military industrial divide: Cold War transformation of the economy and the rise of new industrial complexes, Paper presented at the conference *Network of Innovators Workshop*, Montreal, Canada.

OAKEY, R. (1984) Innovation and regional growth in small high technology firms: evidence from Britain and the USA, *Regional Studies*, Vol. 18, no. 3, pp. 237-51.

PEREZ, C. (1990) Electronics and development in Venezuela: a user oriented strategy and its policy implications, Report to the OECD development centre, October.

ROTHWELL, R. (1989) Small firms, innovation and industrial change, *Small Business Economics*, Vol. 1, pp. 51-64.

ROTHWELL, R. (1990) External networking and innovation in small and medium-sized manufacturing firms in Europe, Paper presented at the conference *Network of Innovators Workshop*, Montreal, Canada, 1-3 May.

ROTHWELL, R. (1992) Issues in user-producer relations: role of government, Paper prepared for the *Six Countries Programme on User Producer Relations in the Innovation Process*, Dipoli Congress Centre, Espoo, Finland, 26-27 November.

ROTHWELL, R. and DODGSON, M. (1989) Technology-based small and medium-sized firms in Europe: the IRDAC results and their public policy implications, *Science and Public Policy*, Vol. 16, no. 1, February, pp. 9-18.

ROTHWELL, R. and DODGSON, M. (1992) Growth and renewal in technology-based SMEs: the role of external technology, Paper prepared for the conference on *Birth and Start-up of Small Firms*, University of Bocconi, 18-19 June.

SOETE, L. (1985) International diffusion of technology, industrial development and technological leapfrogging, *World Development*, Vol. 13, no. 3, pp. 409-22.

STERNBERG, R. (1989) Innovation centres and their importance for the growth of new technology-based firms: experience gained from the Federal Republic of Germany, *Technovation*, no. 9, pp. 681-94.

STOREY, D. (1982) *Entrepreneurship and the Small Firm*, Croom Helm, London.

VON HIPPEL, E. (1986) Large users: a source of novel product concepts, *Management Science*, July.

CHAPTER 16

The Role of Science and Technology Parks in NTBF Development

JÜRGEN HAUSCHILDT AND RALF H. STEINKÜHLER

PRELIMINARY REMARKS: DEVELOPMENT AND DEFINITIONS OF TS-PARKS

Technology parks and science parks were terms which appeared in Continental Europe in the early 1980s during a worldwide recession. In those days governments and regional planners were looking for new ways to avoid economic stagnation. American and British models for industrial development provided us with promising ideas from which the agglomeration of technology-based, young small firms close to a university emerged as an appealing model. The guiding example was Silicon Valley, which grew from a research park near Stanford University in the 1950s (Hisrich, 1985, p. 223). This paper is concerned with German attempts to replicate this early growth in more recent times. Figure 16.1 demonstrates the extensive development in Germany of technology centres (the German equivalent of science parks). Within the territory of the old Federal Republic there are currently about 100 technology centres in existence, with about 2,000

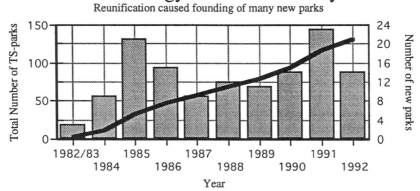

Figure 16.1
Development of technology parks in Germany

tenant firms and about 20,000 employees. In the 5 states of the former GDR, 14 tech-nology centres have been started since 1990, with about 225 tenants and more than 1,000 jobs have been created (Wirschaftswoche, 1992).

There appear to be three factors which determine the success of these industrial estab-lishments:

- energetic local or regional government authority
- interested local industrial tenants
- a university or another institution which provides a technological education.

Already in the early days, numerous different German models were developed. This is reflected by several names for these establishments, including research park, science park, innovation centre, business incubator etc. Since these establishments are the result of independent entrepreneurship, one should not be astonished at the diversity of chosen names. But they all have one attribute in common: the tenant firms in these technology centres are concentrated in one place (in a former barracks, abandoned factories or recently developed industrial estates). As we will see later, this spatial concentration entails variable chances and risks associated with each type of site. In the meantime we have become accustomed to the following typology (see Figure 16.2).

At one end of the continuum we find so-called 'science parks' or 'research parks'. These parks are intended to bring together R&D departments of firms and research insti-tutes of universities. The guiding principle here is the local agglomeration of technolog-ical expertise and know-how. They are often focused on a certain technology; for exam-ple, computer science or medical instruments.

At the other extreme we find the so-called 'business incubators'. These are mostly conglomerations of newly founded, entrepreneurial firms. The guiding principle here is to give support to the business start-up. Sponsors are mainly the local authority or indus-try. In most of these incubators the time span of tenancy is restricted.

Between these two extremes we find a wide variety of so-called 'technology parks or centres'. In most cases the tenant firms pursue different technological ideas. They may be of various sizes and from different industries. They may be spin-offs from universi-ties, management buy-outs, or joint ventures. The guiding principle for admission to the development is their expected business success and the chances of increasing employment in that region or town. The main promoters of such centres are the local communities or regional governments (Monck, 1988, pp. 84-8: Sternberg, 1988, pp. 150-2).

Because true science parks are very rare, we will leave them out of our further con-siderations and focus on 'business incubators', which exclusively promote entrepreneur-ial start-ups and raise a lot of special questions. We concentrate on this 'bread and but-ter' model of technologically and scientifically oriented industrial parks which are called TS-parks for the purposes of our paper.

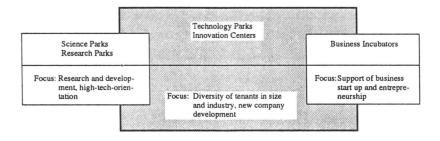

Figure 16.2
Types of technology park

THE PROBLEM

These TS-parks can be entirely private enterprises. Normally they have a mixture of private and public founders, and very often they are supported and subsidized by local government. Corresponding to these different interests, we find different standards of the evaluation of the success of TS-parks. This observation inevitably leads to a political discussion. Should government engage in, or refrain from, the founding and subsidization of TS-parks, or should this be a private initiative driven only by market forces? The defenders of a political involvement will argue that local government is responsible for the long-term economic development in a region. Subsidization is thus not a loss but an investment for the future. However, critics argue that these TS-parks cannot survive independently in the long term, or if survival occurs, they will make a bare living providing accommodation for backyard traders or as repairshop areas (Dose and Drexler, 1988, p. 358).

We believe that this political discussion only makes sense if it is shown that the tenant firms in the TS-parks are as successful as private enterprises elsewhere. Business success, as measured in terms of profit and growth, is a necessary test of any political policy. Moreover, if the firms are successful, one might also ask whether this private success has been bought with public subsidies. However, we must insist that if the tenant firms in the TS-parks are not successful, the entire concept makes no sense. Our contribution to this volume is a summary of our research results which seek to answer the question of whether the tenant firms in TS-parks are successful.

In accordance with this general objective of answering the success of the TS-parks, various questions must be raised (see Figure 16.3).

- Ask prospective tenants what sort of services they actually expect from a TS-park.
- Enter the TS-park and ask park manager for an assessment of his park, or attempt to get an assessment of the TS-park from the tenants.
- Ask former tenants, who have already left the TS-park, their view of the support they received when they were located on the TS-park.
- Evaluate the success of the TS-parks and their tenants by means of an external assessment.

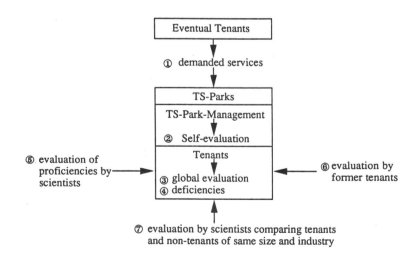

Figure 16.3
Evaulating the success of TS-parks

• Last, but not least, compare TS-park tenant firms with comparative off-park competitors.

These are the tasks that we will undertake to get a valid impression of success, proficiencies and deficiencies associated with a TS-park location.

PROPERTIES OF THE TENANT FIRMS

What do we know about a typical tenant firm?

Although there is much statistical data available, we are content with the findings of Sternberg's investigation (1988) and the work of Steinkühler (1989). Figure 16.4 indicates the main results.

The typical tenant seems to be a small enterprise, very often founded by one or two academics. Having left the university, these academics are typically joined by other junior staff (e.g. graduates). One cannot expect these entrepreneurs to already possess solid business experience. However, they compensate for this lack of experience by enthusiastically going about their work. They prefer independence and entrepreneurial autonomy in their home town, to dependency and working as an employee for a larger firm in another town or region. We suppose that their firms receive their first customer orders partly as a result of minimal social and physical distance from their home-town customers. One may speculate that most of these tenants are service firms, selling industrial products which command high profit margins.

THE PROPERTIES AND PERFORMANCE OF TS-PARKS – AS SEEN BY TENANTS AND MANAGEMENT

Other surveys have provided data on demands of tenants for the services of TS-parks (Allen and Rhaman, 1985; Monck et al., 1988; Smilor, 1987; Steinkühler, 1989; Sternberg, 1988). We can divide these into four groups (see Figure 16.5). Firstly basic support services that are provided by all parks to a certain extent. We call them 'facilities support'.

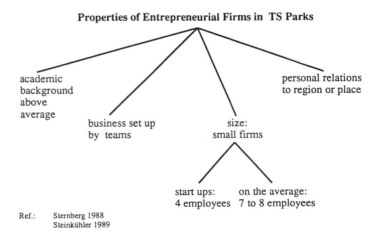

Figure 16.4
Properties of tenant firms

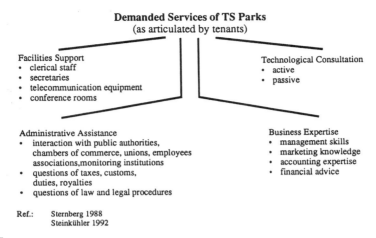

Figure 16.5
Tenants' demands

On top of that most parks provide 'administrative assistance' through the TS-park man-ager's expertise and or that of his/her team. It helps the often inexperienced founders of companies to deal with authorities and banks, and in getting access to public subsidies. A third and fourth category are consulting services in technical and business questions. These services are sometimes provided by third parties with the TS-park manager being an agent. Whilst the first two categories of services are provided almost everywhere, the latter two differ a lot both in quality and quantity from park to park.

Relevant research has evaluated the relationships between the success of TS-parks and their characteristics. It is interesting to note that this type of assessment reveals that strategic aspects are related to success, rather than operational factors (see Figure 16.6). According to these findings, there are three necessary criteria for the success of TS-park management: provision of space, expertise and personal management skills of TS-park managers. Apart from these 'TS-park management factors', a fourth 'external' factor is

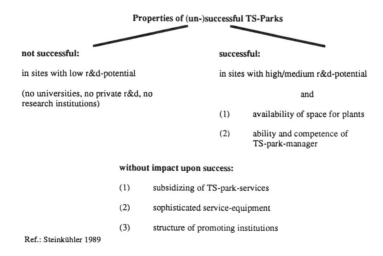

Figure 16.6
Conditions for success

also a pre-requisite for success: the choice of location. If the town/region lacks a certain level of R&D potential or infrastructure (measured by the number of employees in public and private R&D), even the best TS-park management cannot make it a success. On the other hand it is interesting to observe that the rendering of the following services do not seem to be necessary conditions for success, i.e. growth/attractiveness of TS-parks does not significantly differ for the following variables:

- Subsidies do not help to attract a higher number of tenants.
- The degree of provision of special sophisticated services does not enhance the park's attractiveness.
- The structure of promoting institutions does not matter. Parks with public partners only are as successful in acquiring tenants as parks that include private partners.

In summation, success is not dependent upon a sophisticated network of services, but on a robust and simple promotion programme.

HOW USEFUL ARE THE TS-PARKS?

Initially, a global assessment of success, as articulated by tenants in TS-parks, is provided by Sternberg (1989, p. 687). In this study tenants see the following advantages (in order of the importance) (see also Figure 16.7):

1. Reduction of overhead costs, namely administrative costs.
2. Establishing good contact with other tenants, thus enabling an informal exchange of experience on foundation problems, and other formation issues. The status of these other tenants as suppliers or clients is of no importance.
3. Better access to public subsidies. Here they refer to the transfer of the positive TS-park image as a help towards making contacts with banks and venture capital suppliers.
4. A better general image for the company through its location in a TS-park; this being a help in establishing contacts with customers and suppliers.
5. Better access to consultation.
6. Better access to R&D institutions and their personnel.
7. An offer of flexible space provision in case of an increase or decrease in employment.

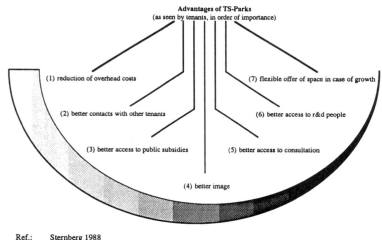

Ref.:   Sternberg 1988

Figure 16.7
Advantages of TS-parks

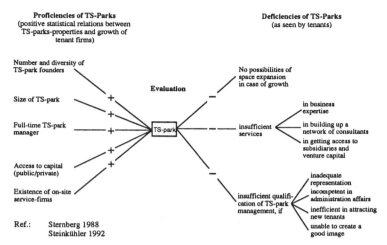

Figure 16.8
Proficiencies and deficiencies of TS-parks

It should be emphasized that, apart from instances where solid cost advantages apply, the personally based cooperation between TS-park tenants seems to be the most important advantage of a TS-park location.

Based on Sternberg's results, a recent survey undertaken at our institute by Steinkühler (1992) provided a somewhat more differentiated assessment of the proficiencies and deficiencies of the Science Parks. We then correlated properties of the Science Parks with performance measures. This provides a picture which refines the above results (see Figure 16.8).

Tenants naming deficiencies grouped them into the following categories (Sternberg, 1989, p. 687):

- No possibility for space expansion in case of growth.
- Insufficient services, i.e. lack of business expertise, inability to build up network of consultants, and no opportunity to gain access to subsidies and venture capital.
- In particular: underqualification of the TS-park management was a major factor (i.e. inadequate representation, incompetence in administrative affairs, inefficiency in attracting new tenants, and inability to create a good TS-park image). We have consciously exaggerated these deficiencies here, since they normally do not coincide and occur in all cases.

The above mentioned assessments have the disadvantage that they were observed by persons who work in TS-parks. Therefore, it can be presumed that they might tend to evaluate the TS-parks more positively than people who are not – or no longer – concerned with a TS-park. This is why our critical examination must extend beyond the approaches used so far. In this aspect, our survey takes two additional steps: first a survey of former tenants; second a comparison of tenant firms of the same size and industry, that have not benefited from a TS-park location.

Let us present some of the findings of these two investigations. Our assessment of the opinions of former tenants reveals the following trends (see Figure 16.9):

- Former tenants considered it to be an important advantage that the TS-parks provide standardized facilities, that they enable contact with other tenants facing the same or similar problems, and that they transmit the TS-park's positive image to the tenant's business partners.

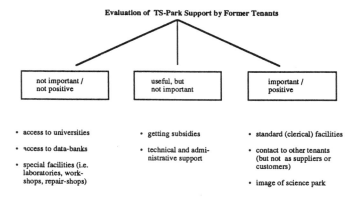

not important / not positive	useful, but not important	important / positive
• access to universities • access to data-banks • special facilities (i.e. laboratories, work- shops, repair-shops)	• getting subsidies • technical and admi- nistrative support	• standard (clerical) facilities • contact to other tenants (but not as suppliers or customers) • image of science park

Ref.:   Steinkühler 1992

Figure 16.9
Evaulation by former tenants

- Former tenants considered to be useful, but not very important, that there is access to subsidies provided, as well as technical and administrative support. Possibly, the experience they have now accumulated has made the tenants forget the problems they were confronted with when they were still helpless beginners.
- It is remarkable that the following services were considered not to be important:
  - access to universities (most of the tenants are graduates, and therefore may be self-sufficient);
  - access to data banks (which were hardly used anyway);
  - contact with suppliers or customers (something which every company has to seek out itself);
  - special facilities, such as laboratories, workshops or repair shops (these are not tailored to the special demand of the different tenants concerned).

According to our survey, the following properties of TS-parks have been detected as proficiencies for former tenants:

- The number and the diversity of science park sponsors: the interaction of at least three particular groups seems to be advantageous (i.e. the local economy, local authorities and local scientific institutions).
- Larger TS-parks were judged more successful. This raises a question about the optimum range of influence and about competition among TS-parks. Furthermore, the size of a TS-park correlates with other factors that influence success (e.g. the size of university towns).
- The existence of full-time TS-park managers. This reveals the great importance of the management component. The management of a TS-park is not a casual job.
- The offer of venture capital was judged to be important by former tenants. Again it becomes evident that the performance of the TS-park requires the interaction of all production factors.
- Establishment of service firms inside or close to the TS-park. It is not absolutely necessary that these service firms (workshops, consultants, emergency services) are located inside the TS-park. But naturally, they must be accessible.

Finally, we should ask ourselves whether the science park tenants are more successful with regard to their growth by comparing them with companies similar in size and sector. At first glance, the results are not very exciting: the tenants in TS-parks tend to show marginally stronger growth (sales growth +33% per year, reference group +24%) (see Figure 16.10).

At second glance, however, it is worthwhile noting that the variance in the results is much larger within the group of tenant companies, than in the reference group. Inside the TS-park-group, we find many 'strong companies that are growing extremely fast compared to the reference group, but there are also some 'weak' companies that show very slow growth. The outside companies are much more homogenous in respect to their success. This leads to the suggestion that the growth of 'promising' companies is accelerated by the TS-park, and that the park's support makes them much more successful compared to firms outside the park. It is also probable that 'weak' firms with a low potential for success are 'propped up' in the TS-park and given help to survive for rather a long time, whereas they would have been out of the market already if founded without TS-park help (Storey and Strange, 1992, p. 26).

In search of the reasons for success in the TS-park group, factors that explain the huge variance between 'weak' and 'strong' firms, three groups of main causes can be distinguished, which also correlate:

- It is in fact the services of the TS-parks that are of use to such companies. It can be proven that the companies surveyed make much more extensive use of consultants than comparable firms do. What is more, they are less experienced than comparable companies and apparently need more help in administration and business.
- However, it is already essential for the success of tenant firms that they were chosen for the TS-parks. The process of selection naturally singles out the most promising firms. This successful examination could be based on the fact that they are better at planning and have a more long-term foresight. Academics are preferred, since they usually come directly from the university with new technical ideas. Indeed on the whole, the selection committees make a wise choice.
- Finally, the behaviour patterns of the tenant firms influence their success. They are capable of better post-formation planning and long-term foresight, which was noted above as influencing their initial selection for the TS-park. Furthermore, they have better connections with local R&D institutions and personnel. Once again, the academics have an advantage here.

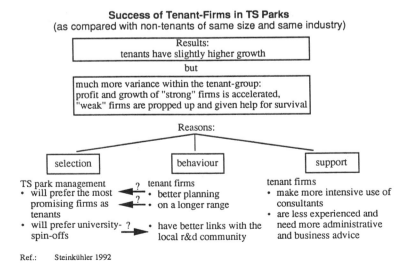

Figure 16.10
Comparisons with non-tenants

If we sum up the overall results from a complex, statistical evaluation, it reveals a completely autonomous and statistically significant influence of the TS-parks on the performance of the tenant firms.

This, then, is the answer to our initial questions: generally it is worthwhile for a company to be a tenant of a TS-park. On average, their size and their growth do not especially differ from companies that are forced to develop on the open market. However, the strong companies have a much better opportunity to develop, and the weak firms are given better chances of survival.

IS THE TS-PARK MODEL ADVISABLE?

Even if the value of TS-parks to business development seems less doubtful now, so far nothing has been said about the assessment of the cost benefits of TS-parks for local authorities and the local industry.

Towns and communities regard the TS-park as an instrument of local economic policy. In Germany, the local authorities are actively involved in about 80% of these centres. They see the chance to improve the regional economic structure through TS-parks. However, they accept that they cannot expect them to provide a short-term solution to all local economic problems. The creation of employment through innovative companies is a long-term issue for everybody. However, one word of warning: it is particularly true that communities in structurally weak regions have great (or even too great) expectations of their TS-parks. They hope to improve their situation in competition with other locations/communitites, and to contribute to the reduction of unemployment.

Critics of the TS-park concept raise the following objections (Steinkühler, 1989, p. 6):

- The employment situation will not improve considerably since the firms are too small.
- The companies privatize the subsidies they receive and thus fund their private costs with public capital.
- Companies that would normally be unable to survive are artificially maintained.
- If the economy slows down, the TS-park will be unable to attract new tenants.
- Finally, a new kind of competition between communities is likely to arise. The towns may seek to outbid each other in offering subsidies. However, it should be noted that TS-parks can only operate successfully in places which already have strong local industrial and scientific infrastructures. Thus, the prosperity of TS-parks might not reduce regional disparities, but increase them.

Local industry also has mixed feelings towards TS-parks. On the one hand, the regions's attractiveness and the economic environment for customer-supplier relations will undergo an improvement. On the other hand, it is evident that the TS-parks represent subsidized competition, and this public financial support puts the established companies at a disadvantage.

These reflections exceed by far the ability of this paper to provide answers to all of the issues raised. From our point of view, however, we can only offer a general word of warning that it is not advisable to found TS-parks far away from established economic centres and local industries.

TS-PARKS: A MODEL OF DEVELOPMENT FOR EASTERN EUROPE?

The transition from a socialistic economy to a market economy may require the establishment of TS-parks. At first glance, it seems to be an ideal instrument for the promotion of young entrepreneurs, and the promotion of young entrepreneurs is a precondition for operation of a market economy. However, our experience in Western Europe gives a clear warning of the need to observe the conditions for success when establishing such TS-parks.

In establishing TS-parks it is advisable to locate them:

• in towns with active local authorities and one or several scientific institutions and local industries,
• where an energetic and qualified manager for a TS-park can be found,
• where robust and simple facilities can be provided,
• where venture capital can be raised,
• where there is enough space for developing companies.

The lack of personal resources could be a bottleneck in the management of such a park, and, as far as may be possible, this missing factor can be provided by a TS-park environment.

REFERENCES

ALLEN, D. N. and RAHMAN, S. (1985) Small business incubators: a positive environment for entrepreneurship, *Journal of Small Business Management*, Vol. 23, no. 3, pp.12-22.

DOSE, N. and DREXLER, A. (eds.) (1988) *Technologieparks: Voraussetzungen, Bestandsaufnahme und Kritik*, Opladen.

HISRICH, R. D. (1988) New business formation through the enterprise development center: a model for new venture creation, *IEEE Transactions on Engineering Management*, Vol. 35, no. 4, pp. 221-31.

MONCK, C. S. P. et al. (1988) *Science Parks and the Growth of High Technology Firms*, Croom Helm, London, New York, Sydney.

SMILOR, R. W. (1987) Commercializing technology through new business incubators, *Research Management*, Vol. 30, no. 5, pp. 36-41.

STEINKÜHLER, R. H. (1989) *Konzeptionen und Erfolgsbeurteilung von Technologiezentrums-Modellen*, Unpublished Master Thesis, Kiel.

STEINKÜHLER, R. H. (1992) *Technologiezentren und Gründungserfolg technologieorientierter Unternehmen*, Diss. Kiel.

STERNBERG, R. (1988) *Technologie- und Gründerzentren als Instrument kommunaler Wirt-schafts-förderung*, Dortmunder Verlag für Bau-und Planungslitératur.

STERNBERG, R. (1989) Innovation centres and their importance for the growth of new technology-based firms: experience gained from the Federal Republic of Germany, *Technovation*, Vol. 9, pp. 681-94.

STOREY, D. J. and STRANGE, A. (1992) Where are they now? Some changes in firms located on UK Science Parks in 1986, *New Technology, Work and Employment*, Vol. 7, no. 1, pp. 15-28.

WIRTSCHAFTSWOCHE (1992) no. 48 dd., 20 November, p. 108.

CHAPTER 17

Policies and Founder Characteristics of New Technology-Based Firms (NTBFs): A Comparison Between British and Indian Firms

MATHEW J. MANIMALA

INTRODUCTION

Though there has been considerable interest in high-technology-based firms (Cooper, 1970; 1973; 1986), specific research focus on new technology-based firms (NTBFs) is less common. The reason may be that many of the attributes of high-tech firms are equally applicable to NTBFs. Take, for example, one of the recent definitions of high-tech firms as those firms having a stronger than usual focus on scientific discovery, innovation and R&D, and therefore characterized by highly volatile environments, unstable workforces, simultaneous demands for flexibility and tight controls, and so on (Gomez-Mejia and Lawless, 1990).

Prior research has identified a few characteristics that are special for high-tech enterprises. Some of these findings imply that it would be more successful to have high-tech or new technology operations organized as entrepreneurial ventures. Some of these characteristics identified in the literature are listed below:

- The need for high degrees of integration both at strategy (Grant et al., 1991) and at operational (Hayes and Jaikumar, 1988; Florida, 1991) levels.
- The need for collaboration among several individuals, agencies and organizations for technology development and commercialization (Freund, 1990; Mock, 1991; Wissema and Eusser, 1991; Manimala and Pearson, 1991).
- The greater degrees of uncertainty associated with new technologies and the consequent need for greater flexibility required for solving the emerging technological problems and securing customer acceptance (Chetty, 1990; Chein et al., 1990; Krishnamurthy, 1991; Meldrum and Millman, 1991).
- The greater susceptibility of new technologies to Murphy's Law that anything that can go wrong, will, and the consequent need for constant monitoring, especially with a view to overcoming customer resistance to new technologies (Chein et al.,1990).
- The special needs of the human factor at work vis-à-vis new technologies, their fears, misconceptions, their obsolescence and the consequent need for retraining and redeployment, and so on (Ettkin et al., 1990; Betcherman, 1991; Thomas, 1991; Cunningham et al., 1991; Hackett, 1991; Krishna, 1991; Yuen, 1990).
- The lethargy and the 'not-invented-here' attitude of large organizations (Drucker, 1985) especially the publicly held ones (Rose and Joskow, 1990), and their resultant inability to make use of the entrepreneurial opportunities presented by new technologies (Holmes and Schmitz, 1990).

The special nature of new technology-based operations as identified by various researchers shows the relative advantage of entrepreneurs over existing firms in successfully introducing new technologies. Hence there is a greater likelihood of NTBFs being entrepreneurial ventures. The need for studying the special characteristics of NTBFs and their founders is therefore evident. The present study is an attempt to identify the policies, traits, motives and background variables that may distinguish between the founders of new technology-based firms and those of old technology-based firms (OTBFs). Comparison is also made between British and Indian NTBFs.

METHODOLOGY

Data for this research were obtained through mailed survey from a sample of 90 British entrepreneurs and 68 Indian entrepreneurs. The questionnaire had five parts. Part 1 was on the general characteristics of the enterprise, part 2 on the policies of the enterprise, and parts 3-5 on the personality traits (personal policies), motives and background of the entrepreneurs respectively. All the data except the evidence on religion were collected on interval scale so that they were amenable to parametric statistical processing.

The sample was classified into NTBFs and OTBFs based on their main products. Firms operating in the fields of electronics, robotics, bio-technology, computer software, lasers, etc. were classified as new technology based-firms. There were 32 such firms among the 90 British firms. The Indian sample was smaller than the British. Of the 68 firms which responded, 20 were classified as NTBFs.

Analysis of the data was done in two stages. In the first stage, NTBFs were compared with OTBFs separately for the British and Indian firms. The second stage involved a comparison between NTBFs of Britain and NTBFs of India. The distinguishing variables emerging in both cases were factor-analysed to find out the major dimensions of the differences between the respective groups. Discriminatory powers of these dimensions were also tested.

FINDINGS: BRITISH NTBFs Vs OTBFs

NTBFs of Britain (N=32) were compared with OTBFs of the same country (N=58) in terms of the policies of the venture and the traits, motives and background of their founders. In the t-test, twelve variables emerged as significantly different. All of them were significant at p≤0.05. Out of the 12 variables, 4 related to policies, 4 to traits and a further 4 to background variables. There was no difference between motives (see Table 17.1). A brief discussion of their implications is given below.

Motives

It is interesting to note that none of the motives were significantly different for the two groups, implying that entrepreneurial motives may not be a factor influencing the choice of technology. The latter is not even related to one's need to do something new and 'leading edge', since the difference between the two groups was negligible. The means differed by -0.030, which is virtually no difference at all. The reason seems to be that for a person to do something new and 'leading edge', it is not essential that such a strategy should be based on new technology. In other words, innovation is not dependent on technology alone. There are so many other areas in which an entrepreneur can (and does) innovate, an observation suggested by an earlier study by this author (Manimala, 1992a). The choice of a new technology may not be influenced by one's desire to innovate. It may largely be on account of having had opportunities to be familiar with a new technology. The significant observed difference in the length of previous employment (see B9 in Table 17.1), with founders of NTBFs having longer experience, is probably an indication of this phenomenom.

Table 17.1: *NTBFs V. OTBFs of Britain:variables that are significantly different for the two groups*

VARIABLE NO. AND DESCRIPTION	MEAN FOR BRITISH OTBFs (N=58)	MEAN FOR BRITISH NTBFs (N=32)	T	P
(i) Policies (P)				
P1 Preference for tried and tested products	4.45	3.69	1.95	0.050
P4 Changing goals for profitable opportunities	4.98	4.06	2.43	0.017
P17 Adherence to strict rules and procedures and non-tolerance of experimentation	3.35	2.56	2.16	0.034
P22 Close supervision and punishing deviations	4.72	3.84	2.32	0.022
(ii) Traits (T)				
T1 Lack of scruples	3.28	2.38	2.46	0.016
T5 Difficulty with unstructured situations (need for structure)	3.85	3.13	2.10	0.039
T18 Challenge in doing difficult tasks	5.43	4.78	2.45	0.016
T19 Complacency about the knowledge of business, and aversion to learning	2.33	1.78	2.28	0.025
(iii) Motives (M) None of the motives was significantly different for the two groups				
(iv) Background variables (B)*				
B9 Length of work experience as employee	3.91	4.43	−2.01	0.047
B12 Family affluence during childhood	4.39	3.80	2.10	0.032
B16 Deep interest in a variety of activities during childhood	5.65	4.80	2.73	0.008
B22 Entrepreneurship through purposeful action	5.67	4.90	2.29	0.024

* The group sizes for this analysis were 54 for OTBFs and 30 for NTBFs.

Policies

The four policy variables that were shown to be significantly different for the two groups were: (a) a preference for tried and tested products, (b) changing goals to accommodate emerging profitable opportunities, (c) adherence to strict rules and procedures permitting very little experimentation, and (d) close supervision with a view to correcting and punishing deviations. The first of these was expected as the classification itself was based on product information. In any case product and technology choices cannot be independent of each other, as was also shown in the author's earlier study (Manimala, 1992a) where both product and process innovations were shown as part of operations innovation.

The second policy that shows difference (P4) suggests that the founders of NTBFs have developed a special interest in, and a love for, the product/technology of their choice, and that their goals are likely to be tied up with their product/technology choices. This is probably why they are reluctant to change their lines/goals even when opportunities present themselves in other products or technologies. Or it may be because these entrepreneurs have their basic competencies in these technologies and so would feel diffident about maintaining the quality of products and services in a different field. Alternatively, they may not enjoy working in any other fields at all. Hence these opportunities may not be presenting any real opportunities for them.

The third and fourth variables in this group (P17 and P22) obviously relate to the way that human resources are controlled in the organization. It is natural that NTBFs cannot become rigid about their rules and procedures. Since the technology is new and probably evolving, there is scope for some experimentation, which has to be allowed. In short, entrepreneurs are obliged to grant autonomy to the people involved, and so close supervision and punishments for deviations are likely to become counter-productive. This conforms with the findings of Burns and Stalker (1961) who observed that an organic structure based on flexibility and autonomy at lower levels is more appropriate in a dynamic environment. Clearly, NTBFs are operating in a technologically dynamic environment.

Traits

Of the four significantly different traits discovered, two are easily explainable. Founders of OTBFs have a higher need for structure. Similarly, their disagreement with the complacency statement is not as strong as that of the founders of NTBFs. These are to be expected because new technologies involve uncertainties and new firms will not be able to easily structure their organisations. Moreover, one cannot be complacent about knowledge in the field, but must keep oneself abreast of the evolving technology.

The two other significant traits are more difficult to explain. One of them is that the founders of NTBFs expressed a stronger disagreement with the statement that everything is fair in business as long as it produces results. It is rather difficult to explain why NTBFs should be more ethical than OTBFs. It may be because of the longer association of the founders of NTBFs with professional organizations as employees (see Table 17.1, section on background). Another supporting factor from the background is the finding that the founders of NTBFs were not as strong as those of OTBFs in their desire to become entrepreneurs through purposeful action. It appears that they are not as 'entrepreneurial' as their OTBF counterparts. They seem more akin to the 'inventor-tinkerer' category of entrepreneurs identified in an earlier study (Manimala, 1988). They are scientists, professionals, inventors, etc. in the first place, and have become entrepreneurs because of some opportunities or constraints experienced in their areas of expertise. They are therefore likely to score lowly in terms of the 'entrepreneurial attitude' of getting things done by whatever means.

The last of the significant trait variables is the attitude of respondents towards difficult, and therefore challenging, tasks. OTBFs are more inclined to take up such tasks, which, as observed above, is somewhat difficult to explain. It is more logical to think that it would be more challenging to build an enterprise based on a new technology than to build a conventional enterprise. The logical force of this argument is likely to be derived from an 'actor-observer' bias (Bruno and Tyebjee, 1982). From the NTBF entrepreneur's point of view, managing the new technology may not be a challenge at all because, as we have observed above, he is probably an expert technician in the new field. Since he is likely to be less of an entrepreneur the real challenge would be in the entrepreneurial function of gaining and retaining a position in the market. The latter part is probably taken care of because the 'technician' was 'induced' to become an entrepreneur by a market opportunity. Besides, as we have noted above, a new technology-based firm is also likely to have a new product which would easily secure a market niche for the firm. On the other hand, when an entrepreneur is in the field with a 'me-too' product, which is often the case with OTBFs, the task of creating and maintaining a position for oneself in the market can be formidable. It may be with reference to this task that the founders of OTBFs show a greater degree of enthusiasm in accomplishing challenging and difficult tasks. In fact, an earlier study by this author observed that entrepreneurs choosing new products (or new technology, by the extension of the argument) do so in order to avoid competition (Manimala, 1992b). They are risk-managers or risk-avoiders rather than risk-takers. This may be the reason for the founders of NTBFs stating that they are relatively less enthusiastic toward the taking up of difficult and challenging jobs.

Background variables

Of the four background variables showing significant difference, two have been mentioned above in support of the differences in other variables. It was noted that the length of previous experience as employees was longer in the case of NTBF founders. Similarly, their current status as entrepreneurs is the result of less purposeful action than in the case of OTBF founders. It appears that NTBF entrepreneurs were motivated more by a desire to be technicians than to be entrepreneurs. Their need for job satisfaction in terms of the development of new technology seems to be comparatively high, and indeed, they would have continued to pursue this goal in their previous employment, but for some constraints therein or opportunities outside. To this extent there is probably a chance element in their decision to become entrepreneurial. It may also be inferred that there is a greater scope for an incubator phase (Smilor and Gill, 1986) in the formation of NTBFs, when compared with the OTBFs' case.

Two other background variables sharing significant difference between the two groups are 'affluence during childhood' and 'deep interest in a variety of activities during childhood'. In both these instances, the founders of OTBFs are significantly more prevalent than the founders of NTBFs. It may be hypothesized that deep interest in a single activity would lead to specialization, whereas deep interest in a variety of activities would stimulate generalist tendencies. Founders of NTBFs are more likely to be specialists in the technology concerned, which might be a major reason for their venturing into the new technology. The influence of material welfare or the lack of it during childhood on the choice of technologies is difficult to explain. It may be that the more affluent individuals might have had better opportunitites for getting involved in a variety of activities and thus to develop generalist tendencies. Alternatively, the enterprising individual with adequate financial support need not go through a long period of employment before he/she could start his/her own venture. As we have observed above, employment with other firms seems to be an important means for a person to acquire new technologies. Affluence in childhood could be a possible explanation for the differences.

Distinguishing factors

The 12 variables that were significantly different between NTBFs and OTBFs were factor-analysed using data from the 84 British respondents who gave information on all variables. There were 6 factors that differed between NTBF and OTBF founders. Juxtaposing these factors with the group means and t-values discussed above, it may be hypothesized that the founders of NTBFs, in comparison with those of OTBFs, are more likely to be low on the following factors:

• Need for structure,
• Opportunism,
• Entrepreneurial interests,
• Affluence during childhood,
• Beaten path orientation, and
• Complacency about the knowledge of one's business.

FINDINGS: INDIAN NTBFs vs OTBFs

The Indian NTBFs seem to be much less differentiated from their OTBF counterparts, when compared with the differences between British NTBFs and OTBFs. In the case of the Indian data, there were three policies, one motive, and one background variable which were significantly different. The t-values and the significance levels of these variables are given in Table 17.2. The fewer number of distinguishing characteristics may be

Table 17.2: *NTBFs VS OTBFs of India:variables that are significantly different for the two groups*

VARIABLE NO. AND DESCRIPTION		MEAN FOR INDIAN OTBFs (N=48)	MEAN FOR INDIAN NTBFs (N=20)	T	P
(i)	Policies				
P1	Preference for tried and tested products	4.71	3.65	2.18	0.036
P7	Talent search and recruiting the best	6.00	5.30	1.92	0.062
P14	Quality at any cost	6.38	5.80	1.98	0.057
(ii)	Traits				
	None of the traits was significantly different at p ≤ 0.10.				
(iii)	Motives				
M10	Deontic motive	5.31	4.30	2.38	0.020
(iv)	Background variables				
B14	Parental care	5.90	4.68	2.89	0.005

indicative of the different conditions under which NTBFs have to operate in the two countries. This is especially true in terms of differences in political environments.

However, one of the distinguishing policy variables is common with the British NTBFs, which is that their 'preference' for tried and tested products and services is weaker for Indian NTBFs than in the case of OTBFs. This may be due to the association between new technology and new products. Alternatively, as we have suggested above, the choice of a new technology may be an outcome of the desire to avoid competition through product novelty or differentiation.

The two other policies that are different are apparently not in conformity with general expectations. OTBFs are more keen on recruiting the best people and maintaining quality at any cost. This may be because in a developing country like India, talents in the new technologies may not be available, and the entrepreneur himself may be one of the best in the field. As for quality, there may not be comparable standards in the country and therefore there may not be any deliberate attempt to keep oneself above an external benchmark. Besides, the lower degrees of competition in the new field would imply that the pressures for maintaining quality may not be as high as in the case of OTBFs.

The motive that emerged as significantly different is the deontic motive. Unlike in the case of British entrepreneurs, the deontic motive was relatively high in the Indian sample, which was to be expected because of the stronger emphasis in oriental cultures on obligations based on loyalties, relationships and prior benefits received. The difference discussed here, however, is not the one between the Indian and the British sample but the one between Indian NTBFs and Indian OTBFs. The deontic motive is higher for the OTBFs. This is possibly because the founders of NTBFs are likely to be driven more by a love for the new technology and the work involved than by a sense of duty. Thus, though duty consciousness may be a general trait of the Indian entrepreneur, apparently it tends to diminish when a person founds a business on the basis of new technologies. However, the inverse may also be true. Does duty-consciousness make the individual act in a particular fashion and restrain him/her from innovating or adopting new technologies?

The last of the distinguishing variables is a background variable. The founders of NTBFs had received lesser degrees of parental care during their childhood. It may be noted that similar observations have been made about entrepreneurs in general (McClelland, 1961). However, no such pattern was observed with regard to the British entrepreneurs in this study. Neither the NTBF founders nor the OTBF founders in the British sample had experienced parental neglect in childhood. There has been, however, an experience of lower degrees of affluence among the British NTBF founders. It appears that innovativeness or adoption of new technologies rather than entrepreneurship per se is associated with conditions of deprivation in childhood.

FINDINGS: BRITISH NTBFs vs INDIAN NTBFs

This section is based on a comparison between the 32 British NTBFs and the 20 Indian NTBFs. There were 12 policy variables, 14 trait variables, 8 motive variables and 8 background variables which were significantly different for the two groups. These differences are likely to be due to the fact that the respondents were Indians and Britons, rather than managers of Indian and British NTBFs.

Four factors emerged from the 12 distinguishing policies. They were named as follows:

- Theory-X orientation,
- Managing risks through information processing,
- Capability building, and
- Financial resource orientation.

The Indian NTBFs had higher scores on all 3 except capability building. It looks as though the Indians are more rigid, cautious and concerned about finances, but less interested in developing organizational capabilities. Alternatively, there seems to be a lack of information, opportunities and resources in the country.

The 14 distinguishing traits also got grouped into 4 factors, which were named as follows:

- Need for structure and conformity,
- Self-confidence,
- Self-employment orientation due to a dislike for authority, and
- Hard-work orientation.

The first two were higher for the Indian NTBFs and the second two were higher for the British firms.

The distinguishing motives also had 4 factors, which were:

- Status motive,
- Self-development motive,
- Super-ordinate motive, and
- Deontic motive.

On all these 4 motive factors, the founders of the Indian NTBFs scored higher.

Finally, there were 3 factors for the distinguishing background variables which were named as follows:

- Psychological deprivations and disappointments,
- Family affluence and nature of previous work, and
- Personal interests and choices.

Founders of British NTBFs had higher scores only on the first of these, implying that entrepreneurship in India, even in the case of NTBFs, is largely hereditary. The founders of Indian NTBFs had greater self-employment traditions in their ancestral families, had experienced greater affluence during childhood, had shorter stints as employees, and had more opportunities to pursue their interests and choices.

Combined factors of differences

The first-stage factors from the 4 variable groups of policies, traits, motives and background variables were factor-analysed again to derive the combined factors of differences. There were 5 of them which were named as follows (see Table 17.3 for details):

- Extrinsic orientation
- Self-worth orientation
- Risk-taking and management
- Work orientation
- Financial resource orientation.

The Indian NTBFs seem to operate more on the basis of external referral points. Social recognition and status, contribution to society, targets and standards, conformity to norms and procedures, etc. are indicative of this attitude. The second factor indicates a self-sufficiency feeling where importance is judged in terms of one's own interests and choices and a feeling of self-worth, even to the neglect of developing organizational capabilities. The third factor relates to the management of risks through information processing. The last two are work orientation, where the British NTBFs score higher, and financial resource orientation, where the Indians score higher.

Table 17.3: *British VS. Indian NTBFs:combined factor analysis of the 15 first-stage factors derived from the distinguishing policy, trait, motive and background variables (N=143)*

FINAL FACTOR NO.	FIRST STAGE FACTORS NO. AND DESCRIPTION		FACTOR LOADING		NAME GIVEN TO THE FINAL FACTOR
DF–I	P–I	Theory-X orientation	0.57	) (	
	T–I	Need for structure and conformity	0.66	) ( ) (	Extrinsic orientation
	T–II	Self-confidence	0.68	) ( ) (	
	M–I	Status motive	0.76	) ( ) (	
	M–II	Skill and target orientation	0.67	) ( ) (	
	M–III	Super-ordinate motive	0.65	) (	
DF–II	P–III	Capability building	–0.70	) (	
	M–IV	Deontic motive	0.58	) ( ) (	Self–worth orientation
	B–III	Personal interests and choices	0.56	) ( ) (	
DF–III	P–II	Managing risk through information processing	0.79	) ( ) (	
	T–III	Self-employment orientation due to a dislike for authority	–0.67	) ( ) ( ) (	Risk–taking and management
	B–I	Psychological deprivation and disappointments	–0.53	) ( ) ( ) (	
DF–IV	T–IV	Aversion to hard work	0.71	) ( ) (	Work orientation
DF–V	P–IV	Financial rather than human resource orientation	0.58	) ( ) ( ) (	Financial resource orientation
	B–II	Family affluence and nature of previous work experience	–0.70	) (	

The power of these 5 factors to discriminate between Indian and British NTBFs was tested through a discriminant analysis. Ninety-two per cent of the respondents were correctly classified, the relative importance of the factors moving from Factor-I to Factor-V in that order. As we have hypothesized earlier, the differences between the Indians and the British were stronger than those between NTBFs and OTBFs. The misclassification in the case of British NTBFs and OTBFs was 28% and that in the case of Indian NTBFs and OTBFs was 33%. Apparently, therefore, the cultural differences are stronger than the differences caused by the choice of technology.

CONCLUSION

Although the differences between Indian and British NTBFs should be attributed largely to the cultural differences, and not necessarily to the technology choices, some of these differences, read with the differences between NTBFs and OTBFs of both the countries, may give rise to certain issues which have policy implications for a developing country like India. A few such issues and their policy implications are briefly mentioned below.

- The relatively low proportion of NTBFs in the Indian sample, their weaker desire to acquire technical knowledge or recruit the best people for developing organizational capabilities, their greater dependence on extrinsic factors to promote their business, etc. suggest that opportunities of technical education are limited in the country. In fact, the present government policy in India is biased in favour of a heavily subsidised general education, which may also be a reason for the founders of Indian NTBFs having higher levels of education than their British counterparts. There has to be a decisive shift in the Indian educational policy in favour of promoting technical and trade-related education which would help the country, not only to keep abreast of the technological developments, but also to evolve indigenously appropriate technologies so that a culture of assimilation and development would replace the culture of continuous borrowing.
- One of the most important stimuli for continuous innovation, especially in the area of developing new technologies, processes and products based on them, is to create a moderately high degree of competition between enterprises. The liberalisation process, initiated in India during recent years, is a step in the right direction. The pace and extent of reforms, however, does not seem to be adequate.
- Founders of British NTBFs were observed to have had longer periods of incubation in existing organizations. In India, such opportunities were curtailed because of the government's policies of deliberately restricting large firms, especially foreign ones, who might play a very vital role of transferring technology to indigenous entrepreneurs and thereby assist the formation of NTBFs (Manimala, 1992c). The experience of countries like Malaysia and South Korea has shown the efficacy of this model of technology transfer (Jha, 1985). It is high time that the Indian government also lifted restrictions on the operations of large, especially foreign, firms in India.
- Availability of venture capital seems to be a problem in India, as indicated by the NTBF entrepreneur's greater inclination for choosing partners for capital contribution. There is a need for the creation of, and/or the promotion of, professionally managed venture capital firms.
- Finally, it should cause some concern that two major characteristics of Indian NTBF entrepreneurs are a higher degree of theory-X orientation (i.e. a strict adherence to rules and procedures and aversion to experimentation) and a greater need for structure and conformity. The latter is likely to have restrictive influences on the entrepreneur's own creativity and the former on his subordinates'. There is therefore a need for changing the general (Manimala, 1992c) and formative (McClelland, 1961) environments which are instrumental in creating such attitudes in the individual. The primary target in an Indian context, therefore, should be the education system which should be reoriented with greater emphasis on unstructured activities, divergent thinking, and a desire for exploration and constant improvement.

REFERENCES

BETCHERMAN, G. (1991) The effect of unions on the innovative behaviour of firms in Canada, *Industrial Relations Journal*, Vol. 22(2), pp. 142-51.

BRUNO, A. V. and TYEBJEE, T. T. (1982) The environment for entrepreneurship, in Kent et al. (eds.) *Encyclopaedia of Entrepreneurship*, Prentice-Hall, New Jersey.

BURNS, T. and STALKER, G. (1961) *The Management of Innovation*, Tavistock, London.

CHEIN, W. B., LEONARD, B. and BOHN, R. E. (1991) Beating Murphy's Law, *Sloan Management Review*, Vol. 32(3), pp. 5-16.

CHETTY, B. S. (1990) Reorientation of the manufacturing managers: agenda in the 1990s, *Indian Management*, Vol. 29(9), pp. 4-7.

COOPER, A. C. (1970) *The Founding of Technologically Based Firms*, The Centre for Venture Management, Milwaukee.

COOPER, A. C. (1973) Technical entrepreneurship: what do we know? *R&D Management*, Vol. 3, pp. 59-64.

COOPER, A. C. (1986) Entrepreneurship and high technology, in D. L. Sexton and R. W. Smilor (eds.) *The Art and Science of Entrepreneurship*, Ballinger, Cambridge: MA, pp. 153-68.

CUNNINGHAM, J. B., FARQUHARSON, J. and HULL, D. (1991) A profile of the human fears of technological change, *Technological Forecasting and Social Change*, Vol. 40(4), pp. 355-70.

DRUCKER, P. F. (1985) *Innovation and Entrepreneurship: Principles and Practices*, Heinemann, London.

ETTKIN, L. P., HELMS, M. M. and HAYNES, P. J. (1990) People: critical element of new technology implementation, *Industrial Management*, Vol. 32(5), pp. 27-9.

FLORIDA, R. (1991) The industrial revolution, *Futures*, Vol. 23(6), pp. 559-79.

FREUND, M. I. (1990) The cost of not investing in new technologies, *Financial Executive*, Vol. 6(6), p. 55.

GOMEZ-MEJIA, L. R. and LAWLESS, M. W. (eds.) (1990) *Organizational Issues in High Technology Management*, 2 vols, JAI Press, Greenwich, CT.

GRANT, R. M., KRISHNAN, R., SHANI, A. B. and BAER, R. (1991) Appropriate manufacturing technology: a strategic approach, *Sloan Management Review*, Vol. 33(1), pp. 43-54.

HACKETT, E. J. (1991) Women's and men's expectations about the effects of new technology at work, *Group and Organization Studies*, Vol. 16(1), pp. 60-85.

HAYES, R. H. and JAIKUMAR, R. (1988) Manufacturing crisis: new technologies, obsolete organizations, *Harvard Business Review*, Vol. 66(5), pp. 77-85.

HOLMES, T. J. and SCHMITZ, J. A. (1990) A theory of entrepreneurship and its application to the study of business transfers, *Journal of Political Economy*, Vol. 98(2), pp. 265-94.

JHA, P. S. (1985) Strategies of growth: where Korea took another path, *The Times of India* (Ahmedabad edition), 3 and 4 June.

KRISHNA, N. V. (1991) Human resource obsolescence in organizations: issues and strategies, *Indian Management*, Vol. 30(3), pp. 45-9.

KRISHNAMURTHY, H. (1991) Service sector in the 1990s: management issues, *Indian Management*, Vol. 30(3), pp. 3-6.

MANIMALA, M. J. (1988) Managerial Heuristics of Pioneering – Innovative (PI) Entrepreneurs: An Exploratory Study, Unpublished Doctoral Dissertation, Indian Institute of Management, Ahmedabad.

MANIMALA, M. J. (1992a) Entrepreneurial innovation: beyond Schumpeter, *Creativity and Innovation Management*, Vol. 1(1), pp. 46-55.

MANIMALA, M. J. (1992b) Entrepreneurial heuristics: a comparison between high PI (Pioneering Innovative) and low PI ventures, *Journal of Business Venturing*, Vol. 7(6), pp. 477-504.

MANIMALA, M. J. (1992c) Innovative entrepreneurship: testing the theory of environmental determinism, in B. L. Maheshwari (ed.) *Innovations in Management for Development*, Tata McGraw-Hill, New Delhi.

MANIMALA, M. J. and PEARSON, A. W. (1991) Hoyle Marine Ltd and the T-disc oil skimmer, Unpublished Case Study, Manchester Business School, Manchester: NIMTECH-LES.

MCCLELLAND, D. C. (1961) *The Achieving Society*, Van Nostrand, Princeton; NJ.

MELDRUM, M. J. and MILLMAN, A. F. (1991) Ten risks in the marketing of high-technology products, *Industrial Marketing Management*, Vol. 20(1), pp. 43-50.

MOCK, A. (1991) Globalization of technologies: strategy of industry, *Indian Management*, Vol. 30(8-9), pp. 70-82.

ROSE, N. L. and JOSKOW, P. L. (1990) The diffusion of new technologies: evidence from the electric utility industry, *The Rand Journal of Economics*, Vol. 21(3), pp. 354-73.

SMILOR, R. W. and GILL, M. D. JR (1986) *The New Business Incubator*, Lexington Books, Lexington, MA.

THOMAS, R. J. (1991) Technological choice and union management cooperation, *Industrial Relations*, Vol. 30(2), pp. 169-92.

WISSEMA, J. G. and EUSSER, L. (1991) Successful innovation through inter-company networks, *Long Range Planning*, Vol. 24(6), pp. 33-9.

YUEN, E. C. (1990) Human resource management in high and medium-technology companies, *Personnel Review*, Vol. 19(4), pp. 36-44.

CHAPTER 18

Regional Influences and Policy in New Technology-Based Firm Creation and Growth

DAVID KEEBLE

INTRODUCTION

Since at least the early 1980s, new technology-based firms (NTBFs) have been viewed in most western industrialised countries as a significant potential source of regional economic and employment growth. This perception, and associated regional and local policy interest, are based both on theoretical debates over the possible role of radical technological innovation and NTBFs as key components of a possible 5th Kondratieff long wave of western economic growth (Hall, 1981; Malecki, 1991, pp. 165-73) and the empirical evidence of dramatic NTBF development in particular regional environments such as Silicon Valley, California. By 1991, technology-based firms in this area were employing 275,000 workers in sectors such as computers, software, electronics, instrumentation, telecommunications, biotechnology and associated advanced business services.[1] In contrast to positive perceptions and USA experience, however, technology-based employment in most European countries has not grown substantially in recent years, 'high-technology' industry[2] employment in the UK, for example, actually falling by 137,000 jobs or 10.8% between 1981 and 1991 (see Table 18.1).

This reflects both steeply rising productivity and restructuring and cutbacks in defence-related sectors such as aerospace and military electronics. Within this context, this paper will review four themes concerning regional development and NTBFs. These focus on whether NTBF formation has been characterised by regional clustering, as in the Silicon Valley or Boston Route 128 models, or by spatial dispersion within an urban-rural framework; on the nature and relevance of the French concept of a territorial 'innovative milieu' (Aydalot, 1986; Aydalot and Keeble, 1988) as necessary or significant in successful NTBF creation and growth; on whether NTBFs offer any hope of economic growth for such 'hostile' regional environments as old nineteenth century 'smokestack' or peripheral less-industrialised regions; and on the role of national, regional and local policy in assisting successful local NTBF development.

NTBFS: REGIONAL CLUSTERING OR DISPERSION?

The experience of successful regional NTBF clusters such as Silicon Valley and Orange County, California, has led many observers to view NTBF development as intrinsically regionally uneven, and concentrated spatially in particular favourable environments.

While usually unplanned and the result of specific combinations of locally favourable circumstances, as in the Cambridge (Keeble, 1989) and Grenoble (Bernady and Boisgontier, 1988) cases, such clusters even appear to be capable of being created by

Table 18.1: *National and regional trends in high-technology industry employment in Great Britain, 1981-1991*

			TOTAL HIGH-TECHNOLOGY EMPLOYMENT	
	1981 '000	1991 '000	CHANGE, 1981–1991 '000	%
East Anglia	32.6	39.8	+7.2	+22.1
Wales	36.1	43.6	+7.5	+20.8
Yorkshire and Humberside	53.3	55.9	+2.6	+4.9
Scotland	90.5	89.2	−1.3	−1.4
South West	106.6	102.9	−3.7	−3.5
Rest of South East	323.9	307.1	−16.8	−5.2
North	49.0	45.6	−3.4	−6.9
East Midlands	81.5	73.8	−7.7	−9.5
North West	149.8	124.4	−25.4	−16.9
West Midlands	111.1	88.2	−22.9	−20.7
Greater London	220.9	163.3	−57.6	−26.1
Great Britain	1271.0	1113.9	−137.1	−10.8

Note: High technology industry is defined as SIC Activities 2514, 2515, 2570, 3301, 3302, 3420, 3441, 3442, 3443, 3444, 3453, 3640, 3710, 3720, 3732, 3733, 7902, 8394 and 9400.

Source: Unpublished Census of Employment statistics from NOMIS.

government policies, as with the Sophia-Antipolis 'technopolis' or science park near Nice on the French Cote d'Azur (Longhi and Quéré, 1993). By 1991, this park, set up on former scrubland near Valbonne in 1972 on the initiative of Pierre Lafitte, the locally-born Director of the French government Ecole des Mines, had attracted over 700 enterprises, most of which are NTBFs. Over 90% of Sophia-Antipolis firms have been set up there since 1980. By 1991, total employment was over 14,000 workers, the majority in high-technology activities such as electronics, computer sciences and telecommunications. While much employment is in research establishments set up by large national and international enterprises, there has also been a particularly rapid growth of new and small firms since 1986 (Longhi and Quéré, 1993, Table 1).

In contrast, however, to this 'orthodox' view of regional clustering, empirical evidence from several European countries now suggests that notwithstanding the relative success of these particular cases, the process of NTBF creation has in fact been markedly more spatially dispersed than clustered, as part of a broad 'urban-rural shift' of economic activity which has been under way, in Europe at least, ever since the 1970s (Keeble, Owens and Thompson, 1983; Townsend, 1993; Keeble, 1993; Keeble and Tyler, 1994). This dispersion is moreover true both for high-technology industry generally, involving large and small firms (Keeble, 1992), and for newly-created firms in particular. This is illustrated by Figures 18.1 and 18.2,[3] which show county-level trends in high-technology employment 1981-91 by an urban-rural classification, and the urban-rural distribution of a large (1,987 firms) sample of small and medium-sized enterprises drawn equally from manufacturing and business services surveyed by the Small Business Research Centre of Cambridge University (1992) in 1991, relative to those 183 firms in this sample which were new (founded 1980-91) high-technology enterprises. The latter shows the clear relative – and absolute – orientation of British NTBFs to small towns (1981 populations of between 10,000 and 149,999) and rural settlements (less than 10,000 population), rather than to Britain's major conurbations and large towns. Figure 18.3 shows the actual pattern of (mainly) rural counties recording the highest rates of growth of high technology employment in Britain between 1981 and 1991, these lying in two broad bands running from Suffolk and Cambridgeshire to North Yorkshire in the east, and from north to south Wales including adjacent Shropshire in the west. Volume increases and decreases in high technology employment are shown in Figure 18.4, which highlights the massive losses sustained by all Britain's major urban areas, notably London, Birmingham, Manchester and Liverpool. Finally, Figure 18.5 shows that the SBRC sample of new technology-based firms is widely dispersed throughout Britain, with only 4 counties (Greater London, Berkshire, Cheshire and Hertfordshire) possessing clusters of more than 5% of the total. Spatial dispersion or 'footlooseness' in NTBF creation, noted also

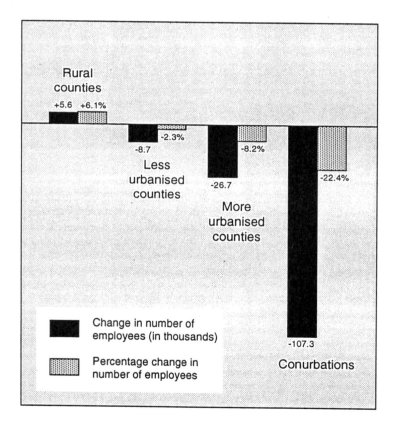

Figure 18.1
The urban-rural shift of high-technology industry employment in Britain, 1981–1991
Source: Unpublished Census of Employment statistics from NOMIS

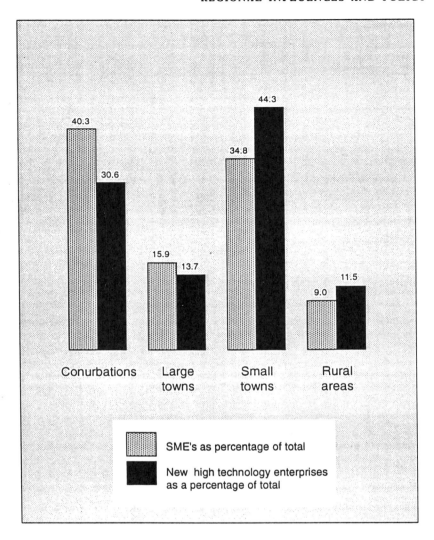

Figure 18.2
The urban-rural distribution of new high-technology and total SMEs in Britain, 1991
Source: Cambridge University Small Business Research Centre Survey, 1991

by Oakey and Cooper (1989) in the specific biotechnology case, is almost certainly true of other countries such as Germany and, perhaps, France. Its significance lies in the opportunities that it presents for small town and rural region development policy, especially in a European context of agricultural policy reform and consequent rural employment decline and economic restructuring.

NTBF's AND TERRITORIAL 'INNOVATIVE MILIEUX'

Recent French research by workers such as Aydalot (1986; see also Aydalot and Keeble, 1988) has proposed and developed the concept of a territorial 'innovative milieu' as a framework for understanding both successful and unsuccessful endogenous small firm high-technology growth in areas such as Grenoble, Sophia-Antipolis and Toulouse. The core characteristic of an 'innovative milieu' is a form of networking characterised both by vertical subcontracting chains and horizontal linkages with the providers of financial, technical, fashion, design, marketing and training services and advice. The consequent

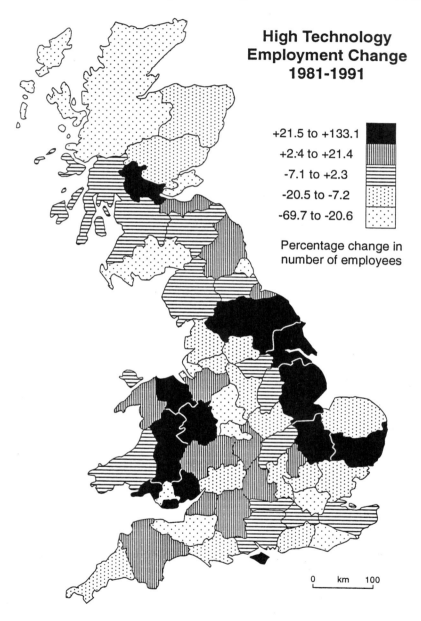

Figure 18.3

The geography of high-technology employment change in Britain, 1981–1991: percentage rates
Source: Unpublished Census of Employment statistics from NOMIS

Marshallian-type 'industrial district' generates economies which are external to the firm, and include specialisation of product and service supply, pools of skilled labour, and synergetic flows of technical, scientific and other strategic information. This concept is seen as illuminating the key processes underlying successful, endogenously-developed, NTBF complexes such as those of Silicon Valley and Route 128 (Hansen, 1992), while

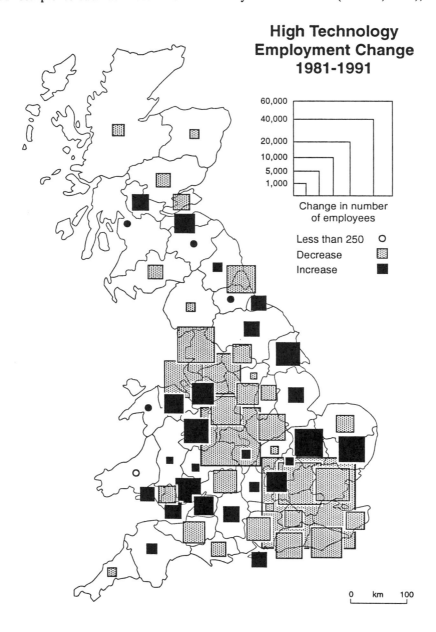

Figure 18.4
The geography of high-technology employment change in Britain, 1981–1991: absolute numbers
Source: Unpublished Census of Employment statistics from NOMIS

it also provides a basis for criticism of supposedly non-interactive NTBF clusters such as Sophia-Antipolis by workers such as Michael Storper[4] as 'fake complexes', which are unlikely to experience sustained growth.

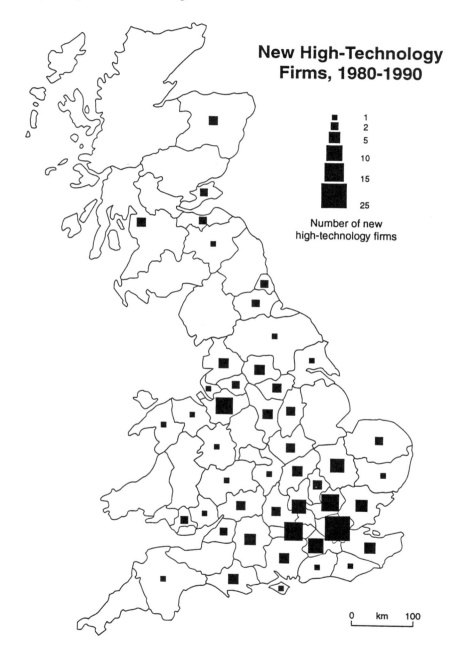

Figure 18.5
The location of new high-technology firms in Britain, 1980–1990
Source: Cambridge University Small Business Research Centre Survey, 1991.

The extent to which the development of a territorial 'innovative milieu' is essential for successful NTBF growth is an important issue for research and policy. Certainly NTBF creation appears to be markedly greater in particular regional environments than others, as for example in the UK, where there is a clear north–south regional differential in both firm formation rates and the success of science park initiatives set up during the 1980s to encourage NTBF growth (Massey, Quintas and Wield, 1992, pp. 16-17). Thus despite the spatial dispersion noted earlier, no less than 72% of the Cambridge Small Business Research Centre survey sample of NTBFs are located in southern (the South East, South West, East Anglia and the East Midlands) rather than northern England, despite random sampling from nationwide Dun and Bradstreet registers (see Figure 18.5). Only 11% are in the nineteenth century coalfield industrial regions of Scotland, Wales and Northern England. This supports Hall's oft-quoted contention that 'tomorrow's industries are not going to be born in yesterday's regions' (Hall, 1981). The high technology employment growth which has occurred in such older British industrial regions as Wales and Scotland (see Table 18.1 and Figure 18.4) is thus almost entirely a result of investment by large firm and multinational branch plants and subsidiaries (Keeble, 1992).

The reasons for regional concentration in new technology-based firm formation – as for the bias to small town and rural environments noted earlier – are, however, more debatable. Key factors cited by previous researchers include the role of spin-offs from, and research linkages with, university and other major research institutions, the importance of residential amenity and environmental attractiveness to highly-qualified scientists and engineers in their role as entrepreneurs and essential brain-power, and access to international communications, especially airports, for NTBFs whose specialised niche market orientation often requires rapid internationalization of sales and technological linkages, at least in a European context. Local availability of essential finance, such as venture capital, is stressed by some workers.

Despite criticism by workers such as Malecki (1991, p. 222) and Cooper (1986), the role of universities as incubator and environmentally-supportive organisations is undoubtedly important in particular cases such as the 'Cambridge Phenomenon', where a recent study by Finnish researchers (Lumme et al., 1993) estimates there to have been a steady flow of NTBFs from university departments and research institutes during the 1980s. Equally, though in a different context, the key role of attractive residential environments is shown by a recent study of small firm formation, including NTBF formation, in accessible rural areas of England to be strongly related to environmentally-stimulated migration of potential entrepreneurs to these areas (Keeble et al., 1992; Keeble and Tyler, 1994). This finding almost certainly underpins the small town/rural bias in NTBF formation noted earlier, as well as the success of European 'sunbelt' developments such as Sophia-Antipolis, which possesses only weak links with the University of Nice. The importance of international airport access is supported by Lumme's finding (Lumme et al., 1993, pp. 117-19) that 37% of the value of Cambridge NTBF sales in 1991 were international exports, and that no less than 80% of founders of these firms regarded 'going international', either already or within the next five years, as 'very important' for the competitive success of their business (compared, incidentally, with only 46% of a comparable sample of Finnish NTBFs). Equally, externally-acquired technological information from international suppliers and customers constituted the second most important source of such information (24% of firms) reported by the Cambridge SBRC national sample of NTBFs, excluding trade or professional journals, after UK suppliers and customers (40%). In this respect, UK universities or other higher education institutions came fourth in the list (22% of firms). Finally, the role of localised venture capital availability in established technology-oriented complexes such as Silicon Valley, argued as significant by researchers such as Florida and Kenney

(1988), is probably relatively unimportant in most European countries, although Lumme's work (Lumme et al., 1993) does suggest that its availability in 'prestige' locations such as Cambridge has been important for post-start-up financing of a small minority of firms.

These judgments do not, however, of course address the question of the possible additional role and significance of local synergetic linkages and inter-firm interaction in the development of successful NTBF innovative milieux, an issue which remains surprisingly little researched. Earlier investigation of the Cambridge Phenomenon, for example, suggests only moderate rather than marked development of such linkages by the mid-1980s, with only 32% of firms reporting significant local input or subcontracting linkages in 1986, and 46% reporting research linkages – usually informal – with the university (Keeble, 1989). So-called 'time-space compression' as a result of modern telecommunication and information technologies since then has led some workers to argue that collaborative linkages are now as likely to be with other NTBFs in Taiwan as in Silicon Valley or Cambridge (Gordon and Kimball, 1991). This issue will be central to a forthcoming research project on territorial clustering and innovative milieux in NTBF development which will form part of the work of the new ESCR-sponsored interdisciplinary Cambridge University Centre for Business Research, to be established from October 1994.

NTBFs AND 'HOSTILE' REGIONAL ENVIRONMENTS

Environmental Elements?

Despite the regionally uneven distribution of NTBFs in industrialised countries, new technology-based firms are to be found even in regions which are generally judged to afford less favourable, or even 'hostile', environments for the successful development of such activities. Such environments are usually conceptualised in terms either of economically-lagging, low-income, rural peripheral regions, or old industrial regions characterised by the decline of nineteenth century 'smokestack' industries and little tradition of entrepreneurship (Keeble, 1991). As such, they are frequently designated by government regional policies for economic development assistance, including initiatives to stimulate technology-based enterprise. In the British case, examples include Wales, Scotland and Northern England (see Figure 18.4).

Explanations for the low creation rate of NTBFs in such regions, as documented for the UK case earlier, usually focus on the same factors as discussed for innovative milieux, but in reverse. However, much less easy to explain is the fact that though much fewer in number, NTBFs established in 'hostile' regional environments often achieve high – and indeed higher – growth rates than their counterparts in more favourable environments. This fact, recently noted in the Netherlands by Vaessen and Wever (1993), is documented for the British case in Table 18.2. This shows that SBRC-surveyed NTBFs in the three peripheral and old industrial regions of Scotland, Northern England and Wales reported percentage employment and turnover growth rates 1987-90 which were on average substantially greater than those for NTBFs in southern England, with employment growth three times faster than in London, and turnover growth five times faster than in the South East outside London. And this difference cannot be explained by, for example, size differences[5] since peripheral NTBFs are in fact on average larger than those in any other region.

The table also reveals that this performance difference in favour of NTBFs in 'hostile' regional environments is accompanied by an appreciably higher proportion of peripheral NTBFs (80%) reporting 'successful introduction of major innovations in products or services during the last 5 years', again compared with those in southern England (only 44% of London NTBFs). Peripheral region NTBF high innovation rates are therefore closely associated with rapid growth, as might be expected. These differ-ences are not however, associated with any great regional differences in the frequency of systematic R&D, or of the importance of export markets. Interestingly, however, the frequency of 'unemployment-push' influences (Keeble, 1990) on NTBF creation does broadly follow the expected pattern, with the highest proportion of firms reporting that their business was established 'as a result of the actual or potential unemployment of its founder(s)' being in the old industrial peripheral regions of traditionally high unemploy-ment (40%), in line with the 'hostile' environment thesis. In contrast, London firms record the lowest percentage (16%).

These findings are of course based on small samples, and may partly reflect sectoral variations with more peripheral NTBFs being manufacturing firms, but more London NTBFs being service firms, for example. But the differences revealed are exactly in line with the independent Vaessen and Wever (1993) findings in the Netherlands, namely

Push factors in NTBF formation

Table 18.2: *NTBF performance and growth in 'hostile' and 'favoured' British regions*

	GREATER LONDON	REST OF SOUTH EAST	OUTER SOUTHERN ENGLAND	PERIPHERAL REGIONS
Mean % employment growth 1987–90	+96	+144	+145	+296
Mean % turnover growth 1987–90	+601	+206	+345	+1085
Mean employment size	23	32	22	40
Exports as % of turnover	15.8	9.2	17.0	15.7
% firms reporting major innovations in products or services, 1986–91	44.0	61.2	65.0	80.0
% firms carrying out systematic R&D into new products or services	56.0	67.2	60.0	50.0
% firms with only 4 or fewer competitors	32.0	47.8	50.0	70.0
% firms with actually or potentially unemployed founders	16.0	35.8	25.0	40.0
% firms seeking advice during last 3 years from:				
Small Firms Service	0.0	10.4	7.5	20.0
Local Enterprise Agencies	4.0	9.0	7.5	25.0
DTI Enterprise Initiative	24.0	29.9	40.0	40.0

Note: Peripheral regions comprise Wales, Scotland and Northern England. Outer Southern England comprises East Anglia, South West England and the East Midlands. Data are for 1990 unless otherwise specified. Sample sizes are London, 25; ROSE, 67; OSE, 40; periphery, 20.

Source: Cambridge University Small Business Research Centre, national SME survey. I am indebted to Diana Day for computing assistance in compiling this table.

that successful NTBF growth is not only perfectly possible in supposedly less favourable regional environments, but may actually outstrip that of similar enterprises in apparently more favoured locations. One possible reason for this is suggested by the further interesting finding in Table 18.2 that peripheral region NTBFs in Britain also differ markedly from their southern English counterparts, and especially those in London, in relation to the number of competitors with which they are faced. Thus 70% of peripheral NTBFs report operating in markets in which there are only 4 or fewer competitors, compared with only 32% of London NTBFs. This competitor-frequency indicator has recently been shown by Pratten (1991) to be closely diagnostic of the degree to which firms serve specialist niche markets, in which technological leadership or the provision of customized products tailored to the specific needs of clients afford SMEs significant non-price competitive advantages. The SBRC survey evidence thus suggests that peripheral region NTBFs have achieved their above-average growth by successfully targeting specialised niche markets with innovative products, a pattern closely similar to that revealed for successful accessible rural English firms in the major rural enterprise study referred to earlier (Keeble et al., 1992; Keeble and Tyler, 1994). This finding is perfectly consistent with Vaessen and Wever's more general argument (1993, p. 129) that small firm success in less favoured Dutch regions reflects pro-active entrepreneurial responses to overcome regional growth constraints, 'either by manipulating them, by becoming immune to their influence, or by adapting to environmental conditions'. In such pro-active – and varied – entrepreneurial responses, nationwide personal and client networks developed by SME founders through previous employment in organisations outside the region concerned were very important in enabling sufficient initial growth for firms to reach a size which provided the internal resources necessary to tackle – and overcome – these regional constraints.

NTBFs AND REGIONAL POLICY

The final set of issues relates to government policies – whether national, regional or local – seeking to stimulate NTBF creation and growth in particular regional environments. Such policies are widespread in European countries, many of which are facing unprecedented levels of localised and growing unemployment. Three points deserve emphasis. Firstly, the Cambridge SBRC survey reveals that the most severe limitations on growth reported by NTBFs focus on 'the availability and cost of finance for expansion', and on inadequate 'marketing and sales skills'. These both rated mean values of over 5.0 on a scale from 0 to 9, in terms of relative severity as experienced during the three years 1988-91. The marketing and sales skills rating is particularly pronounced for NTBFs compared with non-high technology SMEs. Regional capital availability, and the provision of government-subsidised marketing and sales consultancy advice, thus stand out from recent British experience as key areas in which government policy intervention could be important in enabling NTBF growth in particular regions.

Secondly, it has often been argued that nationwide government policies of NTBF assistance may discriminate against less-favoured regions, because of their dearth of enterprises which might apply for assistance and lower rates of application and take-up because of the possibly smaller size and more introverted nature of local businesses. However, Table 18.2 shows that NTBFs in Britain's peripheral regions in fact record the highest rather than lowest rates of take-up of different government schemes for business advice and consultancy assistance, a finding replicating those both of the overall SBRC survey of small and medium-sized enterprises (Small Business Research Centre, 1992), and of Mason and Harrison's recent study (1992) of the regional take-up of the DTI's Enterprise Initiative scheme. More significantly still, Table 18.3, which records the locations of successful applicants over the 3-year period 1990-92 to the Department of Trade and Industry's SMART scheme (Small Firms Merit Award for Research and Technology) of competitive technology grants,[6] shows that there are markedly higher success rates in the UK's 4 most peripheral and regional-policy assisted regions – Wales, Scotland, Northern England and Northern Ireland – than in southern Britain, especially London. Even more strikingly, the absolute number of small firms receiving technology grants under this scheme in these 4 regions (153) is in fact appreciably greater than the number of South East firms (112), despite the undoubtedly much larger number of potential if not actual applicants in the latter region. This suggests that far from being disadvantaged by such national technology-focused schemes, NTBFs in 'hostile' British regional environments are both more aware of and successful in obtaining help from them than their counterparts elsewhere. In turn, this may be explained by the historic importance of government regional assistance in these regions, and resultant more widespread knowledge of and greater willingness to apply for government grants.

Thirdly, British experience lends considerable support to the view that appropriately structured, and especially 'hands-on', local support schemes for fledgling NTBFs can have an important positive effect in enabling viability and survival, if not growth, of such enterprises. This is of course the argument underlying science park development, which has been rapid in the UK since 1980, with an increase in the number of operational parks with membership of the UK Science Park Association (1992) from only 2 in 1981 to 39 in 1991, with a further 5 under construction, and a further 12 planned. Numbers of tenant enterprises operating within these parks grew from 30 to 1,020, with an employment increase from 3,800 to 15,200, over this same period. The possible effects of such parks are illustrated by the case of the St John's Innovation Park in Cambridge, the more recent and NTBF-focused of the city's two science parks. Set up

Table 18.3: *Successful applicants for DTI SMART awards, 1990-92, by UK region*

	SUCCESSFUL APPLICANTS FOR SMART TECHNOLOGY AWARDS	
	NUMBER OF SUCCESSFUL APPLICANTS	FIRMS PER 1,000 VAT-REGISTERED MANUFACTURING BUSINESSES 1990
Wales	49	8.94
Scotland	55	6.93
Northern England	32	6.65
Northern Ireland	17	5.78
South West	58	4.94
East Anglia	27	4.88
East Midlands	49	3.79
Yorkshire and Humberside	42	3.34
Rest of South East	92	3.01
West Midlands	50	2.66
North West	42	2.65
Greater London	20	0.94

Sources: DTI Directories of Winners, Stage 1, SMART Awards, 1990, 1991, 1992, and Business Monitor PA10003, Size Analyses of UK Enterprises, 1990.

only in 1987 specifically to provide a supportive incubator environment for new small technology-based businesses, the park provides exceptional facilities to such firms in the form of small, modern and flexible premises, shared central services (switchboard, fax, telex, photocopying, library, meeting rooms, computer networks and secretarial support), in-house management consultancy and business advice, and direct access to venture capital through the college's own venture capital fund, St John's Ventures Ltd. Since its foundation, and despite severe national recession and high rates of business failures 1990-93, the failure rate of businesses operating within the park has been only 12% (13 failures out of 110 companies over $5\frac{1}{2}$ years, or only 2% per year), with a number of firms achieving sufficient growth to stimulate movement off the park to larger premises elsewhere, leaving 70 currently operating. These have an annual turnover of £20-25 million and employ 5-600 workers on the park. The failure rate includes firms which have failed since leaving the park.[7] This is a far better performance, in terms of crude failure rates, than either for new enterprises generally in the UK (VAT registration data suggest a 50% failure rate for any cohort of new firms over 7 years: see Keeble, 1990) or for mature Cambridge Phenomenon technology-based firms. Garnsey and Cannon-Brookes' recent work (1993) reveals an annual failure rate for the latter of 3.7% over the period 1985-92. Interestingly, the St. John's Park also reports no less than 12 currently operational technical collaborations between different science park companies, involving nearly one-third of current tenants, a level of localised synergy which would seem exceptional and reflects deliberate encouragement and orchestration by the park's Director and professionals. While this success may well of course partly reflect the particular advantages of Cambridge's 'innovative milieu' for NTBF development, it does provide some encouragement for policies of publicly-sponsored 'incubator' provision in less-favourable regional environments, in suggesting that institutional intervention can have a significant and measurable effect on regional NTBF development.

NOTES

1. Dr Stuart Evans, Chairman, Pedagogy, Menlo Park, California, in a research seminar on 'Innovation to Compete: the Case of Silicon Valley', Downing College, Cambridge, 20 October, 1992.
2. As defined in Keeble (1992), following Butchart, the former Chief Statistician in the Department of Trade and Industry: see also Table 18.1.
3. I am indebted to Mr Ian Agnew of the Cambridge University Department of Geography Drawing Office for designing these and later Figures.
4. In a Cambridge University Department of Geography Research Seminar on 'Regional Worlds of Production: Conventions of Learning and Innovation in Growth Regions of France, Italy and the United States', 7 November 1991.
5. Very small firms can sometimes achieve high percentage growth rates simply because of the low base level from which calculation is made.
6. I am indebted to the DTI's Eastern Region office for the original data from which Table 18.3 has been calculated, and to Antonia Sinden of the Department of Geography, Cambridge University, for research assistance. The objectives of the SMART scheme are 'to stimulate small businesses to develop and market new science and technology-based products, to encourage and facilitate the formation of viable and durable science and technology-based small businesses, and to contribute to a climate which encourages investment in highly innovative technology by individuals, firms and financial institutions.'
7. I am indebted to the St John's Innovation Park's Director, Mr Walter Herriot, for this current information.

REFERENCES

AYDALOT, P. (ed.) (1986) *Milieux Innovateurs en Europe*, GREMI, Paris.

AYDALOT, P. and KEEBLE, D. (eds.) (1988) *High Technology Industry and Innovative Environments: the European Experience*, Routledge, London.

BERNADY, DE SIGOYER, M. and BOISGONTIER, P. (1988) *Grains de Technopole: Micro-Entreprises Grenobloises et Nouveaux Espaces Productifs*, Presses Universitaires de Grenoble, Grenoble.

COOPER, A. C. (1986) Entrepreneurship and high technology, in D. L. Sexton and R. W. Smilor (eds.) *The Art and Science of Entrepreneurship*, Ballinger, Cambridge: Mass.

FLORIDA, R. L. and KENNEY, M. (1988) Venture capital and high technology entrepreneurship, *Journal of Business Venturing*, Vol. 3, pp. 301-19.

GARNSEY, E. and CANNON-BROOKES, A. (1993) Small high technology firms in an era of rapid change: evidence from Cambridge, *Local Economy*, February, pp. 318-33.

GORDON, R. and KIMBALL, L. M. (1991) Beyond industrial maturity: planning the future of Silicon Valley, in R. Camagni (ed.), *Les Politiques d'Innovation Technologique au Niveau Local: Articulation des Dynamiques Locales aux Dynamiques Externes*, Paris.

HALL, P. (1981) The geography of the Fifth Kondratieff Cycle, *New Society*, 26 March, pp. 535-7.

HANSEN, N. (1992) Competition, trust and reciprocity in the development of innovative milieux, *Papers in Regional Science*, Vol. 71, pp. 95-105.

KEEBLE, D. (1989) High-technology industry and regional development in Britain: the case of the Cambridge Phenomenon, *Environment and Planning C, Government and Policy*, Vol. 7, no. 2, pp. 153-72.

KEEBLE, D. (1990) Small firms, new firms and uneven regional development in the United Kingdom, *Area*, Vol. 22, no. 3, pp. 234-45.

KEEBLE, D. (1991) Core-periphery disparities and regional restructuring in the European Community of the 1990s, in H. H. Blotevogel (ed.) *Europaische Regionen im Wandel*, Dortmunder Vertrieb für Bau-und Planungsliteratur, Dortmund, pp. 49-68.

KEEBLE, D. (1992) High technology industry and the restructuring of the UK space economy, in P. Townroe and R. Martin (eds.), *Regional Development in the 1990s: The British Isles in Transition*, Jessica Kingsley, London, pp. 172-81.

KEEBLE, D. (1993) Small firm creation, innovation and growth and the urban-rural shift, in J. Curran and D. Storey (eds.), *Small Firms in Urban and Rural Locations*, Routledge, London, pp. 54-78.

KEEBLE, D. and BRYSON, J. (1993) Small firm creation and growth, regional development and the North-South divide, Cambridge University Small Business Research Centre Working Paper, 29.

KEEBLE, D., OWENS, P. L. and THOMPSON, C. (1983) The urban-rural manufacturing shift in the European Community, *Urban Studies*, Vol. 20, no. 4, pp. 405-18.

KEEBLE, D., and TYLER P. (1994) Enterprising behaviour and the urban-rural shift, Cambridge University Centre for Business Research Working Paper

KEEBLE, D., TYLER, P., BROOM, G. and LEWIS, J. (1992) *Business Success in the Countryside: The Performance of Rural Enterprise*, HMSO, London.

KEEBLE, D. and WEVER, E. (1986) Introduction, in D. Keeble and E. Wever (eds.) *New Firms and Regional Development in Europe*, Croom Helm, London.

LONGHI, C. and QUERE, M. (1993) Innovative networks and the Technopolis phenomenon: the case of Sophia-Antipolis, *Environment and Planning C, Government and Policy*, Vol. 11, pp. 317-30.

LUMME, A., KAURANEN, I., AUTIO, E. and KAILA, M. M. (1993) New technology-based companies in Cambridge in an international perspective, Cambridge University Small Business Research Centre Working Paper, 35.

MALECKI, E. J. (1991) *Technology and Economic Development*, Longman, Harlow.

MASON, C. and HARRISON, R. (1992) Regional take-up of the Enterprise Initiative in Great Britain: the Consultancy Initiatives Programme, in M. Robertson, E. Chell. and C. Mason (eds.) *Towards the Twenty-First Century: The Challenge for Small Business*, Nadamal Books, Macclesfield, Cheshire.

MASSEY, D., QUINTAS, P. and WIELD, D., (1992) *High-Tech Fantasies: Science Parks in Society, Science and Space*, Routledge, London.

OAKEY, R. P. and COOPER, S. Y. (1989) High technology industry, agglomeration and the potential for peripherally sited small firms, *Regional Studies*, Vol.23, no. 4, pp. 347-60.

PRATTEN, C. (1991) *The Competitiveness of Small Firms*, Department of Applied Economics Occasional Paper 57, Cambridge University Press, Cambridge.

SMALL BUSINESS RESEARCH CENTRE (1992) *The State of British Enterprise: Growth, Innovation and Competitive Advantage in Small and Medium-Sized Firms*, University of Cambridge, Cambridge.

TOWNSEND, A. (1993) The urban-rural cycle in the Thatcher growth years, *Transactions of the Institute of British Geographers*, N.S., Vol. 18, no. 2, pp. 207-21.

UNITED KINGDOM SCIENCE PARK ASSOCIATION (1992) *Science Park Directory (5th edition)*, UKSPA, Birmingham.

VAESSEN, P. and WEVER, E. (1993) Spatial responsiveness of small firms, *Tijdschrift voor Economische en Sociale Geografie*, Vol. 84, no. 2, pp. 119-31.